YOUR MIND IS NOT YOUR BRAIN

The Science of Multidimensional Thinking: A Medical Doctor's Guide to Unlocking Your True Self

GARY EPLER

E&R

PUBLISHERS OF O.G AUTHOR GENIUSES

Published by E&R Publishers
New York, NY USA

An imprint of MillsoCo Publishing, USA
www.EandR.pub

Your guarantee of quality

As publishers, we strive to produce every book to the highest commercial standards. The printing and binding have been planned to ensure a sturdy, attractive publication that should give years of enjoyment. If your copy fails to meet our high standards, please inform us and we will gladly replace it.

admin@millsi.co

ISBN: 9781945674914 (Hardcover)
ISBN: 9781945674921 (Softcover)
ISBN: 9781945674938 (Ebook)
ISBN: 9781945674945 (Audiobook)
Library of Congress Control Number: 2024933632

First Edition

TABLE OF CONTENTS

ACKNOWLEDGEMENTS

I'm grateful for everyone who has helped me with this book through their knowledge, insights, and writing. They include Simon Sinek for leadership trainings and US Navy SEAL Jocko Willink for his outstanding leadership skills and his book, *Extreme Ownership*, UPenn Psychology Professor Dr. Marty Seligman for creating positive psychology, and Harvard psychologist Shawn Achor for his outstanding contribution to the understanding and teachings of happiness. They include University of Chicago Psychology Professor Mihaly Csikszentmihalyi for being in the flow, Professor Carol Dweck at UPenn for creating the growth mindset, Heidi Sormaz for her work about overthinking and her yoga breathing techniques, and Professor Kristen Neff about her studies of compassion and treating yourself with kindness as well as Kamal Ravikant for *Love Yourself Like Your Life Depends on It*. They include Ismo, the Finnish standup comedian for his insight that negative words are unhealthy, Japanese tech company founder, Naotaka Nishiyama for his insights about gratitude, and author Leil Loundas for her insight about social skills. They include UPenn Sociology Professor Damon Centola for the strong and weak ties social media network research, Dave Allman at the Gallup organization for his outstanding work with global wellbeing, author Dr. Angela Duckworth for her outstanding contribution about grit, business professor, Kenneth Brown for his contribution to understanding influence and persuasion, communication professor Dannagal Young for her perspective on nefarious social media disinformation, and Jo Marchant for her ground-breaking research in the mind/brain-body connection. Lastly, I'm grateful to Jared Rosen for his inspirational editorial guidance and media management and to Simon Mills for helping me create a human civilization.

References

1. Epler GR. Eplerian Philosophy is a Model for Managing Stress at Home and in the Community. *Preventive Medicine and Community Health.* doi: 10.15761/PMCH.1000139. March 2020.
2. Epler G. Eplerian Life Philosophy: Thinking and Feelings from Five Locations. *Open Journal of Philosophy.* 13(2):336–341. Doi:10.4236/ojpp.2023.132023. May 2023.
3. Epler G. Eplerian Life Philosophy is a Model for Being Your Authentic Self. *London Journal of Medical and Health Research.* 23(10):1–6. October 2023.

Chapter 1

Your Mind is Not Your Brain

"The mind is the only place where you can experience true freedom."
— Deepak Chopra

As a lad of nine, I had my appendix removed as part of the typical boyhood experience, but six weeks later, massive belly scar caused another major abdominal surgical procedure which was followed by another four weeks later and one more four weeks after that. I remember being in the back of the car in agonizing pain going to the hospital for the fourth time in four months, and my mother saying to my father, "He's not going to make it."

Fortunately, I didn't know what that meant, and because of that I'm alive today. The brain can be a powerful negative force by thinking from the primitive brain region that I later call the stress center. If I had thoughts of dying generated from this obsolete brain region, I wouldn't be here today. Not knowing the meaning of "he's not going to make it" saved my life.

I'm here today, stronger than ever. Persistent enough to get into medical school despite rejection after rejection. I recall walking down first Avenue in New York after another NYU Medical school rejection, my head hanging so low shuffling along that someone called me out, "The last time I looked that bad, I was at a funeral." Inspired, I drove to New Orleans that day. It was the first day of classes, and I knocked on the door of the Dean of Admissions. He exclaimed, "You're in!" Some one in St. Louis had changed their mind at the last minute. That was the greatest day of my life!

That led me to discovering a lung fluke parasite in the jungles of the South America Colombian jungle during medical school and discovering a lung disease during my training as a pulmonary and critical care doctor in Boston.

My next discovery was going to develop something to improve the lives of millions of people all over the world. After years and years of research, failures, and thousands of rejections, in December 2019, I discovered a novel connection between brain science and a new way of living, which is called the "Eplerian Life Philosophy."

For most of us in this world we have assumed the brain and the mind are interchangeable. What we never learned in high school biology class is that the mind exists outside the brain. Your mind is not your brain.

Where is the mind located? The mind is the universe surrounding the physical body. Thinking from the brain inhibits creativity, innovation, and performance. Thinking from the mind connects you to all information and knowledge in the past, present, and future. Quantum physicists know that time and space are a construct of consciousness, which is the field we connect with when we think from the mind. The Eplerian Life Philosophy helps people shift from brain thinking to thinking from the heart with kindness and from the mind with creativity and innovation.

*　*　*

Eplerian Life Philosophy for a New Way of Life. Know Who You Are Moment by Moment

The idea of knowing who you are goes back 3400 years ago with the words "know thyself" inscribed in granite. Later, Socrates wrote, "The unexamined life is not worth living."

Why has this idea survived for thousands of years? Because knowing who you are and being your true self is the ultimate developmental phase of a person's life that people recognize during the late 30s, 40s, or beyond. However, there are many people throughout their lives who are never their true selves. They're always comparing themselves to others, trying to be someone else, trying to please others, or thinking about what other people think of them.

Thanks to functional MRI studies, I was able to develop a way for people to learn how to be their true selves by knowing where they're thinking from.

> *"Know who you are moment by moment."*
>   *– Gary Epler*

During childhood and grade school, you're told who you should be by your parents and teachers. This is useful for learning social skills. During college, you're told who you are by your professors and friends. Then you're told who you are by your boss so you can do your job successfully. During all this time, you're being told who you are by society so that you will learn regulatory laws and social rules. All of this is necessary, but time approaches where this is stress and you need to be free from this. It's time to become your true self.

In addition to freedom, there are many benefits of knowing who you are and being your true self. It feels good. You're your own person. You're happier, more productive, and a better person. You have high energy. You're creative. You're engaged in life. You enjoy living in the moment. You don't criticize, complain, or blame. You have no guilt, worry, or jealousy. You're trustworthy. People want to be with you.

The historic perspective of the "know thyself" concept shows that scientists and psychologists have suggested this aphorism be abandoned because it's too general and lacks a specific, useful meaning. They're right. People are all types throughout the day such as teachers, students, husbands, wives, friends, lawyers, and accountants. These labels don't help improve life.

To me, the idea of knowing who you are and being your true self is too important to abandon. I have developed a way to bring it to life by adding *moment by moment.*

New brain science and functional magnetic resonance imaging (fMRI) studies provided clarification. Adding three words 'moment by moment' to the concept resulted in the Eplerian Life Philosophy, a new way for a healthy life. "Know who you are moment by moment."

Additional science showed that people think from many locations in the brain. These regions are independent with no communication between them. You can only think from one location at a time.

Furthermore, there are two regions that I consider the crocodile brain located in the primitive brain region. These are the anger center and the stress center. The crocodile only thinks of itself with anger and lashes out if provoked. So, when humans think from this primitive brain region, they're angry and stressed. In addition, the expression, "overthinking" at work or during athletic competition means you're thinking from the stress center.

Knowing who you are moment by moment means knowing where you're thinking from. If you're thinking from the anger center, then you're angry. If you're thinking from the self-centered stress center, you're stressed. An important health issue regarding these two centers is they require no sleep and thrive on junk food. These centers are shut down with exercise. This is why eight hours of sleep, a healthy nutrition lifestyle, and one hour of exercise are useful to help limit thinking from these two regions.

A third region in the brain is the accumbens pleasure center. The issue with thinking from this center is that it's the addiction center as the pleasure is short-lived and followed by a crash resulting in wanting more to sustain the good feeling and avoid the crash. This region can take over a person's life shutting down all thinking from healthy locations.

The pleasure center like the anger center and stress center is powerful especially for people with no sleep. For example, it's more powerful than the gut and belly brain. Order a big plate of fried seafood with fried onion rings or a hot fudge sundae, your belly brain is screaming to stop, but not the head pleasure center. Most of the time, the head wins over the belly.

The prefrontal cortex is the highly advanced human brain. Thinking from this region has become automatic from childhood and acts as a social judge for doing what's right and following healthy social norms. The prefrontal cortex also has the capacity to connect and access the mind, which is outside the body. However, unlike the crocodile brain, this region is sensitive to lack of eight hours of sleep and shuts down. In addition, the crocodile brain with anger and stress will completely override the prefrontal lobe, leaving people making bad judgment calls. In addition to eight hours of sleep, a healthy nutrition lifestyle and one hour of daily exercise will keep this region healthy and alert.

What's the alternative to thinking from the anger and stress centers? Additional science has shown neuro tissue with decision making capability and feelings in the heart and the abdominal organ system. We've known about this for centuries. Phrases such as "listen to your heart" or "having a gut reaction" are common.

Expanding the philosophy of knowing where you're thinking from includes a total of five locations you can think from moment by moment – your head, your heart, your gut, your body, and the fifth is the mind, which is outside the body. Remember, you can only think from one location at a time.

Let's reconsider the head. The primitive crocodile brain has an anger center and stress center. This brain region saves your life every day through instinctive actions such as getting you in the safest situation during a serious automobile accident, keeping seconds away from a falling tree branch, or preventing you from stepping in an unmarked street repair hole.

The advanced prefrontal lobe is for positive social judgment and doing what's right.

Using the Eplerian Life Philosophy, we can learn to limit your time thinking from the anger center and stress center to six to eight seconds. You do this by feeling the anger and stress, letting the feeling peak, and then moving on in six to eight seconds. Distract yourself with the body, exercising or going for a walk. Shift your thinking to the heart or to the mind.

Try this. Something triggers your anger center – someone yells at you, offends you, or makes you feel bad about yourself. First, you need to remember that the person is angry, not you. Someone has been cruel or nasty to the person or the person has been betrayed or swindled. Use empathy from your heart, don't react from your head, respond from your heart by listening.

If you find yourself thinking about your money problems, relationship problems, or you're having negative thoughts about work, then these thoughts are from the stress center. You can have these thoughts for six to eight seconds, and then change. Think from the heart about being kind to yourself with self-compassion and kind to others. Think from the mind with creativity to develop a next step solution.

You can also think from the gut or the belly brain. Take advantage of your belly brain for healthy nutrition and risk management. Listen to your belly brain for eating the right foods in the right amount at the right time. Do you have a decision about a potential risky situation? Listen to your gut for the right choice.

The body is the fourth location to think from. When you're exercising, running, or doing yoga, you can't be stressed out because you can only think from one location at any given moment. For a competitive event, use visualization and feel from the muscles for the upcoming event. This will give you an edge over the competition.

The mind is the most compelling and powerful location to think from. Need to solve a problem at home or at work? Need to create a new way of doing something? Need to make a new discovery? Use the mind. The mind is outside the body. Are you feeling low or out of energy? Use the mind. The feelings from the mind include total calmness, acceptance, and unconditional love.

There are numerous applications of the Eplerian Life Philosophy. Learning to be your true self with courage is the fundamental application.

Health is also a major application. The traditional meaning of health has been the absence of disease which does not fully represent health.

Health is a state of mind and feelings. My definition is living an invigorating life filled with high energy, creativity, enjoyment, positive experiences, and extraordinary friends. This means eliminating bad health habits such as stress, complaining, and not enough sleep. This means having good health habits such as always being engaged in life, living in the moment, and being your true self.

Other applications include learning to eliminate the unhealthy effects of stress and anger. Developing successful personal leadership at home and at work. Increasing productivity and performance at work as well as increasing creativity and innovation. Increased happiness level. You'll make instant decisions and enjoy taking on responsibility.

You're always engaged in life, which means knowing what you want, where you're going, and what you're doing with no negative mobile devices. You develop meaning in your life outside yourself. You are a better friend, family member, and citizen.

You'll use self-healing for restoring your health. You have self-compassion and compassion for others. You're grateful. Worry and guilt are eliminated. You learn new healthy habits to replace unhealthy habits.

You'll have close personal relationships because you will be your true self, open and thinking from the heart with kindness and giving.

You'll sustain three fundamental requirements for a healthy life. These include a healthy nutritional lifestyle by eating the right foods in the right amount at the right time and prepared in a healthy manner. You'll have eight hours of sleep every night. You'll do one hour of exercise every day.

* * *

Courage to Be Your True Authentic Self. At the core, knowing who you are moment by moment is about having the courage to be your true authentic self. Often, we put on a performance for others, trying to fit into their ideas of who we should be. But our lives can be fuller, richer if we have the courage to be who we really are. Embrace your true self and learn the skills to tap into the core of who you are.

Being your true self is fundamental for an extraordinary and enjoyable life. The benefits are endless and continue to develop during a lifetime.

Being your true self brings freedom with no complaining, criticizing, or blaming. You have no negative feelings about yourself. There are no feelings of guilt or worry. There is no resentment, no jealousy, and no retaliation. There is no anger and no stress. You don't need to compare yourself to anyone. You don't need to try to be anyone else, especially the perfect person you've developed in your mind. You don't need to please anyone. You don't need to listen to anyone tell you who you are.

During childhood, you're told who you are by your parents and teachers. During college, you're told who you are by your professors and friends. During your first job, you're told who you are by the boss or else you get fired. You're continuously told who you are by society by following all the rules and regulations. None of this may be a problem during your teenage years and during your twenties. However, being told who you are can cause stress.

Stress is not recognized at first, but over the years, the feeling begins to permeate your conscious thinking, and you don't like it. This becomes a life-changing turning point. You have two options. You can continue to try to be someone else or you can become your true self.

For some people, the feeling of stress from these life forces is never recognized, and they go through life with a negative outlook always stressed out by trying to be someone else and trying to please others. They complain, criticize, and blame. They live in the past and fear the future.

There are others who recognize the situation but don't want to take the risk of being themselves because they don't believe in themselves or don't have self-confidence. Being your true self can have unpredicted and uncomfortable consequences.

Another way to look at the situation is the idea of people 'identifying' themselves with a location, a group, or a job. This makes people feel important and better than other people. This is unhealthy thinking from the cingulate self-centered stress center.

For example, people who are living in New York City or Los Angeles use the location as a feeling of importance because they're living in these big cities. People who are managers, executive officers, doctors, lawyers use these titles to identify themselves, giving them credibility.

People in certain prestigious groups will use these labels to give themselves confidence. This is self-centered from the stress center taking away from enjoying life. None of this is your true self. These labels are a distraction taking you away from being your true self and moving on to an enjoyable life.

My story can serve as an example of knowing when you've become your true self. At a certain level, I have always been my true self since childhood and maybe everyone is at the beginning. The behavior is labelled as being stubborn or rebellious because you do what you want to do. You learn to suppress these feelings and adjust so you can have friends and succeed at school and in your job. This is what I would call the 'identifying with' stage.

During high school I identified myself with the football team and a school club. During college, it was the name of the college. During medical school, I was so thankful for being there that I was my true self and didn't identify with the name of the school.

After that, I recall identifying with Boston which gave me confidence. Incidentally, I recall taking the internal medicine certification board examination. I thought to myself that they had to pass me because I was an assistant professor. I believed this at the time. Looking back now, I can see this is total nonsense. The grading is done by a computer. A line is drawn at one-standard deviation. Everyone above the line passes and everyone below the line fails. Fortunately, I passed.

I don't think I'm alone in this thinking. During this identifying phase of human development, almost everyone uses this in one form or another.

The final phase for me was identifying with the 'Chief of Medicine' title. At the time, this was a dream come true. At work, in social gatherings, and in writing, I acted as a 'Chief of Medicine' and not my true self.

My friend Bob woke me up. He said, "You gotta get out of there." I was surprised and confused; how could he say I had to leave? This is the greatest thing in my life. Why would I want to do anything else? "It's holding you back," he told me.

Fortunately, they threw me out as the result of a merger. It was the best thing ever!

I was faced with two options. Do I become my true authentic self or get another job title? My initial feeling was one of terrifying fear. I didn't know anything. I wasn't smart enough to be my true self. I can't succeed on my own. I needed someone else. I needed an institution. I needed a job title. The excuses went on and on. But I took the right path. I chose to become my true authentic self and started a healthcare business and began a life of freedom.

Many people never make the transition. People go through their lives never being their true selves. They're acting. They're trying to act like someone else. They're trying to be someone else. They're their job title. This causes stress, unhappiness, and lack of trust. You can't trust people who aren't their true selves because you don't know who they are.

People may want to be their true selves, but they don't know how. There has been no answer for thousands of years of 'how' to be your true self until fMRI tech, new brain science, and the Eplerian Life Philosophy.

Knowing who you are is too general. We're all types of people, parents, husbands, wives, teachers, students. However, this can be specific by added the words "moment by moment." you can know who you are moment by moment because it's where you're thinking from.

Random thoughts occur throughout the day without your control; however, people can control their second thoughts, moment by moment. Thoughts are slow, compared to uncontrollable instincts, and require energy so they can be controlled. You can stop thinking thoughts. You can move thoughts to another location. You can have new thoughts. Building negative thoughts from the first thought can be stopped.

Negative thinking becomes a habit. Most thinking during the day is a habit. Research has shown that up to 98 percent of thoughts are the same thoughts as yesterday, and 70 to 80 percent of the thoughts are negative. Remember, you control the second thought and prevent building a negative story leading to stress.

There are plenty of positive thoughts that pop into your head. In this situation, think a second thought and build a story for a few seconds. If it's about a past positive memory, it feels good and the good feeling will last a long time. For example, it may be a thought about a magical time with someone you love.

There are several separate brain regions that are independent with no communication between them. You can only think from one brain region at a time. So, you know who you are moment by moment because you know what brain region or other location you're thinking from.

There are three unhealthy brain regions to think from that include the anger center, the self-centered stress center, and the addiction center.

By now, you're familiar with the anger center. It's called the amygdala. Anger is defined as something that has been being taken from you, usually in a personal manner and maybe in an intentional, cruel way. You get fired, you get thrown out of school or more commonly, your enjoyment is taken away, your time, your opinions, or even your autonomy.

Something is taken from you in a rude manner which triggers the anger center. This causes the adrenal sympathetic nervous system response with increased blood pressure, heart rate, shutting down the immune system and digestive system, and causes inflammation resulting in heart disease, diabetes, high blood pressure, and a shortened life. That's why you need to transfer out of the amygdala anger center and stop thinking from there. You're allowed six to eight seconds before these harmful effects begin. Learn to eliminate the anger trigger.

So, everyone knows prolonged anger is not good for you or for anyone else. How do you stop anger? The traditional way of hitting a pillow or something else prolongs the anger and you might get hurt. Suppressing anger is not healthy as this also prolongs the anger and outbursts will come later. Distraction from thinking about something can be effective.

Another way to shorten the anger is the six to eight second method. Feel the anger, let it peak, and move on. Staying there for longer time causes the cortisol adrenalin response that is unhealthy, causing inflammation, and disease. Another way out of the anger center is to think from the heart. Do the opposite, instead of taking, give. Give your time, give your energy, or give your help.

What's the stress center? Let's find out. Take 100 people, put them in a functional MRI machine, which shows the brain region where a person is thinking from. Give them a simple task, "Don't think about yourself." If they do, a red light will go on. Within a few seconds, they start thinking about their problems or a mistake they made. The red light goes on. They feel sorry for themselves because they're not doing as well as someone else. The red light goes on. They have negative thoughts about other people, resentment, retaliation, or jealousy. The red light blinks furiously. For three weeks, these subjects learned to keep the red light off by learning how to stop thinking about themselves.

What's going on? The fMRI technician behind the glass wall watches the scan screen. Whenever the posterior cingulate cortex (PCC) lights up, then the technician pushes the button for the red light. When this cingulate region no longer lights up, the technician turns off the red light. The technician had no idea that whenever people were thinking of themselves, they were thinking from the cingulate region, and they were stressed. I use an easier name for this region. It's the stress center.

People in the fMRI learned to stop thinking about themselves after three weeks. What happens six months later? They're healthier, more productive, three times more creative, and enjoy life more. They're happier. They're better friends and better citizens. All of this without pills, specialized equipment, and long and expensive consultations. It's free without life-threatening adverse reactions.

How can people learn how to be their true selves? Like the people in the fMRI, train yourself to limit thinking about yourself from the stress center. Limit the time to six to eight seconds. This is not harmful to you or to anyone else. If you're stressed, feel it, let it peak, and it will pass. Don't think about the events that's causing the stress. Feel the stress and move on. Think from the heart with kindness or the mind with creativity.

Understand the science that whenever you think about your problems or think about yourself in any way, you're going to be stressed. Realize that if you are stressed, then you're thinking from the stress center. One quick way to get out of the stress center is to be kind to yourself. Instead of thinking negative thoughts about yourself, do the opposite, think positive thoughts from the heart with kindness to yourself.

If you make a mistake, acknowledge it, try to learn something, and move on to thinking from somewhere else. Think from the mind about creating something better.

> "The less you think about yourself, the more you are your true self."

If you're thinking unhealthy thoughts toward other people such as blame, criticism, judgment, jealousy or even retaliation, then acknowledge the thought. Try to learn something and move on. These are taking behaviors, so give.

Give from the heart with expecting nothing in return. It feels good for a lifetime.

People say what they want, and they do what others want. This is living from the primitive brain region. Be your authentic self, think like a human from the heart and the mind. Do what you want. It's good for you. It's good for the world.

* * *

Attention. You might be familiar with the phrase mind over matter. What we give our attention determines the course of our day and our overall health and wellbeing. Learn about training our attention from the mind on the things that matter.

Attention means total concentration on the task with no other thoughts. For concentration, know where you're thinking from. Learn to stop thinking from the head stress center because you can't think from anywhere else and think from the mind for success. Mastering total attention will lead to your success more than you can ever imagine by not thinking from the head and thinking from the mind.

For example, attention can be used to become the best baseball pitcher. Typical baseball pitchers always shake off the catcher's sign as if it's part of the show. They think about the batter's stats. They think about being in the big game. These pitchers are thinking about the opposing team, the ballpark, and even the standings. All these thoughts are from the head self-thinking stress center taking away from concentrating on throwing their best pitch.

The baseball pitcher who uses total attention becomes the best in the league. The pitcher sees the sign from the catcher and throws the pitch. Nothing else. No other thoughts. The pitcher doesn't know who the batter is, doesn't know the team, and whether the team is playing in the final World's Series game.

The best pitcher throws the pitch with no other thoughts. This is concentration. This is attention. This wins World Series games. This means not thinking self-centered thoughts from the stress center. This is thinking from the mind with concentration and attention.

Thinking from the mind means you're not thinking from the anger center and you're not thinking from the stress center about thoughts of not being good enough, about having a difficult day, or that the other person is better than you.

Remember, you can only think from one location at a time. If you're thinking about your problems, then you can't pay attention from the mind for your performance. In addition, when you're thinking about your problems, then you're thinking in the fast beta-brainwave state and not from the mind. You need to be concentrating in the "zone," in the slow alpha-brainwave state for paying attention.

The best quarterback in football wins important games like the playoffs and the Super Bowl. Other quarterbacks may be faster or smarter and win games, but not when it counts. What's the difference?

The winning quarterback focuses on the play as the ball is hiked. There are no thoughts about the opposition players, the last game, the last play, the stadium, the importance of the game, or how many seconds are left. The best quarterback uses the mind, not the brain. In the mind, this quarterback visualizes where each opposing player is on the field, and where each player is going to be. That's why the pass is thrown to the right receiver at the right time without an interception.

How do you pay attention to what you're doing? The clue comes from examples of these athletes. They don't think from the head. There's a saying in sports, "get out of your head." They think from the mind. Attention is from the mind.

This means they have no thoughts about themselves, about losing the game, or making mistakes. These are self-centered thoughts, thinking about themselves from the head stress center. They only think about throwing the pitch, the football, or any other athletic skill from the mind, not from the head. Laser attention comes from the mind, which is outside the body, and in a slower alpha-brainwave state.

Paying attention applies to the home. This makes chores enjoyable. Give total attention to fixing a leaky faucet, washing dishes, or carrying out the trash without complaining, being angry, or criticizing. This turns these tasks into something positive. It's not doing work or a job washing the dishes, it's giving your time and contributing to the family from the heart with no stress.

Complaining and criticizing about these chores is thinking about yourself. This not only causes you stress, it causes stress in the family and everyone near you. Think about helping the family from the heart with kindness and giving.

Paying attention is especially helpful at work. At work, this means "staying in your lane." Do your job, no one else's. Do your job, don't think about anyone else's job. The CEO pays attention to creating a successful company not with thoughts of day-to-day management. The CTO pays attention to tech with no thoughts about operations. Employees focus on their specific task with no complaints and criticism of others.

For example, the job of a startup board member is to help build an organization, not to be concerned about making money. The board member who only thinks about making money is toxic and will destroy the company. They force decisions based on money, not on developing and improving products and services that are going to make people's lives easier or improve their lives.

Paul was an enthusiastic investor in a new healthcare startup. After several months, he began to exert pressure on the CEO by requesting spending information about his investment. The CEO wanted to hire an important person that could advance the company; however, Paul demanded he not hire the person because it was money from his investment. He soon stopped the CEO from spending his money on anything. The company soon failed, and Paul lost all his money. The CEO manages the company, not the board.

These board members analyze every expense and block the CEO from hiring key people or spending money for capital raise because this means losing the board member's money. This egocentric board member is thinking from the self-thinking stress center. They're not thinking from the heart to help the organization, and they're not thinking from the mind with innovative ideas and solving problems.

There are many other examples such as egocentric CEOs, managers, and top performers who only think of themselves. Thinking from the mind and not the head stress center can make the difference between success and failure. Use the mind for attention.

Paying attention can be helpful to your community. Focusing on the task with no self-thinking thoughts about criticism, seeking power, or judgment results in completion of the task and a positive, enjoyable experience working with others.

Here's a call to action: Give total attention to tasks at home and at work with no self-centered thoughts from the head stress center. Reframe tasks and jobs, it's giving and contributing to the family or the company. Think from the heart with kindness and giving. Think from the mind with focus, concentration, and attention.

*   *   *

Innovation. I use innovation as developing a new product or service that is used by billions of people worldwide. CEOs, executives, and employers can innovate through the power of creative thinking from the mind.

What's the difference between a global innovative product and other products? An innovative product is used by billions of people throughout the world making people's lives easier or improving their lives.

Innovators are what I call trial-and-error people. These are people who try something new. It fails. They try again. It fails. They repeat and continue to repeat until they develop an innovation.

Planners are organized, methodical people. They plan product development and continue to plan until they get the plan right. Then they develop the product. There are no failures.

Planners bring stability to the organization through operations and regulatory management. Trial & error people create innovative products and services.

Having both types of people in an organization is optimal. This discussion is about innovators.

What does it take for successful innovation? There are two fundamental requirements, the right person and the right governmental structure.

Innovation comes from a team of people with distinct cultures and from various parts of the world with ideas from the periphery, from the edge. A UPenn study showed that teams from within a company have massive amounts of similar information, and they quickly develop good products. However, teams with geographic and cultural differences take a long time to develop a product, but these teams develop the best products.

A governmental structure that creates an environment for innovators is the right mix of personal freedom and business regulations. For example, a country in the far distant past developed innovations that continue to be used to the present time, but self-centered governmental structures developed that resulted in shifting innovation from that country to another part of the world. Governmental regulations are needed for intellectual property protection and for uniform accounting rules with no interference with personal choices. Innovation creates the strongest, most vibrant countries in the world.

There are three components of developing an innovative product or service.

Frist, apply the Eplerian Life Philosophy principle of abandoning thinking from the head cingulate stress center. Practice this every day. If you think about your problems, upset with yourself, trying to be someone else, or thinking about failing, then you're thinking from the stress center. If you're stressed, you're thinking about yourself. You can only think from one location at a time; therefore, if you're stressed and thinking about your problems, then you can't think from the mind with innovation.

Second, learn to think from the mind quickly and automatically. The mind is outside the body and has unlimited knowledge about the past, present, and future. Because the mind is outside the body, you need to be in a slow alpha brainwave state, not in the everyday highspeed beta brainwave state. Learn to be in the slow brainwave state naturally for innovative ideas.

Third, develop an egalitarian team with five to seven individuals who have strong ties from different cultural backgrounds and geographic locations. Centralized teams with similar members can quickly develop good products. They make choices that are familiar, not necessarily the best. Egalitarian teams develop innovative products.

As the company grows, it's important to include frontline people and people from the fringe when making decisions. For example, a study of major league baseball teams showed that using the opinions of the established, entrenched scouts produced good teams but having an equal voice for all scouts and coaching staff who each see something different creates championship teams.

The typical lifestyle of trial-and-error innovators is a life filled with failures, and they often have negative cash flow. They never retire. Innovators have failure after failure, but also extraordinary international successes. Innovators are not discouraged by failures. These failures provide energy to try something new. Not so with investors, they are deterred by failures and quickly take away the money, but that's part of the path to innovation.

Being a trial-and-error person is filled with enormous risk and entrepreneurial fear in exchange for an exciting and invigorating life.

Innovation is fundamental for products and services that make life easier and improve the lives of people all over the world. Innovation is creating a product or service that is entirely new. This requires thinking from the mind for creative ways to help people and innovative ideas to improve people's lives.

*   *   *

Trust. If you want to be someone people trust, then be your true authentic self. You trust people who are their true authentic selves. They do what they say, every time in all situations. They're consistent with their actions. You believe the person will do what is expected. The person will do the right thing. There is no uncertainty. You can rely on them. You know they will have your back no matter the situation.

Trust increases the quality of interpersonal relationships and makes social life more predictable and enjoyable. Trust creates a sense of community. Trust makes it easier for people to work together.

Loyal friends and coworkers tell you they'll support you for an upcoming proposal at a high-level meeting. If they're being their true selves, they will support you regardless of what happens. They won't criticize you. They won't blame you. They won't make you look bad or embarrass you.

False friends with self-thinking controlling personalities will make themselves look good by making you look bad. If the presentation goes poorly, they'll attack you and publicly humiliate you without hesitation.

People are their true selves when they know who they are moment by moment. This means they always know where they're thinking from. They don't think from the head anger and stress centers. They think from the heart and the mind.

There's no self-centered thinking trying to one-up someone or put someone down to make themselves look better. Self-centered people thinking about themselves feeling good by making others look bad by criticizing them, blaming them, or making them look weak. If people are thinking from the anger center and stress center, then there's no trust. If you're thinking from the heart with kindness, empathy, and giving, then there's trust.

The reason why people have this injurious behavior is this behavior gives them a tiny dose of what I call dopamine chemical pleasure from the accumbens addiction brain center. These people have learned this behavior since childhood because this behavior gets them what they want. When it comes to lack of trust, people are thinking from the primitive anger center and stress center as well as the accumbens addiction center. People need to stop thinking from these centers.

If you're thinking from the stress center, it feels good to blame someone else because this gives chemical pleasure from the pleasure center. But it feels so much better to think from the heart with kindness or the mind with creativity. Take responsibility. If you make a mistake or do something wrong, then take personal responsibility. This comes from the heart.

It may feel good for some people to criticize and point out faults, but it feels so much better to give, because this is from the heart. A harsh example is revenge. If people are thinking from the stress center, revenge will make them feel better. This is toxic chemical pleasure. Forgiveness is so much better because this comes from the heart. A final example, negative thinking by always talking about problems is toxic chemical pleasure. It's short-lived, addictive, and unhealthy. This creates no trust. The feeling from the heart with kindness and empathy is not from a chemical. It's a positive feeling. It's healthy and creates trust.

Can people change thinking from the stress center and chemical pleasure center to thinking from the heart? It's difficult because thinking from the cingulate stress center is from a lifetime of conditioning using this for pleasure. If you challenge this, they will respond with anger and rage because you're taking away pleasure. They need to realize this is fake pleasure. It's a chemical pleasure and not healthy.

People need to realize that thinking from the heart with kindness and empathy will give them a good feeling for a lifetime that is so much better than the tiny amount of fake, chemical pleasure. Thinking from the heart feels good and puts a smile on your face. You stand tall with shoulders back, chin straight, and eyes bright. You see the good in all things. People can trust you because you're not trying to be anyone else. This is a great feeling compared to the chemical pleasure from criticizing and blaming others.

Trust is fundamental for close personal relationships. Remember, a close personal relationship is one with someone where you can be yourself without having to think about what you say or worry about what you do. There is no judgment, no criticism, and no blame. You always have each other's back no matter what happens. Trust is a natural part of healthy close relationships.

Simon Sinek talked about the Navy SEAL's boat six described in US Navy SEAL Jocko Willink's book, *Extreme Ownership*. Boat six always wins, and Jocko said there are no bad crews, only bad leaders. Simon wanted to know, "How does the commanding officer pick the boat six team? He explained this using a horizontal and vertical line graph. He wrote the word "Trust" below the horizontal line and the word "Performance" on the vertical line.

The worst team leader is at the top of the performance scale but has no trust. These are self-centered people thinking about themselves and are toxic team members. These top performers are good at high visibility and being praised by management or the board; however, this is at the superficial level. They are toxic to the company by breaking the rules and destroying all other employees with their manipulative, lying behavior.

The best leader is at the top of the performance scale and top of the trust scale. The high-performance and high-trust people lead with concerns for all team members, each with a different assignment, but working together. They're the boat leaders that come in first place quietly cooperating and sending positive encouragement to each other. You can hear the last place boat coming in a hundred yards away as the leader is yelling at the team, and the team yelling at each other or yelling about being too slow or too weak.

The high-performing, low-trust people are not being their true selves. They only think about themselves, and how everyone or everything can help them get what they want, which is money, power, or victory. They're not high performers to help the organization. They're high performers to get what they want.

High-trust people are the opposite. They are being their true selves and always consider how they can help others and the organization succeed. They consider what's best for each team member to work together to accomplish the task. They consider what's best for the organization.

Simon Sinek continues by pointing out that there are unlimited measures of performance such as the sales quotas, number of clients, and the amount money brought into the firm. However, there are no easy measures for trust. This can be difficult, sometimes taking months or even years. By then, it may be too late because they've done irreversible damage to the organization. This is because the high-performer low-trust people are aggressive and self-promoting, blinding management with their over-the-top performance and persuasive skills.

How can you recognize the no-trust people when making a hiring decision or team leader decision? Listen to their words and ask questions. Are they self-centered thinkers? Do they think of others?

Listen for clues to their personality. They are self-centered and narcissistic. They will do anything to get what they want. They have no remorse about their actions. They're manipulative and will lie as part of their conversation, and they'll make elaborate excuses if you catch them in a lie.

They use many negative words. They're life's attitude is pessimistic, seeing everything as a problem and seeing the future as negative. This attitude is often masked by their aggressive behavior and not recognized. The fundamental characteristic is they're not their true authentic selves. They're trying to be someone else such as someone with power or someone with enormous amounts of money.

They always have their cell phone in their hands. They brag about only needing five hours of sleep so they can gain sales. They have elevated levels of stress because they only think about themselves. They think from the mind with creative ideas to get what they want, not with creative ideas to help others.

How do you recognize high-trust people? They're rare as many people are trying to be someone else instead of their true selves. You can look for personality clues during the conversation. They're self-confident in a quiet manner. They know what they want, where they're going, and what they're always doing. They're not fake in any way. They have opinions but have a flexible mindset and allow others to express themselves fully. They're committed and reliable. They take responsibility and the consequences of a bad outcome by admitting immediately they made a mistake.

Develop trust by being your true self. Know where you're thinking from. Build trust by eliminating thinking about yourself and thinking from the heart with feelings of kindness, empathy, and giving. Think from the mind with creativity to solve problems and help others. Thinking from the heart is fundamental for trust. It's healthy and feels great.

Chapter 2

Exploring the Five Locations for Thinking and Feeling

"The heart is the compass of the soul."

— *Rumi*

You wake up tired and miserable from working all night preparing for an annoying team growth meeting. You're forced to go to the office, and a car cuts you off triggering an angry shout out the window at the driver. Your lunch plans with a friend fall through causing a grumbling response to yourself. That night you're doing tasks that could have easily been completed at the office, but coworkers and outdated office policies kept you from finishing your work. You're too tired to do any work at home so you find yourself looking at video clips for hours. You go to sleep upset about yourself, but the next day, you repeat the same stressful day.

You are in charge of your life. Stress is a self-generated bad health habit. The bad habit is thinking from your primitive brain region. Stop the habit, and your life will be free of stress and anger. Functional MRI research changed my way of thinking about the brain forever. There's not only the head to think from, but you can think from the heart, gut, body, and the mind. Use them. They're for thinking like a human. They're for being your true authentic self.

The head is social judgment. The heart is kindness. The gut is risk management. The body is strength. The mind is creative. Let's explore the function and feelings of these five locations. My friend from Australia suggested thinking of them as five brains.

* * *

Head. The head has positive and negative functions. The feelings from the head include anger, stress, and chemical pleasure.

The brain hippocampus is for short-term and long-term memory. The advanced prefrontal lobe is for social judgment and making the right choices in society and also for connecting with the mind. The head primitive amygdala and cingulate brain regions provide instant life-saving response to dangerous and life-threatening situations. None of these require thinking. They're either instinctive or learned conditioned responses.

Let's talk about the negative functions of the head brain. You need to avoid thinking from three negative brain regions because these three regions cause anger, stress, and addiction. The anger center is triggered when something has been taken from you such as your enjoyment, your confidence, or your values. The stress center is triggered when you're thinking about yourself in a negative way such as thinking about your problems, comparing yourself to others, or thinking about the negative past or future. The addiction pleasure center is triggered by drugs, alcohol, sugar, and self-centered narcissistic behavior.

Thinking from these regions is unhealthy for you and others, and takes you away from enjoying life.

Traditionally, the brain has been considered the center of creative thinking and happy feelings. New functional MRI technology has turned this notion upside down. The brain consists of primitive reptilian regions that are for instinctive reactions to danger, but thinking from these regions causes anger and stress. The head is selfish and self-centered. Thinking from these primitive brain regions will make your life miserable, and you'll be unhappy. You'll never achieve the satisfaction of a fulfilled life. You'll never live a healthy life.

Why would anyone think this way? The human brain starts out as a pod of cells and evolves into the primitive brain which is useful as an infant for nutrition and a diaper change. The brain continues to develop enabling individuals to be independent and eventually, the prefrontal lobe becomes fully developed by age 25 propelling people into interdependent, productive adults making positive contributions to society.

The instinctive life-saving response from the primitive brain remains active and intact for a lifetime. However, thinking from this reptilian brain needs to be left behind after infancy because thinking with anger, stress, and additive pleasure is not needed for living an enjoyable fulfilling life. This brain region doesn't require sleep and thrives on junk food. If you let it happen, this primitive brain region with anger, stress, and addiction will take over your life.

What ae the negative emotions and feelings from these negative head brain regions? Thinking from the head anger center makes people angry that may worsen to rage and destruction. Thinking from the head stress center makes people complain, criticize, blame, and feel sorry for themselves. They feel guilt, resentment, and jealousy. They can be narcissistic and manipulative. In the extreme, they'll do anything to anybody or organization to get what they want, and they have no remorse or kind feelings toward other people.

This negative thinking may begin during childhood by throwing a temper tantrum to get a toy. This leads to lying and manipulation as adults to get what they want. They learn to get what they want through this taking behavior. It's bullying. They don't care about the pain for other people and how harmful it is to themselves and others. This behavior causes stress, which is a natural warning to educate and convince people to stop this unhealthy and harmful behavior. However, people don't make this connection and keep thinking this way causing stress, not realizing all they must do is stop self-centered thinking and stress goes away.

Self-serving thoughts cause stress, and if you're stressed, then you're thinking about yourself.

This is what happens when you interact with individuals whose life is dominated by primitive brain thinking. At first, you don't feel anything, but the stressful feeling is registered at the subconscious level. As the conversation escalates to anger and stress, you begin to feel stress, you're uncomfortable. It's a bad feeling in the stomach. You want to back away. These people purposely make you feel bad about yourself because this makes them feel good. This triggers the addiction pleasure center and gives them four seconds of pleasure.

The conversation increases with complaining, criticism, and blame. These unhealthy feelings you're experiencing intensify. You start to defend yourself. Your heart rate and blood pressure increase. Your muscles tighten. This can happen with a family member, a boss, or a coworker. In rare situations, the conversation can escalate to the extreme with accusations and rage causing physical pain, exhaustion, giving up, and the feeling of losing interest in enjoying life. You need to recognize this extreme as soon as possible and seek a solution before serious physical injury.

> *"The pleasure from kindness and giving from the heart lasts a lifetime."*

Unfortunately, these individuals don't want to change because taking behavior feels good to them, and they get what they want. Changing to healthy behavior requires them to give up their rewarding behavior. It's too big of a loss for them. It's easier to continue using this taking behavior. It's a habit. Any challenge to this taking behavior results in anger, and they'll shut you down. They don't want to lose the pleasure they obtain from this behavior. Remember, this is chemical pleasure from the brain addiction center, toxic and short-lived lasting four seconds. They need to learn that the pleasure felt thinking from the heart with kindness is so much better than pleasure from the head and kindness from the heart lasts a lifetime.

Almost everyone has head-thinking behavior during their lives especially without enough sleep or feeling ill, but it's mild and transient. For example, how do you feel if you've only had a couple of hours of sleep? In addition to feeling tired and groggy, you don't have the brain energy to be patient with people. You only have enough energy to think about yourself, so people and trivial things irritate you. This is primitive, non-human thinking. Fortunately, eight hours of sleep and recovery from the illness will reverse this negative thinking.

Let's talk about eliminating anger and stress. Anger comes from the primitive amygdala anger region. Stress come from the primitive cingulate stress region. Angry or stressed? You're thinking from the non-human primitive brain. Learn to stop thinking from these two regions by stopping anger and stress triggers.

Prolonged anger and stress are unhealthy. They cause the adrenalin cortisol response which increases blood pressure, shuts down the digestive and immune systems, and causes inflammation which results in heart disease, strokes, cancer, and a shortened life.

Anger is a natural response to something that's taken from you. One way to limit your time in the anger center is to feel the anger, let it peak in six to eight seconds, and move on. Feel the anger, don't think. Don't think the second thought about the cause. Don't build a story. Feel the anger, let it pass.

Do the same thing with stress. You're in a stressful situation, feel the stress, let it peak, and move on to thinking from somewhere else.

Why do anger and stress stop after six to eight seconds from no thinking? The anger response is triggered by a potential threat, and if there is no thinking about a threat, then there is no threat which in turn activates the parasympathetic calming system and neutralizes the response restoring calm. Thinking about yourself initiates the stress response; therefore, stop thinking about yourself and calm will be restored by neutralizing the stress response by the calming system.

You need to stop thinking from the anger and stress centers because you can't think from the heart with kindness or forgiveness. You can only think from one location at a time. You can't be stressed and think from the mind with creativity to solve problems and help others.

The primitive amygdala and cingulate brain regions are always scanning the environment for threats and categorizes them as pleasant, neutral, or unpleasant. This is automatic at the subconscious level, and you're not aware of it. These unpleasant thoughts are going to come into your head throughout the day. Studies have shown that in some people up to 80 percent of these random thoughts coming into your brain are negative. Do not react to these thoughts.

Do not give these unpleasant negative responses a second thought. This second thought will lead to a story, and the story will have a bad ending. You will be stressed during this whole time as you're thinking about yourself from the stress center. The second thought can be eliminating by saying "love and peace" to yourself instantly or feel the negative thought, let it peak in six to eight seconds, and move on. You can use a yoga breathing technique, go for a 12-minute walk, or drink water.

You can confirm the feeling of zero stress with the cold shower technique. After your typical warm shower, turn the dial all the way down to just before the water turns off. This will be cold, so cold, it'll take your breath away. This only requires a few seconds. After you recover from this built-in cold-face reflex, how do you feel? You have no problems. You feel like you can deal with anything that comes your way. This is zero stress.

You now know how to manage anger and stress so it's not harmful; however, this is not enough. You need to eliminate anger and stress. After you've learned to limit the anger and stress to less than ten seconds, now learn to eliminate the triggers. Recognize the trigger and stop it from activating the anger and stress centers. Instantly think or do something positive.

For example, you get mad at the computer because it is too slow or crashes during a Zoom call or loses your report. This ignites the amygdala anger center causing the anger response by yelling at the computer. You know this behavior is not necessary. It's a waste of energy and time, and you might break the computer. So, stop the trigger from activating the anger center, and you'll eliminate anger.

When anger trigger happens, recognize, and instantly think from somewhere else, preferably, a positive event such as thinking from the heart with kindness or thinking from the mind with fixing the problem. Say "stop the trigger" over and over for a few times and then "love and peace" for 30 seconds. Look at a positive image or listen to positive music, play a positive game, talk to a friend, or take a 12-minute walk.

Better yet, explore your own method. Something that will not activate the primitive brain region.

Use the positive conditioning technique. Repeat this sequence with every anger trigger every day for three weeks. Here's what's going to happen. Nothing the first day, second day, or the third day. During the next few days, you might notice you don't react with one of the minor triggers. During the second week, you will not react to more of them, and after 21 days, you will not response to any anger triggers. You will live a life with no anger. This is an extraordinary feeling.

Do the same thing with stress. This is going to be more difficult than anger because we've thought about ourselves forever and the primitive stress region is large. Recognize when you're stressed. Instantly change thinking about something positive.

Here's a final consideration, live in the mind at a slightly lower brainwave frequency, and you won't be able to think from the primitive brain with thoughts of anger or stress. Thinking from the primitive brain requires a higher brain frequency at 14 cycles per second. Live in the mind, and there are no negative thoughts from the primitive brain.

> *Imagine a world where there is no anger and no stress from the primitive brain region. It's a new human civilization with thinking from the heart with kindness and thinking from the mind with creativity for solving problems to help people, innovation to improve people's lives, and inspiration to make the world a better place.*

Let's talk about the positive functions of the head brain. The primitive amygdala and cingulate brain regions will save your life in a life-threatening situation by instinct. You're unaware of this because the actions are instant, and so fast they don't register in your conscious thinking. This sets you up in the safest position in a severe car accident. This moves you an inch away from a falling tree or an inch from an unmarked hole in the street or sidewalk. These two primitive brain regions are good for saving your life.

The hippocampus is a small structure that looked like a hippopotamus to the scientist that named the brain region. Its major function is short-term and long-term memory.

There are two types of short-term memory. The first is at the subconscious level that remembers how to walk, get dressed, and all requirements of daily life. We cannot live without this capability. The second short-term memory has seven slots for remembering current action like people's names, an automobile going by, or the grocery list. These memories last for ten to twenty seconds and then are replaced after seven events by something new. Long-term memory requires memory techniques to move some of these short-term memories into long term.

There is a useful feature of short-term memory with anger and stress. When these two primitive brain regions are triggered, if you feel the anger and stress without thinking for less than ten seconds, the cause of these emotions will be forgotten because not thinking about the cause for a few seconds, the memory of the cause will be replaced and eliminated from seven new events such as new images, new sounds, or new distractions.

Keep the hippocampus memory brain region healthy and functioning at peak performance with a healthy nutrition lifestyle, eight hours of sleep every night, one hour of exercise every day, and daily meditation.

The prefrontal cortex brain region is the human brain. The function is social judgment. This means interacting in society in a socially accepted positive way. For example, a CEO who does an injustice to customers for short-term financial gain is thinking from the self-centered cingulate brain region and not using the prefrontal lobe. Not doing your daily exercise, eating unhealthy food, not returning phone calls, ghosting, not showing up for a meeting, being consistently late, and negative social interaction are all examples of not using the prefrontal lobe.

The major function of the human prefrontal cortex is accessing the mind, which is the universe outside the body. Human beings with their prefrontal cortex are the only species on the planet that can connect with the mind. Remember, slow the brainwaves down to experience the profound knowledge and transformational feelings in the mind.

Eight hours of sleep every night are especially important for a peak function prefrontal cortex because two hours of dream sleep or rapid eye movement (REM) sleep are required every night to recharge tis brain region. These two hours occur at the end of the eight-hour cycle; therefore, there is no functioning prefrontal region with only six hours of sleep. In addition, as with the memory center, the prefrontal lobe region needs to be functioning at peak performance with a healthy nutritional lifestyle, one hour of exercise every day, and daily meditation.

Access the mind. The most important function of the human brain is the ability to access the mind. No other living species can do this. That's what makes humans human!

I'm talking about your brain using the mind. The mind is the space surrounding the body that contains all past, current, and future information and knowledge. The brain can access the mind while in a slow-brainwave state for creativity and innovation, and feelings of calmness, belonging, and bliss.

The brain's ability to access the mind gives us attention, discipline, and persistence. For example, I blew out my knee during a ten-mile training run for a half-marathon in Boston. At mile six, there was a slight pain in my left knee and at mile eight, I had to call my wife, Joan, to drive me home because I couldn't walk. Research showed this was weakening of the quadriceps muscle, specifically the vastus lateralis part of the quad on the left side.

The pain resolved, and I continued my training for another week, but then I awoke with a huge swollen knee, not the size of a grapefruit, but the size of a cantaloupe. Fortunately, there was no bleeding in the knee, but the pain was severe. It was so bad, I felt like I would never run again with Joan. This was a bad feeling. However, the mind, not the selfish and negative brain, can turn this into a positive and better situation.

With the help of the mind, I began what I call a three-week 1000 rep physical therapy program. Every morning for 45 minutes, I did ten left knee exercises with 100 repetitions each for a total of one-thousand reps. This was painful and extremely difficult for the first few days, but soon the pain disappeared, and the sessions became easier. Within two weeks, I could walk without pain or knee weakness, and began my running workout with a one-mile walk.

The reason I tell this story is to show the brain can access the mind for life-changing solutions. The selfish and negative brain cannot do this. It's the mind that gives you attention, self-discipline, and persistence. Attention from the mind is required to think from the quadriceps muscle and the gluteus muscle while doing the exercises for creating a healthy knee. Discipline from the mind is needed to have the determination to do exercises every morning regardless of the situation and how you're feeling. Persistence from the mind is needed to do the 100 reps for each of the ten exercises.

This applies to all aspects of your life. Use the mind for attention, discipline, and persistence for success.

The placebo nocebo effect. Recent scientific research has produced new insights into placebos and nocebos. The London journalist Jo Marchant has summarized these findings in her excellent presentation through *Wondrium*. The most important new findings are related to the positive effects of the placebos and the powerfully negative effects of nocebos.

The term 'placebo' is now a commonly used word and means using a treatment with no active biological medical substance to improve symptoms. This is often thought of as a sugar pill.

In the past, placebos were used in double-blind studies for testing new pharmaceutical drugs for effectiveness. The newly tested drug must be more effective than the placebo. However, in some of these drug trial studies, doctors realized the placebo itself was 25 percent to 35 percent effective which was often more effective than the drug being tested and in some situations more effective than conventional medications that had been used for many years.

As a result, doctors and scientists are now studying the use of the placebo effect as a treatment or as an adjacent treatment along with conventional medications to reduce the dose and adverse reactions. Studies show placebos can induce the same chemical reaction in the brain as conventional medications. These substances include endorphins, dopamine, and prostaglandins.

Further studies show it's not only the pill that produces the placebo effect, it's the ritual associated with the placebo. For example, using a green drink mixture that tastes like peaches or taking the placebo at specific times during the day, and showing a caring feeling or using positive words.

A group of individuals were told there will be a slight pain with a needle injection and another group told the injection will strengthen the arm. Individuals in the first group felt the slight pain, which is the nocebo effect, and none of individuals in the second group felt pain, which is the placebo effect.

These studies show that being kind, paying attention, and having a loving hand can increase treatment effectiveness. These are all feelings from the heart and from the mind, and not from the head. A healing environment, wearables, or virtual reality (VR) can have a profound impact on managing and healing disease.

The term 'nocebo' is less well known and shows the negative effects the brain can have on the body. Nocebo is the opposite of placebo. Nocebo is the negative outcome of someone who believes something will harm them. If you're told there will be a slight pain with an injection, you will feel pain.

This negative effect can be powerful and even life-threatening if not detected and eliminated. For example, the story of a man whose father died at age 51 on a certain date, and the man dying at the same age on the same date may or may not be true, but you may be aware of a similar situation. You may have friends or family members who are constantly talking about their illness or injury to anyone who will listen, and the symptoms worsen over time leading to more diagnostic testing and potentially life-threatening medical or surgical treatments.

There's an experiment of putting a fake hand on the table and having the subject put the real hand under the table. The fake hand is probed a few times and soon, the subject reports feeling the sensation of the probe on the fake hand. Then a hammer is brought out, and the fake hand is lightly hit with the hammer resulting in a scream from the subject and disbelief when visualizing the perfectly normal real hand. There are many similar examples of the negative power of the primitive brain on the body.

For a healthy life, do not think from the primitive brain region with negative thoughts. Be your true authentic self and think from the heart with kindness and the mind with creativity to creative successful solutions.

*   *   *

Heart. The function of the heart is to keep itself healthy. The feelings from the heart include kindness, giving, appreciation, gratitude, forgiveness, and empathy.

The heart keeps itself and the body healthy by making decisions that are best for your health and with feelings of kindness, appreciation, gratitude, forgiving, empathy, and giving. There are 40 million neurons in the heart to do this. Your job is to listen to the heart and use the positive feelings from the heart replacing angry and stressful thoughts from the head.

> *"The heart keeps itself healthy by making decisions*
> *that are best for your health."*

You've heard the idiomatic expressions, "What's your heart telling you?" "Follow your heart." "Out of the kindness of your heart." Apply them, they hold a science-based truth with 40 million neurons. The function of the heart is to keep itself healthy. This is through making decisions that are best for your health, so ask. This is through positive feelings of kindness to yourself, appreciation, and gratitude. Feel them. Shift away from negative feelings from the head and embrace feelings from the heart with kindness, empathy, and giving. The heart is kind.

The new way of life is knowing who you are moment by moment. Think from your heart as giving not from your head as taking. Thinking from your heart is giving. The heart expects nothing in return.

Thinking from your heart is good for your job, your coworkers, and the community. You think from the heart with kindness, giving, and empathy. You think from the heart with gratitude, appreciation, and forgiveness. People will trust you because you're being your true authentic self.

You'll know when you meet someone who thinks from the heart. It's calming, enjoyable, and uplifting. It makes you feel grateful and look forward to enjoying the day. It puts a smile on your face. It's healthy. They want to help you in any way they can, and they never expect anything in return.

People who think from their hearts give. They are at the top of the success ladder in life, much above people with taking behavior; however, people who give are also at the bottom of the ladder. Why? Because giving without considering yourself will have unhealthy consequences.

Giving without considering your own situation is the same as the expression, 'being taken advantage of' by people. This is stressful, unhealthy, and makes you feel bad about yourself. You need to be your true self and take the consequences. Takers will take advantage of you. Takers want something from you. They want your time, your enjoyment, or they want you to feel guilty. They only think about themselves, and they have no personal feelings toward you. If you're trying to be kind or trying to help them, they'll turn it around to make you feel bad about yourself. They feel better making you feel bad.

You need to recognize the head-thinking taker to avoid being taken advantage of and landing on the bottom of the success ladder. There are many situations where you're dealing with a taker. For example, they want to talk with you, not for a positive conversation, but so they can complain. You're someone they can complain to, it makes them feel better. They don't want to listen to you.

In the worst situation, the complaining escalates to criticism, and then to blame. You'll be the target for blame. You don't need these negative conversations in your life. They're unhealthy. If you can, avoid these people in your life. If you can't do this, know that you can't change their behavior. You need to recognize when you're in a toxic situation and talk your way out or physically leave.

The taker will be nice to you so you will do favors for them. They're being nice expecting something in return for them. Yet, they never do anything for you, and if they do, they'll expect something big in return. After you do several favors for them, if you refuse because you don't want to or you don't have the time, they'll get angry at you and go into a rage making you feel guilty and bad about yourself.

This negative attack is stressful and unhealthy for you. You need to know when this situation is developing and stop it. Be yourself and take the consequences, which may be additional verbal abuse or threats. They're just words, acknowledge the stress to yourself, let it peak in six to eight seconds, and move on. Continue being yourself, do not do any favors. The head-thinking taker will be angry but will eventually stop asking you for favors and find someone else to intimidate.

Another way to spot a taker is that the taker will never pay for anything. They'll make up some intricate excuses, "You get it this time, I'll get the next one" or "My Venmo has a technical problem." Become aware of the pattern and don't pay every time and limit situations with this person.

There's an expression: "don't let people walk all over you." This is head-thinker behavior. Head-thinkers are the ones who will walk all over you if you let them. They will use you in any way possible to get ahead, sometimes at your expense leaving you in a terrible situation. They have no feelings of remorse about your outcome. For example, your so-called friend, a head-thinker, talks you into lying about something at work. It backfires, the head-thinker comes out unharmed and may even be praised, but you lose your job. Beware of this behavior. Avoid these people.

If you're a heart-thinking giver, what can you do when head-thinkers try to take advantage of you or try to walk all over you? The single best thing you can do is to be your true, authentic self and take the consequences. When head-thinkers realize they can't manipulate you, they'll intimidate, make you feel guilty, and go into a rage to reverse the situation and get you back in their command.

This can be mild, lasting a few minutes or extremely intense lasting for hours. There may be a situation that needs attention through professional help. However, you may be able to manage the mild response by acknowledging the stressful situation to yourself and confirming to yourself that you're a good person, the other person is the problem. Let the stress peak in a few seconds and move on. The head-thinker will find someone else to manipulate.

The best way to deal with toxic head-thinkers is to eliminate all interaction with them because they'll never change, these relationships are unhealthy for you, and sooner or later you'll be hurt.

There are situations where you can't eliminate the interaction. Sometimes, a head-thinker is your family member including parents, children, or siblings. What can you do? In addition to being yourself and limiting the caustic interactions by physically excusing yourself.

You can try the neuro bypass technique by visualizing the person, feeling the pain from stress, and saying "love and peace" to yourself for two minutes once daily for two weeks. If you are successful with this technique, future interactions will result in calmness within you and no stress or anger. Your calmness with no fear may be enough to discontinue the head-thinker taking behavior, as the person will find someone else.

Do you go through the day doing things from the head or the heart? For example, grocery shopping. Thinking from the head means you go by the list, absent-mindedly picking out three apples, four bananas, and three avocados. Thinking from the heart, you realize the food you chose needs to be healthy for yourself and your family, and each item needs to be as high quality as possible. You take the time to select the best individual apples, oranges, or avocados. If the food is not up to high quality, it's not added to the basket.

This applies to many other situations at home and at work. Consider a fast-order cook and an award-winning chef. The cook does the work according to the orders as fast as possible. The chef considers each customer enjoying the food and thinks from the heart with love.

Consider cooking and cleaning dishes at home with the family. If you approach cooking from the head, you'll not like it and dread doing the cooking. You'll be angry and stressed. You'll be complaining and not paying attention so mistakes will be made. This is not only miserable for you, but unfortunately, it's stressful and not enjoyable for everyone else. Think from the heart. You're contributing to the family. You're being kind to the family and helping them. You're grateful for your family. This way there is no stress, no complaining, and food will be enjoyed by all.

Washing dishes? Exact same thing. You think of washing dishes as a messy job that you're forced to do. You complain the whole time, and don't do a good job because you're not paying attention. Pay attention from the mind when you wash dishes, then you're contributing to the family and helping the family.

Taking out the garbage? It's not a forced chore. It's giving and contributing to the family from your heart. Giving from the heart with nothing in return feels good.

Think from the heart with kindness, appreciation, gratitude, and giving. Think from the heart with love and grace.

*   *   *

Gut. The function of the gut is healthy nutrition and risk management. The feelings of the gut include fear and a positive and negative sensation.

Have you ever had a *gut feeling*? That deep knowing that you can feel to your core that communicates valuable information to you. This is the science of our "belly brain," that gut feeling for healthy nutrition and risk management. For a happy life, keep your belly happy.

For many years, scientists have known the digestive system is filled with a massive amount of nerve tissue, which is needed for the millions of complex metabolic activities required every day for converting foods into energy. This is automatic, at the subconscious level, and we aren't aware of these processes.

New science has shown there are also the same neural cells found in the brain making the gut capable of decision making and having feelings. This explains the expressions, "gut reaction" and "what's your gut telling you?"

I call this the belly brain. The belly brain is the healthy nutrition and risk management center. Since ancient times, its primal purpose has been to stop you from eating poisonous food or drinking poisonous fluids.

For example, when you look at unhealthy fatty or sugary food, your belly brain will send you a loud message not to eat it by creating an unpleasant sensation in your stomach. You don't hear words. You feel the answer. Pay attention, the belly brain knows unhealthy foods. The belly brain also knows how much you should eat in one sitting. Don't let the head brain talk you into eating unhealthy food and too much food.

The belly brain goes beyond knowing nutrition. The belly brain tells you about risk of a dangerous action you're considering and will send you a message not to do it. It's a discomforting feeling in the belly. Pay attention. On the positive side, the belly brain will tell you that a potential action will improve your life such as taking on responsibility for a positive undertaking. Do it, it will be the right thing to do.

Go with the "gut feeling." Sometimes it's the best. The American and British intelligence community talks about electronic and AI signal gathering will eventually replace the need for humans. Many people disagree saying that robotic thinking will not replace the need for humans because of intuition. There's a saying among the intelligence community, "If your head says something different from your gut, go with your gut."

In addition to the feeling from the stomach telling you not to eat unhealthy food, there's another major feeling the belly brain communicates. You know it well. It's fear. Think about it, how do you feel when you're suddenly frightened or scared? It's an uneasy feeling and tightness in the stomach, not the head. It's the belly brain. The belly brain is sending you a message to be aware.

You can neutralize this feeling instantly by taking three belly breaths to calm the situation. You have a stressful presentation, a meeting with the boss or a job interview, and you're nervous. Take three belly breaths. Place your hand on your stomach, breathe in moving your hand up and out. This will calm you. This is from an inborn reflex. This opposite motion of the abdominal muscles triggers the parasympathetic calming response.

Another way to eliminate acute fear is to feel it, feel the sensation in your stomach, feel it, let it peak in six to eight seconds, and it will disappear. Then start thinking from the mind for a solution and a next step.

If you're constantly nervous and filled with fear, then your belly is always going to be tense and upset, which is unhealthy. Manage this by managing the episodes of acute fear that develop with belly breaths. If the feeling of fear is constant, then this feeling may be triggered by the stress center thinking about your problems or negative thoughts about the future. Be your true self by thinking from the heart with kindness to yourself and others, and from the mind for creative solutions to problems. A happy belly makes a happy life.

Learn the function of the belly brain. Learn the feelings from the belly brain. The belly brain will tell you healthy food choices and tell you the risk or benefit of an action you're considering. The belly brain will protect you.

* * *

Body. The function of the body is strength. The feelings from the muscles and joints include the good feeling from exercising and the tired feeling from a sufficient amount of exercise. Think from your body for healthy muscles, joints, and organ systems.

The body provides you with the ability to enjoy positive experiences and accomplishments. The body protects your heart, lungs, and other vital organs. The muscles need to be lean and toned for optimal healthy performance.

Muscles contain proprioception neurons signaling the body to maintain balance. This is at the subconscious level so you're not aware of its actions. The ability to maintain optimal proprioception and balance decreases each decade of age and can become limited. The feeling associated with proprioception is imbalance, especially going downstairs in the middle of the night. Too many times, you read headlines about someone falling down the stairs causing an irreversible severe head injury. This can be prevented by adding balancing exercises (standing on one leg) to your daily exercise routine, especially after age 60.

The positive feeling from working the muscles is the release of feel-good neurotransmitters and hormones including endorphin which can be felt with prolonger muscle exertion. An important part of exercise is to use the mind to visualize the specific muscle you're working on as you do the repetitions. This helps strengthen the muscle and helps prevent injury during the exercise.

The opposite of feeling good from the muscles is muscle fatigue from reaching enough muscle stress. Surprisingly, with over-the-top intense muscle exertion as in a televised athletic competition, the brain will overrule the body and shut the body down by passing out sending the person to the hospital before irreversible damage occurs.

For athletic competition, using the body and the mind (not the brain) connection will result in Olympic gold medal winners and football or baseball champions. Use the body-mind connection for weekend athletes, senior athletes, and working out in the gym every day. Eliminate all self-centered thoughts from the selfish head, and keep the cell phone in the locker.

The best quarterback in football wins important games like the playoffs and the Super Bowl. The winning quarterback uses the mind and reviews the opponents video plays so often that the quarterback can visualize where all the opposing players are going to be at the time of throwing the pass. If the linebacker is going to intercept the pass, the ball is not thrown to the receiver who appears to be open. There is not a single thought from the head. The is the same situation for the winning pitchers in the World Series and players in the World Cup.

Think from the body while exercising for energy. Think from the body and the mind for successful athletic performance.

*   *   *

Mind. Your mind is not your brain. The function of the mind is creativity and innovation. The feelings from the mind include total calmness, universal belonging and acceptance, and joyful bliss.

The mind is outside the brain with unlimited knowledge and information containing everything about the past, present, and future. You need to slow down the brainwaves to access the mind.

> *"The head is selfish. The heart is kind. The mind is inspirational."*

How do you know the mind is outside the body? Consider this. Think about when you solved your most recent complex problem. In the past, you would likely tap your head and think the process is going on in your head. However, with your knowledge of the Eplerian Life Philosophy, give it further thought, and you'll realize the answers come from outside your head. The brain has limited information for solving complex problems.

In the context of the Eplerian Life Philosophy, the brain and the mind are separate and distinct.

The brain is the physical organ system in the head that has several independent brain regions with anger, stress, and chemical addictive pleasures. This primitive brain region operates at the beta-brainwave frequency at fourteen cycles per second.

The mind is outside the body, and the mind contains all universal past, present, and future information and knowledge. Access to the mind requires slower brainwave states such as alpha brainwaves at ten cycles per second and theta brainwaves at seven cycles per second. It may be possible to connect with the mind in the slow delta brainwaves at four cycles per second.

Our brain is limited to 86 billion neurons, which is sufficient to navigate through life, solve minor problems, and advance the community in small ways.

The mind is limitless providing answers to massive problems and ideas for innovative products and services that are used by billions of people throughout the world.

Consider where you're thinking from when you're being creative or brainstorming, or when you're trying to solve a problem, or you're developing a new product or a new company. Where are you thinking from? Try it now.

Are you thinking from your head? Maybe to some extent, but it's from more than your head. It also feels like you're thinking from the heart, the gut, or the body. Ultimately, it feels like you're thinking from outside the body, and that's the answer. The mind is outside the body.

Use the mind for creativity to solve problems and help others, and innovation to improve people's lives. Experience the feelings from the mind with total calmness, acceptance, and unconditional love and joy.

You've returned to your home after a two-week vacation and find one-inch of water covering your carpeted basement from a broken rusted-out water heater. Your immediate response is anger, your pleasure has been ripped away from you. This is anger from the primitive brain.

Instead of having anger for hours, feel the anger, let it peak in six to eight seconds, and begin to think about solving the problem. Better yet, don't let the episode trigger the anger center.

Your second thought is stress from thinking about how you're going to pay thousands of dollars for a new hot water heater and replacing the carpet plus everything else that was destroyed by the water leak.

Instead of stress for days and weeks and telling everyone about the problem, feel the stress, let it peak in six to eight seconds, and begin to think from the mind about the next step. Next time, don't think about all the problems so you don't trigger the stress center.

With no anger and no stress, you think from the mind by doing the research for hot-water heater companies. You call your homeowner's insurance company. You find the most convenient and reasonably priced company and have the new hot-water heater installed.

During the week it takes to dry the carpet and complete the work, you've had zero-level stress. You've enjoyed your life completely forgetting about the problem. You don't talk about it. You don't complain. You don't blame. You have no thoughts from the anger center or the stress center.

What happens if you don't stop the anger and stress?

First, you would be telling everyone you talk to about the terrible home catastrophe explaining the hot water tank in detail and exaggerating the damage. You would also say this horrible event ruined your whole vacation.

You would repeat the story incessantly for weeks, each time triggering the anger center and stress center to the point of driving away your friends and coworkers. This causes increased blood pressure, increased weight because of inefficient digestion from stress, shuts down the immune system and causes inflammation from the cortisol release.

Second, you wouldn't be able to think about solving the problem because you can only think from one location at a time. If you're angry and stressed, you can't think about the best solution and pay twice as much for a faulty new water heater.

Because of the anger, you would be yelling at the people trying to help and blaming them for the problem, which continues to trigger your anger center.

You would be continually frustrated and angry about having to call so many people, waiting on the phone, and being impatient about the usual delays and issues that develop.

Third, if you're continually complaining about the old water heater, ruining your vacation, and causing thousands of dollars in damages, then you wouldn't be able to think from your heart with kindness toward others and giving. You wouldn't be kind to yourself with self-compassion.

If you complain, criticize and blame, then you have no access to the mind to learn something new, clean the basement, and turn the situation into a positive outcome. Thinking from the mind requires eliminating thoughts from the anger center and stress center. Thinking from the mind allows you to solve day-to-day problems.

Imagine you're at work, and you've discovered a new product or service. What's the next step? Your head brain can't give you the answer, it's too limited.

This is a complex issue requiring researching the advantages and disadvantages of an almost infinite number of options. Many options will lead to failure while choosing the right path can lead to a massive success for you and the company.

After you've gathered as much knowledge as you can from reading and analyzing other people's work, then you need to think from the mind for weighing the options and choosing the right path.

How to think from the mind? Learn to be in a slow-brainwave state at will. One way to do this is through traditional eye-closed meditation or eyes-open meditation while walking, hiking, or working out on a treadmill or an elliptical. You can do this by visualizing yourself on a mountain walk or at the beach counting down from 25 wooden stairs to the meadow or the water's edge.

Now that you're in the slow wave state, let the mind provide the answer based on your research and asking the right questions. It's like the online AI programs, asking the right question is fundamental for success. Asking the wrong question will lead to no answer or worse, to a poor solution.

Take time to ask the right question and try several options. Do you have a new product? What are the next step options? Talk with the CEO? Talk to the executive committee? Find a partner? Write a business plan? Leave the company and develop a startup? Asking the right question will provide an instant answer for the next step. Then complete the next step before returning to the mind for the next phase.

In addition to finding creative solutions and innovative ideas, explore the mind for feelings. The positive feelings from the mind are described in thousands of reports of near-death experiences including a book, *Proof of Heaven* written by the neurosurgeon, Dr. Eben Alexander.

The reason people experience these feelings is they're not in the fast beta-brainwave waking state at 14 cycles per second. They're in the slow brainwave state such as alpha at ten cycles per second, theta at seven cycles per second, or even the slow delta at four cycles per second.

These feelings include the absence of the body, serenity, security, harmony, and warmth. Others include peace, extreme well-being, and no sensation of pain. You can also experience intense feelings of acceptance, unconditional love, and incredible joy.

These feelings can be experienced through psychedelic drugs such as psilocybin in mushrooms. These have been popularized on social media, podcasts, TV shows, and movies. They are being used in medical and scientific research to further the understanding of the mind. These agents can be extremely dangerous and hazardous in poorly controlled situations.

The feelings and visualizations from the mind can be experienced without any external substance by slowing down the brainwaves and meditation. Buddhist monks have been doing this for thousands of years.

Guided visualized meditation is one way to experience these feelings from the mind.

For example, visualize yourself traveling on the outside of a rocket ship going toward space. You're hanging on going slowly and gently at first, then you speed up, going faster and faster. It's so fast that you soon find yourself only in your mind with no arms, body, or legs.

This is a pleasant sensation going from being connected to your local physical environment to a limitless connection. As you continue to fly and becoming the universe, you pass through two tall pillar guards. You've arrived. You're in the mind. Everything stops. Experience the total calmness and serenity. While you're there, you can search for answers to questions you may have.

Some of these journeys may lead to intense negative feelings. You might sense the question of why you exist or what good are you? If this happens, you might learn something such as humility. You can stop the experience by counting down 5, 4, 3, 2, 1 back to the normal beta brainwave state.

In addition to calmness, you can experience the feeling of total acceptance and unconditional love, which means that you're accepted for who you are with no criticism and no judgment.

Feelings from the mind. The feelings and visualizations from the mind have been described in stories, myths, and legends for thousands of years. New medical technology and methods have been developed for confirming these descriptions and discovering new feelings.

Calmness is one of these feelings. When you're in the mind, calm your joints and muscles, then calm your cells and then the nucleus. Calm the DNA, this is total calmness and quiet, and it feels great.

The second feeling while in the mind is the feeling of total acceptance and belonging with no judgment or criticism. In the beta state, you are always being criticized and judged with everything you do, which is stressful giving you an unpleasant feeling. Not so in the mind, you are totally accepted with no judgment, and it feels good.

The third feeling is unconditional love and joy beyond daily living. It's a continual feeling of being loved and the feeling of bliss.

Courage is another feeling of the mind. For example, it takes courage to be your true authentic self because you need to accept the consequences unequivocally. Most consequences are good because you will have positive accomplishments and improve people's lives. On some occasions, you may be criticized, judged unfairly, or rejected. Having the courage to be your true self gives you an extraordinary life.

The feeling of awe comes from the mind. Awe is experiencing some massive outside yourself like a 300-foot 1000-year-old red wood tree, a raging lightning storm, and the reds, oranges, and yellow trees during a walk in the fall. This feeling balances the brain connections by eliminating isolated regions of stress, improves the hippocampus memory and prefrontal lobe judgment regions, and induces the parasympathetic calming system.

Inspiration comes from the mind in contrast to motivation which comes from the head. The feeling of success and accomplishment comes from the mind.

Attention, discipline, and persistence come from the mind. Pay attention for enjoying the task. Use discipline to do what you need to do regardless of the situation or how you feel. Use persistence to keep doing something now that will show a positive result way into the future.

The mind is outside the body, so you need to slow the brainwaves. Here's another self-visualization guided meditation for being in the slow-brainwave state. Look at the tops of your hands and think about the individual cells. Then visualize the cell nucleus and go smaller to the molecules making up the nucleus.

Visualize the amount of space between molecules and then the massive amount of space between the nucleus of the atom and the cloud of electrons. Position yourself between them and feel the energy.

Breathe in the powerful energy between the center of the atom and the electrons swirling at near the speed of light. Feel the energy. You're in the slow alpha-brainwave state. If you wish to go deeper, you can visualize the huge empty space and massive energy of the subatomic particles like the photons and gluons, and the even more powerful energy of the open strings in the subquantum universe that can move planets.

Another visualization is the opposite of going smaller. Visualize yourself as an eagle flying above your town, then flying above your state and the earth, then above the solar system, above the milky way and to the edge of the expanding universe. Put yourself between the milky way and the edge of the universe. Sit in a comfortable chair and feel the speed flying in your hair. This speeds up your life accomplishments.

In the mind, you can also have the feeling of being safe. No one is going to hurt you. No one is going to threaten you.

The mind is a wonderful world to live in. In the past, I thought you had too leave this world of the mind by counting down 5, 4, 3, 2, 1 back to reality; or sit in silence meditating or live in a cave as a hermit, but I was wrong. You can live in the mind with high energy, creativity, and experience all these wonderful feelings all day. You can be in the middle of a roaring city, a quiet suburb, or living on a farm and feel the profound knowledge and joy of being in the mind.

If you're feeling low, you can't stop thinking about your problems, or you're feeling sorry for yourself, then experiencing calmness, safety, and belonging will eliminate these negative feelings. The problems will lose their strength. Negative concerns about other people will disappear. The future will appear positive and enjoyable.

Here's a final example of showing the difference between the brain and the mind. Take two people sitting in a chair. In one chair is someone who had a bad day, criticized, blamed, and yelled at all day. This person is complaining over and over about the horrific events of the day. This person sees everything as a problem, criticizes anyone near, and blames everyone for the terrible life. This person may take pills to feel better.

You're in the other chair. You've had the same bad day being criticized and yelled at. People have made you feel bad about yourself. However, you've learned to not let these events trigger the anger center or the stress center. You're free to enjoy the day and positive events and use the mind to solve problems and help others.

In addition, you experience the feelings of total calmness, security, and unconditional love. You have everything you need. You have the courage to be your true self. You have no need to complain, criticize, or blame. You enjoy who you are. You don't need to change anything. You don't need to be anyone else.

Time passes and you look at the person in the other chair. Lifeless with a blank look on the face with head down and slumped shoulders, and not engaged in this phenomenal life.

How are you? You're filled with high energy, feeling good, and enjoying life every moment of the day!

The next time you see a group of people, realize that most will be like that other person in the chair. There will be one person who knows who they are moment by moment, and that person is extraordinary. That person is you.

Chapter 3

Feelings

"Our feelings are our most authentic form of communication."

— Brené Brown

Everyone has had a broken heart. Feelings from the heart are real. Feelings of kindness, appreciation, gratitude, and love make you feel good and other people too. The feeling from an emotionally broken heart is real too. It's sadness which means you've lost someone or something you love, and love comes from the heart. Over time, the loss and sadness will always be replaced with love for an open heart once again.

In a world where chaos and negativity dominate our daily lives, there is a simple truth that can transform everything: "Know who you are moment by moment." These seven words hold the key to living a life of authenticity, kindness, and love.

Have you recently found yourself on the receiving end of an unexpected harsh word or scathing comment? A family member, friend, coworker, or the media have lashed out leaving you feeling bad about yourself. It's in these moments of anguish that you have a choice that can profoundly shape your life and the lives of people around you.

The first choice is anger. This is a natural response deep within our primitive brain region caused by having something cruelly taken from us such as our values, opinions, or our enjoyment. However, holding onto this anger for more than a fleeting moment can have destructive unhealthy effects. Research shows that prolonged anger triggers the adrenalin cortisol response that increases blood pressure and causes inflammation and heart disease. Unchecked anger can cause irreversible harm to others. History is filled with global leaders whose uncontrolled anger has destroyed the lives of millions of people.

The second choice is believing the malicious words hurled at you. It's internalizing the hurtful words and allowing them to define you. When someone labels you as a bad person because of who you are, remember these words have no meaning to you. But these hurtful words can be so overpowering that some people believe them leading to a negative spiral of self-doubt. This can have catastrophic consequences leading to tragic stories of school bullying claiming the lives of innocent children.

The malicious use of social media can threaten people and society. Egocentric world leaders can set up thousands of fake social media accounts where trained users deliberately craft messages to make people feel bad about themselves and guilty for fabricated past actions. This form of disinformation and propaganda is hidden and ignored for many years. However, community leaders may eventually soften and cooperate into believing this manipulation, which makes them feel so guilty, they unknowingly divert funds away from keeping the community clean and safe sending the city into an abyss.

The third choice is to be your true authentic self, the healthy and sustainable response. Being your authentic self will instantly stop destructive response to disinformation. When you live as your authentic self, you cannot be shamed or manipulated by those who use social media to control you. Cyberbullying can be stopped by being your authentic self and resisting manipulation.

Be your true authentic self, regardless of the situation. Stand tall with your chin straight, eyes forward, and palms out and receptive. Being your authentic self means accepting the consequences that come with it. In almost all situations, the rewards far outweigh any transient discomfort. While there is going to be verbal abuse, especially from self-centered individuals, you must recognize these are shallow words with no meaning to you.

Becoming your authentic self frees you from pleasing people and the exhausting pursuit of trying to be someone you're not. By embracing your true self, you eliminate the need to complain, criticize, or blame. Trust is a major benefit of being your authentic self. People know who you are and want to be with you.

The next time someone hurls their anger or negativity your way, remember to deal with it for six to eight seconds. Then, let your true self emerge and shift your focus to thinking from your heart with kindness and giving. This begins the transformative journey of being your true authentic self that leads to a life filled with genuine connections and profound joy.

Why do some people live their lives filled with stress and negative feelings, while others live a positive invigorating life filled with high energy and enjoyment?

New brain science studies are providing the answers. People think from distinct brain regions, and they can only think from one location at a time. These brain regions are associated with specific functions and, most importantly, *feelings*.

Emotions and feelings from three brain regions have a profound influence on our life every moment of the day. The first is being angry. Where does this feeling come from? It's from the head brain region called the amygdala anger center.

The second is stress. It's from the head too and called the cingulate stress center. Whenever you're thinking about yourself, you're thinking from the stress center. Whenever you're stressed, you're thinking about yourself.

The third feeling is pleasure, which is from the accumbens addiction center. This feeling is dopamine chemical pleasure. It's from drugs, alcohol, sugar, and other addicting substances. It's toxic, short-lived, and followed by a crash.

Everyone at one time or another experiences the feelings of anger or stress from these head regions. You may say that you don't get angry that much or you may think your stress levels are low, but any amount of prolonged anger or stress can have devastating adverse health effects such as cortisol-induced inflammation and heart disease. If these locations don't seem like a good place to think from, you're right. They're not. Everyone experiences these feelings, and you're going to find and learn a new path.

Research shows that you can only think from one location at a time, so if you're thinking from the anger and stress centers, then you can't think from the heart with kindness. Constant and prolonged thinking from the anger center and self-centered stress center causes the adrenalin cortisol response resulting in inflammation, heart disease, stroke, cancer, and a shortened life.

How do you learn to limit your thinking from these regions? That's where the heart comes in. Thinking from the anger center and stress center is a natural response of the primitive crocodile brain and is not harmful if limited to six to eight seconds. You do this by feeling the anger and stress, letting these feelings peak, and releasing them. Then think from another location. Think from the heart with kindness and giving.

Science has shown the heart has neuro tissue capable of feelings and decision-making. The heart has forty million neurons that are like neurons in the brain. This explains why people have been saying things for thousands of years like *Listen to your heart* or *What does your heart say?* There are, in fact, enough neurons in your heart to have feelings of kindness and giving, and to make decisions that are good for your health.

The function of the heart is to keep itself healthy. The heart does this with positive feelings and making healthy decisions. The feelings include kindness, empathy, and giving. Other feelings include happiness, gratitude, appreciation, and forgiving. These feelings keep the heart healthy and other people healthy too because these feelings can be transmitted outside the body.

Being nice is good, but in some situations, being nice may come from the head, and people may subconsciously think they'll get something in return, a thank you, a gift, or a returned favor. This is usually not true for being kind, because kindness comes from the heart with expecting nothing in return. This feels good for a long time. You don't have to say the word. Feelings from your Heart are transmitted outside the body and can be felt by other people without saying the word.

Empathy comes from the heart. This means feeling what the other person is experiencing. It's putting yourself in the other person's situation. This is a feeling from the heart. For example, a spouse, friend, or co-worker may want someone to listen to them and their feelings without asking questions or offering solutions. Following this request with empathy means listening to the words and feelings without interrupting by asking questions. It means listening without absorbing the negative feelings or trying to help.

Trying to sell something? Use empathy. Before talking about what you're selling, listen to the other person's situation, problems, and needs with empathy. Sometimes they don't want a solution – they want to be heard. They want someone to listen to them. Be patient, think from the other person's perspective. Listening to the person with empathy gives you a good feeling and the other person too.

Empathy can also be used to prevent triggering the anger center. If someone yells at you, don't automatically trigger the anger center, consider the other person's situation, and feel empathy from the heart. You may not respond with anger.

The positive feeling from giving with expecting nothing in return comes from the heart. I developed the Eplerian Life Philosophy which involves shifting thinking from the head to thinking from the heart with kindness and thinking from the mind with creativity to help people understand how thinking from the heart and mind will result in living an extraordinary life.

This Eplerian Life Philosophy is for a new healthy way of life. It's *know who you are moment by moment* which means knowing where you're thinking from, and that's who you are.

There are five locations to think from that include the head, heart, gut, body, and the mind, which is outside the body. Furthermore, you can only think from one location at a time. If you are thinking from the head stress center, then you can't think from the heart or the mind. That's why it's important to know where these positive feelings come from.

Each feeling comes from one of these five locations. Anger and stress? Functional MRI brain studies show these are from the head. Fear? It's from the gut. Innovation? It's from the mind.

People experience feelings in their own unique way. So, it's useful to review your feelings and consider where they come from. In general, you will likely find that negative feelings come from the head while positive feelings come from the heart.

Some may come from two separate locations depending on the context. For example, giving expecting something in return is from the head while giving wanting nothing in return comes from the heart. This can be slightly more complicated in that giving and expecting something in return where the other person is not adversely harmed is not a problem. Giving a party so that you can connect with someone who can help you is not an issue as no one is hurt except you if you don't get what you want.

Returning to feelings from your Heart. Giving with expecting nothing in return comes from the heart. It's a good feeling and the feeling can last a lifetime. This is not like giving to get something in return. This comes from the head, from the self-centered stress center and the feeling lasts for a few seconds.

When a person gives expecting something in return, the person knows it, and you do too. You can always tell when someone is being nice to you or giving you something, and they want something in return. That's thinking from the head stress center. Give from the heart, no need to think about receiving something in return. Give your time. Give your energy. Volunteer. It feels good. It's from the heart.

Happiness is from the heart. One definition of happiness is being content with your current situation. It's calmness and acceptance.

Pleasure comes from the accumbens chemical pleasure center in the head. It's from drugs, alcohol, and sugar. It's toxic, short-lived, and followed by a crash of energy. It's from the addiction brain center. The purpose of the accumbens is the intoxicating pleasure from reproducing the species. It's not for toxic pleasure from drugs and alcohol.

The good feeling from being grateful and appreciating people or events comes from the heart. Forgiving comes from the heart. If someone has intentionally harmed you or betrayed you, you can't let go of the anger toward them. Forgive them for your own health.

You can't forgive from the head stress center because you're thinking about yourself with resentment, stress, or even revenge. Forgive someone from the heart with no negative thoughts from the head. This will let the unhealthy memory disappear forever.

The heart can make decisions. The ancient expression of "what is your heart telling you to do" now has scientific confirmation. The heart can make decisions. The heart will make instant decisions for you. Why? Because the function of the heart is to keep itself healthy.

The function of the head is different. The function of the primitive crocodile brain is by instinct to save your life in a life-threatening situation. There is no thinking, it's too slow. So, asking your head to make a life-changing decision will result in endless days and nights reviewing the positives and negatives, and no clear answer. Not so with the heart.

The heart provides a unilateral single answer instantly, and that answer is usually the best for your health. For example, are you considering taking a new job? The head brain will be in a continuous loop of questioning the advantages and disadvantages with no answer, but the heart makes a simple, fast decision that is best for your health.

Looking to continue a new romantic relationship? Listen to your heart. There will be a clear and immediate answer, the one that is best for your health and an enjoyable life.

For close personal relationships, think from the heart. The Harvard Study of Adult Development showed that having two to three close relationships is at the top of the list for living a long and healthy life.

A close relationship is with someone where you can be your true self with no criticism, judgment, or blame. You have each other's back no matter what happens. The successful way to have a close relationship with someone is thinking from the heart, not from the head. Feelings from the head can lead to arguments, resentment, and retaliation, which have no place in a close relationship.

For close personal relationships, think from the heart with kindness and giving. Being kind to each other by giving not taking. Listen to the other person's stories and what's going on in the person's life without interruption or awkward questions that take away the enthusiasm or enjoyment of the conversation. Give your time and your attention. The person who is your close personal relationship needs help, listen with empathy from the heart to fully understand the problem and pay attention to the details of the problem so you can provide meaningful help instead of superficial conversation.

Being grateful and appreciating moments and experiences together comes from the heart. You've had a wonderful day together going on a hike, visiting a new location, or seeing friends, talking about being grateful and being able to appreciate being together to share the enjoyable day.

Consider the following. Say to yourself, "I'm going to be nice to someone today." Now put your hand over your heart and say, "I'm going to be kind to someone today." Saying the word "kind" feels like it comes from the heart, not from the head.

Here's another example: Think about your biggest problem right now. You might start to feel bad, agitated, or upset. Where do your thoughts feel like they're from? It's the head, not your heart. Thinking about your problems feels bad because it's from the cingulate stress center, the crocodile brain.

Now think about doing something kind for someone, bringing them a cup of coffee or a surprise gift. How does this feel? Where's the feeling from? You're giving. It feels good. It's from the heart.

If you're feeling low or the future looks bleak, try the following guided visualization to experience the feeling of kindness and giving. Take a deep, calming breath. Use your mind to visualize going into space. You can be sitting quietly with your eyes closed or your eyes open while walking or hiking. With your mind, you're going to travel toward the Andromeda galaxy, our nearest galaxy neighbor. As you go by Mars, think about the past – what was it like on Mars? Was there a strange life, a civilization? What's there now: a silicon-based life? What about the future – a new civilization, will we be there? Consider these events for a few moments.

You leave the planet and now you're going toward the Andromeda galaxy. As you approach, you begin to visualize a new planet. It's magenta in color. On your way to explore the planet, you're surrounded by swirls of vibrant dark blue and dark red colors. With your mind, you land on the planet, and you see people everywhere, all types of people, all types of shapes and sizes, and all types of personalities.

In this visualization, unlike earth, on this magenta planet none of them are going to take anything from you. They won't take your peace, your thoughts, or enjoyment. Experience this feeling. It's kindness. It's a feeling from the heart. You can relax. You have no fear. They won't take your money. They won't take enjoyment from you. Not one of them will take your time, your energy, or your integrity. No one will criticize you, blame you, or make you feel bad about yourself. There are people everywhere, and not one single person will take anything from you. Experience this feeling. It's a comforting feeling. It's a good feeling. It's kindness from the heart.

Your journey is ending. Your final visual is seeing people extending their hands to you palms up, giving. Experience this feeling, giving you some-thing from the heart expecting nothing in return. You leave the journey, 5, 4, 3, 2 ... 1, feeling good and looking forward to an enjoyable day.

Try this right now. Think from your heart for the next hour. If anger is triggered, release it in six to eight seconds. Feeling sorry for yourself? Be kind to yourself with self-compassion from the heart. Thoughts of resentment or retaliation? Give. Be kind to someone. Think from the heart. The heart knows best.

A healthy life is filled with positive feelings. Knowing how you feel moment by moment means knowing you're thinking from one of five loca-tions that include the head, heart, gut, body, and the mind. How does this apply to feelings? Each feeling comes from one of these locations. Learn the feelings from each location so that you can enjoy good feelings and mini-mize unhealthy feelings.

Feelings come from where you're thinking from, and you make that deter-mination. Try this, think about a feeling, and ask yourself where is the feel-ing coming from?

You've likely never thought about this, and you'll be surprised by your answers. For example, feel kindness, where's this from? The heart. Feel fear, where's this from? It's the gut.

Explore feelings by starting with your head. There are three unhealthy locations that include the anger center, the stress center, and the addiction center. The anger center is triggered by someone taking something from you, your job, your enjoyment, or your autonomy.

An important thing to remember about the anger center is that this feeling can be neutralized quickly by feeling the anger, letting it peak, and moving on. If you keep thinking about the anger rather than feeling the anger, these thoughts will continue to trigger the anger center with the feeling of anger.

Someone yells at you and cuts you off in traffic. This will trigger the anger center because your personal space has been invaded and taken away. If you think about the driver and develop a story about how terrible this person is and should be punished, then anger will not go away. Telling the story over and over to people at the office, the family, and anyone who will listen continues the feeling of anger.

This is because the primitive anger center is triggered by something being taken from you which then triggers the adrenal response to fight back. But, if you don't think and only feel the anger, the parasympathetic system kicks in to neutralize the adrenal response as this is not a life-threatening situation. There is no reason for a fight. Anger is triggered. Feel it, let it peak, and release. No thinking, no second thoughts, and no story.

The stress center is triggered by thinking about yourself such as self-destructive thoughts, self-pity, resentment, or jealousy. Thinking negative thoughts about money, the past, or the future; or negative thoughts about relationships or the job will trigger the stress center. This also triggers the adrenal response with increased blood pressure, rapid heart rate, and tense muscles. As this is a crocodile brain response, feeling the stress, letting it peak, and moving on may eliminate the feeling because the calming response will neutralize the adrenal response.

The third feeling from your head is pleasure. How can this be unhealthy? Because it's from the addiction center. I call this chemical pleasure. It's the dopamine chemical released by drugs, alcohol, and sugar. It's short-lived and unhealthy.

Eating a hot-fudge sundae can result in an instant feel-good response. If you think about it, this feeling only occurs during the first few bites and only lasts for 20 seconds. About 90 minutes later, you don't want to finish the report or send out the emails. You have no energy to do anything.

The insulin surge for the sugar and glucose load from the hot fudge sundae results in too much insulin that metabolizes glucose causing energy loss. The intense pleasure from alcohol and drugs is also short-lived, but in this situation, the brain wants to continue to feel this pleasure and not the crash, so more alcohol or drug is needed to sustain the feeling leading to severe addiction.

Determine the feelings from the heart by putting your hand on your heart. You'll come up with feelings like kindness, giving, and being grateful. When you're being your true self, you're thinking from the heart. People will trust you because the feeling of trust comes from the heart, not the self-centered head.

Although a negative feeling, sadness is a feeling from the heart. Sadness means the loss of someone or something you love. It's always transient and resolves over time by replacing the loss with love from the heart.

What's the feeling from the gut? Imagine that you are hiking in the hills during a pleasant afternoon. It's getting dark, you have a long way to go home. Suddenly you're surrounded by a harsh wind and a crashing tree. What do you feel? It's fear.

Where does the feeling come from? For many people, it's a quick and sharp pain in the belly. It comes from the gut, not the head or the heart. When you're scared or frightened, where do you experience the feeling? It's in the belly. As with anger and stress, manage this fear by feeling the fear, learn from it, letting it peak in a few seconds, and let it go. Then you can think about your next move before it's too late.

What are the feelings from the body? It's the positive feeling from exercising the muscles and the negative feeling from muscle fatigue telling you to stop. Stressing the muscles with exercise is good for the body. This keeps muscles toned and prevents loss of muscle mass.

Stressing the muscles needs to be balanced. This means the stress from each muscle group needs to be neutralized by working the opposing muscle group. For example, if you stress the biceps, then you need to do an equal amount of stress for the triceps. Stress the back muscles, do an equal amount of core muscle work. Stress the quads, be sure to do an equal amount of hamstring work.

Surprisingly, the surface of your hands can express feelings. Hold your arms with elbows at 45 degrees and palms facing out. This says welcome and stay. Put your palms face down, and this says go away. Pointing with your index finger means a command.

What are the feelings from the mind? Although doctors and scientists have studied the function and feelings of the brain, systematic studies of feelings and even the names of feelings from the mind have not been conducted. Information is from anecdotal reports and observations. Therefore, you're free to explore the mind to its fullest.

The feelings from the mind are like the feelings from your heart but at a much deeper level. This is because these feelings are experienced outside the body and during the slow alpha brainwave state.

For example, with your mind, you can experience total calmness which is the total silence of the physical surroundings and calmness of every part of your body including the cells and DNA.

The feeling of universal acceptance and belonging with no judgement, criticism, or blame comes from the mind.

Courage and awe are from the mind. The unusual feeling of not needing to do anything occurs in the mind, and there's not a name for this yet. Maybe the word could be carefree or whimsical.

Attention to a task, a project, or an athletic event comes from the mind. The feeling of accomplishment and success comes from the mind.

Feelings are useful in conversation. If you want to tell a good story, keep people interested in your conversation, or sell something, use feelings. Go from feelings to feelings, not words to words.

There is a connection with your voice and feelings. Roger Love is a Hollywood speech coach and says to breathe through your nose, so you don't lose your voice. Try it, take a deep breath with your mouth wide open and your tongue and throat become dry. This eventually causes inflammation and a raspy voice producing negative feelings in the voice.

Roger also says to breathe in and imagine filling up a balloon in your stomach and emptying the air evenly as you talk being able to express feeling in your voice. Speaking in a monotone produces no emotion or feelings. Use melody with your words, go up and down the stairs with your voice.

Do not end a sentence going down as this will cause people to be sad. In addition, a loud voice using monotone means a command and not pleasant to the listener. Using a loud voice with melody creates persuasion.

Remember to pronounce plosives which are words ending in t, k, p, or d. For example, say "pleasant not pleasan," "elegant, not elegan," "quick, not quic." Through speaking with feeling, you'll connect with people emotionally.

Feelings come from distinct locations. These feelings include kindness from the heart, fear from the gut, calmness from the muscles, and acceptance from the mind. Experience these feelings for a healthy life.

Welcome to the world of the Eplerian Life Philosophy where feelings from your heart thrive, and everything falls into place.

*　*　*

Dangers of extreme feelings. Extreme feelings from any of the five locations, head, heart, gut, body, or mind can be dangerous and hazardous to your health. Extreme feelings from these regions with exclusion of other considerations can have unhealthy consequences.

Extreme feelings from the head are well known to everyone. Anger and rage can destroy the lives of millions of people. Extreme stress can cause heart attacks. Drug addiction can be fatal. All feelings from the head must be eliminated.

Listening to the heart for a decision is healthy because the decision is based on what's good for your health, but in complex situations, input from the gut for risk and the mind for creativity is needed.

Totally relying on your gut feelings can sometimes lead to a wrong choice, in complex conditions, you need to also consider feelings from your heart and the mind.

Extreme thinking from the mind with exclusion from the heart, the gut, and the body can result in retreating from society and not sharing innovative ideas with society.

Let's talk about extreme feelings from the head. Prolonged thinking from the anger center, stress center, or addictive pleasure center is dangerous to your health. Extreme thinking from these regions can result in media headlines by destroying lives from anger and dying from drug overdose.

Extreme thinking from the anger center can have serious short-term and lifelong consequences. Extreme thinking from the stress center can have immediate health effects and long-term effects from stress-induced inflammation leading to heart disease, high blood pressure, strokes, cancer, and a shortened life. Extreme thinking from the chemical pleasure center leads to addiction with severe short-term adverse health effects and long-term irreversible health effects.

How can thinking from the heart with extreme kindness be a problem? This can happen if people don't consider their own best interest first. For example, a doctor is being kind by listening to a person's misconduct, mistakes, and wrong behavior toward others. However, the doctor takes this to the extreme by personally experiencing these feelings rather than letting them pass through. This causes stress and when repeated over and over every day can lead to cortisol inflammation. Let these negative feelings pass through without absorbing them.

How is extreme giving a problem? People can be givers or takers. Givers are on top of the success ladder, far above takers; but givers are also on the bottom. That's where extreme thinking by giving is unhealthy. Giving without expecting anything in return is healthy and feels good for you and others. However, giving without regard for your own well-being is hazard-ous. People will take advantage of you. When you give, consider your own well-being, and if there is no harm, then give freely. If the action is going to be harmful to you, then create other ways to help.

Empathy from the heart is more complex; however, it's the same as kindness, extreme empathy can be hazardous to your health. I recently talked with a someone who grew up in a home filled with giving and love, so he became empathetic. However, he took this to the extreme. Later when he was con-fronted with an angry person yelling at him, he was so empathetic that he felt anger with the same intensity as the angry person.

This was repeated over and over through adult years into his 20s and 30s that eventually led to poor health with loss of enjoyment in life and loss of creativity. He eventually talked to a psychologist friend who told him to let these negative feelings from the other person pass through without absorbing them. The man's health and productivity soon returned to normal.

Sadness is a feeling from the heart. How is this a healthy feeling and what happens with extreme sadness? Traditionally, sadness is classified as a neg-ative feeling like anger and stress from the head; however, sadness means that something loved or someone who is loved has been lost. If the feeling is related to love, then the feeling comes from the heart, not from the head.

Loss is a natural event in people's lives that occurs randomly out of their control, but over time the loss will be replaced by something or someone because the heart will do anything to keep itself healthy and that includes love. The loss will be replaced because it's healthy for the heart.

Extreme sadness occurs when people stop feeling love from the loss and begin thinking from the stress center. They turn to thinking about themselves by feel-ing sorry for themselves. People need to allow time to heal from the loss, which may take weeks or months, and continue to think from the heart with love.

The hazard of thinking with extreme fear is panic. Everything shuts down. Thinking is turned over to a primal instinctive response. This can be good in a rare life-threating situation, but a disaster in a non-threatening daily life.

You can't think from the mind with creativity to solve the situation. You can't think from the heart with kindness and giving. You panic, putting yourself and others in danger. Keep your fear in control and use it to manage risky situations successfully.

Creativity and innovation are a wonderful part of the mind helping solve problems and improving people's lives all over the world. How can extreme creativity be a problem? There are two situations.

For the self-centered person, extreme creativity is used to manipulate people to get what they want at the expense of others. They use the mind to develop creative ideas to get what they want.

For some people, extreme creativity can lead to spending their lives in the mind withdrawing from life. They become disengaged and refuse to share their thoughts that could improve people's lives.

Everyone knows how extreme courage from the mind is hazardous. Heroes who don't think about themselves lose their lives. Too much courage without consideration from the risk perspective from the gut and feelings of self-compassion and kindness from the heart can be unhealthy. Courage needs to be accompanied by feelings from the gut and the heart for consideration of action.

Feeling total calmness from the mind all day could result in withdrawing from life. The feeling of total calmness, acceptance, and unconditional love from the mind during alpha brainwave time or meditation is healthy for several minutes, but not longer.

The law of diminishing returns applies to extreme feelings. This means there is a flow of events that follows a natural bell-shaped curve. A program is developed to improve a situation. The improvement begins at the baseline and quickly improves the situation over time. Then the benefits slow and peak at the top. During this time, the law of diminishing returns begins because the benefits are replaced by reversing the initial problem.

For example, solutions are developed that greatly improve an inequality. However, extreme feelings develop because the solutions are not enough to make the problem completely go away. This leads to the law of diminishing returns because extreme thinking with anger and stress leads to the opposite inequality. People take this new change personally and show more anger and stress sometimes resulting in dangerous consequences.

How can people stop from being caught up in the law of diminishing returns? It's helpful to understand this naturally occurring situation and know you cannot control the ebb and flow of cultural change. You can control your response by limiting self-thinking personal thoughts and thinking from the heart and the mind about others.

It's important to accept and adapt to cultural change and social norms by learning new skills, thinking from the heart with kindness and giving, and from the mind with creativity to solve problems and help others.

It's useful to understand the extremes of feelings so you can enjoy life and adjust to changes in a healthy way. Extreme feelings are unhealthy, balance is healthy.

*   *   *

Feelings aren't facts. Eliminate overthinking. Sometimes our feelings seem to rule our lives by overthinking. How can we escape these feelings that shape our day in and out? We need to find a way to eliminate overthinking.

Overthinking is a bad health habit that stalls progress, causes stress, and takes away enjoyment. Overthinking is when you keep reviewing problems or embarrassing moments over and over, or being obsessed about someone said or did. A big component of overthinking is weighing the pros and cons of a situation so many times that a decision is never made. Not deciding stops all forward action and allows time for something bad to happen.

Overthinking is a habit. Most thinking during the day is a habit. Up to 98 percent of thoughts are the same as yesterday, and 70 percent to 80 percent of thoughts are negative.

Yale-trained psychologist Heidi Sormaz talks about overthinking in her *Overcome Your Overthinking* course, and why people develop the habit of overthinking and how to stop the habit.

Types of overthinking include worrying about what-if questions and outcome predictions based on fear, not on probability and fact. Rumination is overthinking such as repetitive negative thoughts, often self-focus thoughts from the stress center, and angry rumination takes the form of blaming others rather than yourself. A third type is an excessive or unnecessary emotional reaction based on exaggerated self-centered thoughts rather than facts.

The many forms of yoga can blunt the overthinking response by engaging the body and distracting the mind from overthinking. Self-compassion will also stop overthinking by diverting thinking from the heart by being kind to yourself.

Knowing and labeling your emotions is important for recognizing and stopping over thinking. The Mood Meter is a chart developed by Dr. Marc Brackett at Yale. Moods are arranged from low energy and less pleasant such as despair, hopeless, and despondent, to high energy and more pleasant such as ecstatic, elated, and exhilarated. The Mood Meter is helpful for recognizing your emotions and emotions in others so that you can get out of the red zone of negative emotions into the green zone of positive emotions.

Feelings aren't facts. Your emotional reactions can lead you to errors, making you believe things that aren't true. For example, you become upset and stressed because you think you're going to lose your job, lose a close relationship, or lose out on a life-changing opportunity. Recurrent and constant thinking about these issues causes high stress. These feelings need to be confirmed by facts. You may assume a threat or predict a catastrophe. Checking the facts can improve this perspective lessening stress.

Treating feelings as facts can create overthinking. For example, the imposter syndrome is when people feel they're an imposter and not good enough for the job, and they doubt their own talent. This is from internalizing your feelings that are not based on facts. You convince yourself that you are not as competent as others think you are because you base this on your feelings of fear and insecurity, not on facts.

> "Feelings aren't facts. Explore all information before judging."

Overthinking results in people believing their single interpretation as truth, and they don't consider alternative explanations. This can lead to errors and overthinking resulting in fear and loss of enjoyment. For example, you hear a noise at night and think someone is breaking in. That's an interpretation, not a fact. Someone doesn't reconnect with you, and you think you're being ghosted. This is an interpretation. You make a mistake, so you think you're not smart or you'll get fired. That's an interpretation. Interpretations are not facts.

Thinking that leads to overthinking and inefficiency include polarizing thinking. It's an all-or-nothing approach and jumping to the worst-case scenario for every problem, big or small.

Overgeneralizing happens when we predict the outcome of something based on one occurrence. This is an easy trap, especially if the occurrence was severe and memorable. This depends on the situation and facts. It's likely that situation will never happen again, and the current situation has nothing in common with the bad occurrence.

Personalizing involves blaming yourself for a situation involving many factors or was out of your control. This occurs in givers and not egocentric takers. For example, you blame yourself for having to cancel a corporate event or a meeting because of a storm. This is out of your control, and there is no need for stress or self-pity.

People often assume what other people are thinking, which is not based on fact. For example, you're considering applying for a job but talk yourself out of it because you think the other person is not going to like you, your resume isn't good enough, or you didn't go to the right school. Apply for the job, do not assume what other people are thinking.

In some situations, people can be convinced that feelings matter more than facts. This overthinking can be used to influence and persuade people to believe a dangerous leader or misguiding policy leading to harming millions of people. For example, using falsely made-up stories and facts to create positive feelings toward a world leader can be so convincing that people cling to their emotions even when told the stories and facts aren't true.

Overthinking is a habit leading to inefficient decision making or no decision at all and causing stress by continuingly thinking about negative events. Feelings aren't facts. Be your true authentic self by eliminating self-generated thoughts and think successfully from your heart and the mind.

*   *   *

Enjoy life's magical moments. Think of the moments when you were with someone you love, and you both experience the feeling of calmness and acceptance with no external negative forces taking away the joy. These moments are rare but are lifelong memories.

You've had them. Recall a magical moment in your life. Hiking in the mountains with someone you love enjoying cranberry nut bread and listening to Mozart. Just the two of you skating on a frozen pond during a moonlit, winter night. Playing your first round of disk golf on a college campus with three extraordinary people during a beautiful early summer day. These are lifelong memories.

The day is filled with experiences that are bad, neutral, or good. Limit the bad experiences that are going to happen to a few moments and enjoy the good. Then, there are the rare, random moments or days every few years that are magical. Cherish these. They're lifelong happy memories.

Bad experiences are destructive social interactions with people involving complaints, criticism, or accusations. These interactions are caused by thinking from the anger center or the stress center. It's unhealthy to absorb these toxic exchanges. Let the hurtful words pass through with no reaction. Use social clues such as a facial expression or body language to show the other person you're uncomfortable with the topic. Try to neutralize the situation with thinking from the heart with kindness or forgiving. If the conversation escalates, physically leave the situation.

Neutral experiences are most common. They're the daily interactions with no feelings while driving, going on errands, shopping, and working.

Good experiences can be planned such as a vacation, a sporting event, a concert, or a festival. For example, giving an experience as a gift has become an excellent option. Success of these events depends on flexibility and people thinking from the heart with kindness and giving and thinking from the mind with creativity. The good feeling from these events occurs when thinking about the event, the actual event, and post event conversations.

However, one person with self-centered thinking and opinions can disrupt and cancel any good feelings at any time. They're the bad house guests or the bad traveling companion. You know the type, head thinkers, complaining, criticizing, and blaming. Go with thinking from the heart and the mind for an enjoyable experience.

Magical moments are different. They're random and rare, only occurring every few years. Sometimes, you don't realize they're magical until a couple of days have gone by. You have a special feeling of joy every time you think about the event.

These are magical moments sharing with someone where you both are your true selves thinking from the heart with love and kindness. You have no feelings of outside negative pressures or thoughts.

You're in the flow with the person or people you're with, all connected with a warm feeling of joy. These are lifelong memories. You'll experience the pleasant feeling over and over each time you recall the story.

You can't plan a magical event, but you can set up your life to have them occur more frequently by living a healthy life by being your true self and thinking from the heart with kindness and love.

* * *

Empathy. It can sometimes seem like triggers for negative emotions are everywhere. A boss who is constantly unimpressed with our work. A spouse who doesn't listen to us. A random driver who cuts us off on our way to work. The triggers for negative emotion lead us down a dark path of anger. This section shows how to blunt these triggers by tapping into thinking from our heart.

Empathy involves experiencing the feelings of others. People can be mean and judgmental to each other during day-to-day social interactions. But we can learn to communicate with empathy and kindness.

Realize that people yell at you or are mean to you, not because of you, but because of the way they're thinking and feeling. They're thinking from the anger center or cingulate stress center, not from the heart. They're mad at their boss, mad because they don't have enough money, mad because someone disagrees with them, or they're blaming the job, the government, or their spouse for their problems. You're not the cause of the angry yelling.

However, the natural response to being yelled at is to be angry in return, which is a response from the head brain anger center. There's another way to respond. Bypass the anger response, think from the heart with empathy. Put yourself in the other person's situation, they're upset, not you.

Here's a call to action: the next time someone yells at you or is mean to you, don't think from the head, think from your heart with empathy and let it go. And, over time, the bypass response will happen automatically. You'll find yourself thinking from the heart, not from the anger center.

This response is for a normal situation on an occasional basis. What if yelling is hurtful? What if someone yells at you every day? This is abnormal behavior and not healthy. This is when you need to be your true self, let the yelling go through you, and take a stand. At this point, physically distancing yourself is an optional consideration.

Why do people get angry at a door because their finger gets jammed or mad at the computer because it doesn't respond? Everyone does this. Why? These annoyances trigger the anger center because your calmness or enjoyment has been taken from you. Feel the anger, let it peak in six to eight seconds, and then think from the heart with empathy, or better, learn to not let the event or action trigger the anger center. This time, empathy is for yourself, be kind to yourself. Use self-compassion.

How can people have deep conversations about relationships, jobs, and politics without anger and stress? It's a skill that needs to be learned. The natural response is getting mad, angry, and yelling. It's a learned response from childhood. You need to learn how to have deep conversations that may be painful short-term, but long-term, they're healthy and more productive. Without these deep conversations, people will continue to hold anger and resentment.

People need to use empathy from the heart for these conversations. Listen to the other person's perspective without thinking from the anger center or self-centered stress center. These conversations are about feelings. Listen to the whole story about the person's feelings and opinions.

You'll find out why the person feels this way, and they'll find out why you feel the way you do. This will bring closure, so both of you can move forward instead of not knowing what's going on, continually thinking about the problem, and wrongly deciding how the other person feels. None of this is healthy; it takes away enjoyment in your life. Learn to use empathy for deep conversations by thinking from the heart.

Why are people so easily offended? Because people are thinking about themselves by comparing themselves to others or trying to be someone else.

Two people are having a conversation about working in an office and one of them gets angry and demands an apology. Why? The person who gets angry claims the other person knows working in an office is an upsetting topic and shouldn't be talked about. This is abnormal behavior. People can't have a normal conversation with people acting this way.

People who are self-centered and only thinking about themselves are socially weak and fragile, they interpret every conversation as a personal attack against them. You can't be your true self with these people because they'll interpret a normal conversation as an assault on their personality. You've lost your freedom to think and talk. Thinking from the heart with kindness, forgiveness, and empathy is so much better than thinking about yourself.

Listen to understand, not to talk. For example, people are talking with each other, the person not talking is thinking about themselves and not listening. This person is thinking about what to say next without paying attention to what's being said, or the person is judging the other person. These people won't understand how the other person feels and may miss learning something new that can make your life better.

Listen from the heart with empathy for improved understanding. Listen from the mind to solve problems and help others.

How can empathy be useful for a romantic breakup or a business partnership breakup? If "you gotta break up," break up with a deep conversation using empathy from the heart.

The easy way out is ghosting. Stop answering texts, emails, or calls. This is weak. This is cingulate, self-centered thinking. This leaves the other person angry and not knowing what's going on and feeling bad about themselves. They'll blame and criticize themselves. There is no closure. The first person gets over this in a few hours. The second person can hold bad feelings for days and maybe even years, and some situations lead to serious long-term health consequences.

Meet up, person to person. Discuss the issue from the heart with empathy. This will be painful for one or two hours for both people, but life will go forward with no continual unanswered questions and unhealthy stress.

Learn to bypass the brain anger center and the brain cingulate stress center by using empathy and kindness from the heart. Someone or something triggers your anger center, use empathy, and think from the heart.

Need a deep conversation, it's always about the other person, use empathy from the heart with kindness and understanding.

*   *   *

Living moment by moment. Have you ever heard the saying *you can't be two places at once?* The same is true for feelings. When we experience feelings, we can only experience them from one of the five locations. This suggests that we can train ourselves to tap into good feelings by living in the moment. Engage in life. Be in the flow. Pay attention. Eliminate stress. It seems like there's always something that wants to steal our time, our moment. Learn how to eliminate stressful thoughts and live in the moment.

Think from the heart with kindness and giving, and from the mind with courage and success. Before discussing positive, healthy feelings, it's helpful to know why people have bad, unhealthy feelings.

Unhealthy feelings occur when you think from your head. You're angry? You're thinking from the head amygdala region. You're stressed? You're thinking about yourself from the cingulate stress brain center. Do you have bad health habits? You're thinking from the chemical pleasure, accumbens region. None of these thoughts are healthy, and they take away from enjoying life.

For the feeling of stress, you should strive to live your life at zero-level stress every day. Level-ten stress is the death zone. Level-four to -six stress is the disease zone with heart disease, diabetes, and cancer. Level-zero stress is the alive-with-life zone. Live your life with zero stress. Everyone knows the serious consequences of out-of-control anger and addiction, think from the heart with kindness.

You need to learn to transfer your thinking from these regions. Start thinking these unhealthy thoughts? Acknowledge them. Learn something from them. Eliminate them in six to eight seconds or eliminate triggering the anger center and the stress center. Think from the heart with kindness, and from the mind with creativity and success.

Can negative feelings be healthy? Yes, fear is a negative healthy feeling. Fear is the feeling from the gut. It's an uneasiness, distressed feeling. This feeling tells you about risk. Beware, proceed with caution or don't proceed at all.

Fear protects your health. Fear is telling you not to do something. Do you want to climb a steep mountain? Go swimming during a storm? Your gut is telling you no. Stepped on a hornet's nest? Your gut is telling you to get out of there fast. Fear helps you make healthy choices.

Sadness is a negative feeling, yet it's healthy because it's from the heart. Sadness means you've lost someone or something you love, and the feeling of love comes from the heart. Sadness is always transient because over time, the loss is replaced by someone or something that you love.

Sadness does not come from unhealthy head feelings. Sadness is healthy and comes from the heart. Move through sadness with time, being patient with yourself, and self-compassion.

For example, you've lost someone you love. At first, you feel upset, you're angry. Acknowledge these feelings and move on. Then you're sad. This is a feeling of emptiness. It's a void. It's not unhealthy, it's a feeling that will be replaced over time with someone you love.

Positive, good feelings come from the heart. Good feelings of kindness and giving come from the heart. For example, say to yourself, "I'm going to be nice to someone today." Now say, "I'm going to be kind to someone today." Being nice comes from the head, a conditioned response since childhood, and usually expecting something in return. Being kind comes from the heart. You can feel it from the heart and so can others, a shared good feeling with someone, not wanting anything in return.

People thinking from the head who give something always expect something in return. Giving from the heart with no expectation feels good for a lifetime.

> "Give from the heart expecting nothing in return."

Positive, good feelings come from the mind. Good feelings of total calmness, belonging, and unconditional love come from the mind. The mind is out-side the body, so you need to slow down the brainwaves, like daydreaming or meditation. Go for a hike or a walk or sit quietly. Go into the slow alpha brainwave state by counting down from 25 to one or through eyes-open meditation. Then imagine being surrounded by quiet. This is a pleasant feeling, a good feeling.

Calm yourself starting with your head and then shoulders, arms, belly, and legs. Visualize your cells and calm them. Good feelings from the mind for a healthy life.

*   *   *

How to live in the moment. The expression "live in the moment" has been around for thousands of years. What does this mean? How do you live in the moment?

For me, living in the moment means being engaged in life at all times. This means knowing what you're doing, what you want, and where you' re going. It means paying attention. You can only do one thing at a time. Pay attention to the moment.

This means putting away the mobile phone when talking with friends and family. Put away the mobile when interacting with people at work and in public. Put away the mobile when working out.

If you're not living in the moment, you're stressed. You're having negative thoughts about the past or about the future. You're upset with yourself about mistakes you've made. You're feeling sorry for yourself. You feel guilty about something. You worry about not finishing a big project. You think about failing at your presentation or losing your job. All these thoughts mean you're thinking from the stress center, and you're not experiencing the moment.

If you're thinking about negative problems in the past or unknown events in the future, then you can't enjoy the moment. You may not experience a magical moment connecting with someone you love. A commencement speaker told the graduates that he let his dying father's calls go to voice mail, rather than taking a moment away from work, to talk. He still regrets not hearing his father's live voice one last time.

A major benefit from living in the moment is having zero-level stress. You can only think from one location at a time. If you're thinking about past and future problems, then you can't think from the heart with enjoyment and kindness. You can't think from the heart with giving. It feels good to give. You're free to think from the mind with creative ways to solve problems and help people.

How do you live in the moment? Be your true self. Use the Eplerian Life Philosophy of knowing where you're thinking from and eliminate thinking about yourself from the stress center. Think from the heart with kindness and giving and think from the mind with creativity to solve problems and help others. This is your true self.

This begins with being healthy, which means having a healthy nutritional lifestyle, eight hours of sleep every night, and one hour of exercise every day. These three health habits will provide the energy for living an extraordinary life with no negative thoughts or self-doubt.

This means having compassion for yourself and others. This means having a high level of happiness by being content with your current situation. This means learning something new every day.

This means positive social communication every moment where both people feel better after the interaction. This means experiencing the feelings from the mind with total calmness and universal acceptance of who you are. This means being in the flow when you're doing something you love.

Being in the flow is an example of living in the moment. You've experienced a wonderful day where everything goes well or you're enjoying something when you forget about time or surroundings. You're happy. You're content.

This is being in the flow, and it's related to skill and challenge. When your skills and challenges are equal, you're focused on the activity with no distractions. You don't think about failure. You have no thoughts about yourself. You don't care what other people are thinking about you. Time is distorted. It feels like ten seconds doing a triple jump at a track meet that takes only a second, or it feels like minutes working on a new discovery that takes hours.

The activity becomes so enjoyable that you want to do it again and again because it's pleasurable and brings you happiness. It's living in the moment.

Paying attention allows you to live in the moment. You and a friend volunteer to build a house for a nonprofit hurricane rebuilding organization. There are 15 new houses to be built from the foundation up, and about 100 people are helping in the project.

You arrive and find sleeping arrangements, and report to the group leader for your assignment. All during this time, you are living in the moment because you are only thinking about what you're doing with no negative thoughts about the past or the future.

You're assigned to the carpenter group with two other volunteers, and you're asked to move a storage room from one location in the house to another. You plan and design the project with your team and then do the sawing and hammering nails. This is the most enjoyable day of your life. You're doing physical work with no thinking from the head. You're having enjoyable feelings of kindness, giving, and helping. You're living in the moment.

Living in the moment means being engaged in life, being in the flow, and paying attention. This means no stress in your life.

Here's a call to action. Remember that at any given moment in time during the day or night doing whatever you're doing or activity you're engaged in, you're safe, you're secure, and you're healthy.

Learn to have no thoughts about yourself from the stress center, and no negative thoughts about past problems and unknown future events. Think from the heart with kindness and giving. Be your true authentic self.

Chapter 4

Foundations for Optimal Health

"Eat right, sleep tight, exercise bright."

– Unknown

Eat sleep and move! John finds himself eating surgery foods, too much food, and one big meal late at night all resulting in inflammation and excess weight. He gets five hours of sleep not having enough thinking power for the day and worse, he's irritable, short-tempered, and mean to people. He doesn't make the time to exercise and is too tired to enjoy the day.

For optimal health, it's a healthy nutritional lifestyle, eight hours of sleep every night, and one hour of exercise every day.

Healthy nutrition lifestyle. What we eat, our overall nutrition, impacts everything about us. Let's take a fresh look at the science of nutrition with the basic tenet of excluding foods that cause inflammation. It's a healthy nutrition lifestyle for living a long and healthy life. An understanding of food metabolism, healthy foods, and unhealthy consequences of unhealthy foods serves as a useful foundation for nutrition.

It's important to continually learn about foods and nutrition because technology and research are updating our knowledge about personal metabolism, sometimes completely reversing traditional thinking.

People often think that diets are the best way to lose weight. They're right. You can lose 20, 30 or 50 pounds, but diets are also the biggest cause of weight gain. It's all gained back plus an additional 10 to 20 pounds. This is because diets reset the brain eating thermostat to a higher level, and it's permanent.

The diet approach leads to trying the latest fad diet every few years with swings of weight loss and weight gain, which leads to diabetes, high blood pressure, and heart disease. A healthy nutritional lifestyle is the better choice. Food needs to provide energy to the brain, heart, and muscles without causing harmful inflammation. My way is the "healthy nutrition lifestyle" that can break the hazardous cycle of diet fads.

> *"Eat the right foods in the right amount at the right time and prepared in a healthy manner."*

The right foods will give you energy for the entire day. The wrong foods will cause inflammation of the arteries and organs. The wrong foods will leave you lacking energy, and some foods will drain your energy leaving you non-productive and lethargic.

What are the right foods?

Foods with no added sugar, no added salt, and no processed foods. Here are three of them: lean protein, omega-3 polyunsaturated fats, and slow-burn low-glycemic or low blood sugar carbohydrates. Let's look at each of these in detail.

Lean protein gives you energy and doesn't cause inflammation or fat deposition. Animal and fish protein are useful sources. Skinless chicken trimmed of fat, boiled in water, and rinsed with water is an excellent source of protein. The taste can be improved with anti-inflammatory herbs and spices such as turmeric, rosemary, and ginger, and by adding low-glycemic colorful vegetables.

Fish such as salmon and cod are excellent sources of pure protein and have the extra advantage of containing omega-3 fatty acid, the protective anti-inflammatory fat. Use caution with farm-raised salmon because the white strips are omega-6 fat that can cause inflammation. Wild-caught salmon has no omega-6 fat.

People should be aware of mercury in fish as this could be an issue in some situations. Mercury is a common element in the Earth's surface, and as fuel is burned around the world, mercury can become airborne, settling in rivers, lakes, and oceans. Fish and aquatic plants such as plankton and algae ingest mercury as part of their feeding cycle.

In addition, larger fish absorb mercury as they eat smaller fish. For people, and especially pregnant women, eating large amounts of certain types of fish could result in accumulating high enough mercury levels to cause the symptoms of mercury poisoning. Sensitivity to mercury varies from person to person; however, the amount of mercury in a person can disappear over time as less mercury is ingested.

Which fish have high mercury levels? The ones with big mouths that live the longest such as shark, blue-fin tuna, and swordfish. Low mercury levels are found in salmon, trout, sole, and cod. The latter group can be eaten during the week; the big fish should be eaten less frequently. Shellfish have low levels of mercury.

Vegetable proteins are an excellent source of energy. Raw vegetables need to be thoroughly washed to eliminate hazardous bacteria and unwanted chemicals. Steamed vegetables are excellent because the healthy nutrients are not destroyed. Some vegetables such as spinach can be sautéed at low heat with olive oil or avocado oil without losing benefits.

Salt does not need to be added to vegetables or any food. Salt was used thousands of years ago as a preservative and is no longer needed. Salt causes inflammation. Added salt needs to be eliminated. There is sufficient sodium in naturally occurring foods. Anti-inflammatory herbs and spices such as ginger, rosemary, or turmeric in curry powder can be added to vegetables for taste.

High-protein plant foods include legumes such as chickpeas, pinto beans, kidney beans, and lentils; and nuts such as almonds. These foods contain a large amount of protein. Grains such as whole oats, whole wheat, quinoa, couscous, and barley also contain high protein.

Whey is a remarkable protein. More than 8,000 years ago, it was found that aged milk separates into liquid whey and solid curd. The whey was discarded, and the curd was made into cheese. However, 5,600 years ago Hippocrates demonstrated that whey could be used for growth and strength. During the 1500s, Swiss pig farmers realized their pigs grew faster and bigger when they ate whey, so they tried it themselves with dramatic results. In the 1600s and 1700s spas sprang up throughout Europe touting the strength-giving powers of whey. In the early 1900s, a digestible powder form was developed, in the 1960s, the sugary lactose was removed, and in the 1980s, the fat was removed so now pure whey protein is available.

Whey has low sodium and high potassium levels. It contains all 20 essential amino acids and has one of the highest scores for ease of digestion.

Whey has a high level of lysine amino acid, which is a fundamental growth protein for children. This is why giving cow's milk to babies and children can result in growing into adults who are 12 inches taller than babies and children who were not given cow's milk. Cow's milk for babies and children remains the optimal choice for healthy tall adults.

Whey protein has appetite-suppressant and anti-inflammatory properties, and it's a low-glycemic food that does not increase blood sugar. The hydrolysate form is often used by athletes because of its rapid absorption. Some people may have whey protein sensitivity and are not able to consume whey.

Fats are the second source of energy food. The right fats are omega-3 fats and polyunsaturated fatty acids. They can give you a huge amount of energy and prevent inflammation of the arteries, especially the small arteries feeding life to the heart.

Food research has shown a balance of omega-3 and omega-6 fats is required because too much omega-6 causes inflammation, especially the manufactured omega-6 that is added to foods. The omega-3 fatty acids circulate in the blood as high-density lipoproteins (LDH) and protect your blood vessels because they have anti-inflammatory properties.

Fish oil has two common omega-3 fatty acids: docosahexaenoic acid or DHA, and eicosatetraenoic acid or EPA. For supplements, DHA has been shown to have more anti-inflammatory effect. Plant oils from seeds such as flax contain the omega-3 fatty acid, alpha-linolenic acid or ALA. Other foods containing omega-3s include cold-water fish such as salmon, cod, mackerel, trout, and herring as well as walnuts, flaxseed, and green leafy vegetables such as spinach and broccoli.

Too much omega-6 fatty acid causes inflammation. The typical American diet may have 15 to 30 times more omega-6 fats compared to omega-3 fats, so it's important to strive for a balance of omega-3 to omega-6. Processed foods may contain too much of the omega-6 inflammation-type fatty acids and should be limited or eliminated.

Omega-9 fatty acids are found in animal fat and vegetable oils, and omega-3 fatty acid is considered a good anti-inflammatory food. Olive oil and avocado oil contain oleic acid, a common omega-9 fatty acid. Read the labels or research to consume foods with the most omega-3 fatty acids and limit or eliminate processed foods with manufactured omega-6 fat.

Carbohydrates are the third food group for energy. These foods are available everywhere 24 hours a day, and they're cheap, which is the perfect combination for overconsumption of the wrong sugar-based carbohydrates.

For healthy carbohydrates, it's helpful to understand the difference between slow and fast metabolism carbohydrates as they relate to blood sugar levels and insulin release. Insulin is produced by the pancreas and is a powerful, life-sustaining hormone that regulates blood sugar levels. It's fundamental to nutrition management because too much insulin turns carbohydrates into fat deposition and inflammatory triglycerides.

Focus on slow metabolism carbohydrates because they don't cause a surge in blood sugar. These carbs include vegetables such as spinach and broccoli and legumes such as beans and peas. Fruit such as apples contain fructose, the sweet-tasting sugar metabolized in the liver. Fructose in natural foods in moderation does not cause a blood sugar surge. Manufactured high-fructose corn syrup causes inflammation and should be avoided.

Fiber is a carbohydrate that binds with toxic substances to eliminate them. Fiber in foods moderates blood sugar peak levels. Insoluble fiber is the woody portion of plant-based foods, such as broccoli and asparagus stems, and can regulate bowel function and keep things moving. Soluble fiber is the gummy substance in oatmeal and red beans. The beta-glucan in soluble fiber can decrease the blood level of low-density lipoprotein or LDL, which is a fatty transport protein in the blood that at elevated levels causes inflammation and thickening of the arteries.

Added sugar causes inflammation. They're sugar foods such as pastries, cakes, pies, candy, and sugary drinks, but added sugar is added to many packaged and processed foods. Read the label for healthy choices. The label now has the amount of added sugar in food products. Choose zero added sugar.

Insulin-inducing fast metabolizing carbohydrates cause inflammation. You may not think about these foods as they are the white starchy foods such as white potatoes, white rice, and white bread. Eating too much of these foods will cause a blood sugar spike.

The problem with sugary foods and potatoes is that it is almost impossible to eat in a small enough amount to prevent triggering the insulin response. Try eating one French fry or one chip. The insulin release is going to trigger two events: cortisol release causing fat deposition and high blood triglycerides causing inflamed arteries. Both responses can be harmful.

Added sugar in foods requires special attention. Added sugar can be considered the single most harmful food. The FDA has recognized this and now requires food labels to have the amount of added sugar. Read food labels, if there is any amount of added sugar, purchase a different food.

Added sugar causes an insulin spike that results in overwhelming the energy-glucose system and dysfunctional metabolism. This results in inflammation throughout the organ systems and the body. Everyone knows this also causes weight gain from developing too much hazardous fat.

Added sugar instantly triggers the accumbens pleasure center releasing the dopamine chemical for tasty pleasure. For example, the first few bites of a hot-fudge sundae or a piece of cake taste delicious and may give you a wonderful pleasure feeling, but this only lasts for 20 seconds. The next few bites and finishing the sugar treat results in nothing. They do not cause ecstatic pleasure feeling. In addition, 90 minutes later, you don't feel like sending out the email, working on the project, or doing anything productive. To prevent this crash, people continue to snack on added sugar foods throughout the day. This tells you the pleasure feeling from added sugar is from the accumbens habit or addiction center.

Eliminating added sugar is difficult because people have developed an automatic and subconscious habit through childhood conditioning. However, if you eliminate added sugar in your life, the outcome is extraordinary and can save your life. Your skin feels healthy and your immune system functions at peak performance. You feel good about yourself. You can prevent inflammation-causing events such as diabetes, heart disease, strokes, and a shortened life.

Eliminate added sugar. Try this for a week. This is what happens. The first day is easy. You'll get through the day, but for two or three nights, you may dream about eating sugary foods, like that hot fudge sundae or chocolate. For the next two days, you're going to have an intense craving for chocolate and all types of sugary foods. Drink lots of water to stop the craving. After that 48 hours, the craving completely stops. You begin to feel good. In three months, you'll notice your skin is healthier, it's smooth and feels good because the skin immune defense system has been restored. Your digestive system improves.

You don't want to tell anyone you're doing this because it's boring to other people, and it will take away your discipline. However, you don't want to be anti-social. Our cultural norm calls for celebrations with cake and ice cream. Occasionally eating the right amount of a celebration dessert without bingeing is not harmful. There is no need to feel guilty. This makes everything worse and shuts down the digestive system. It's a celebration, feel happy for everyone involved. Enjoy the piece of cake and return to your no-added sugar lifestyle.

Remember the sugar feeling is from the accumbens addition center so if you eat surgery foods for a couple of days. Repeat the process of going through the dreams and craving for 48-hours and returning to your added-sugar free life. It's worth it. You'll thank yourself. You can repeat this pattern as long as you want. Not eating added sugar feels great and gives you a long-lasting healthy life.

The right foods are high-quality foods. They're simple, non-processed foods. They're grown naturally with personal attention. They're fruits and vegetables grown organically from well-cultivated fields without pesticides. They're from free-range chickens. They're free-swimming fish in rivers, lakes, and oceans.

They're non-processed carbohydrates that have not been fructose-condensed by a manufacturing process, and olive and avocado oils that have not been hydrogenated. Too much high-fructose corn syrup and hydrogenated fat in oils will cause increased triglycerides and inflammation of the arteries. Whether shopping or eating, seek out high-quality foods.

The right foods have anti-inflammatory properties. For example, flavonoid colors in foods are anti-inflammatory. They make up a group of naturally occurring compounds found in colorful yellow, red, and purple fruits, and vegetables such as spinach, eggplant, and kidney beans. Red, orange, and yellow peppers are good choices. They can keep your blood vessels flexible by inhibiting synthesis of the low-density fatty lipoproteins that cause inflammation. Citrin can, too. It's the most active flavonoid in lemons. Herbs and spices can be anti-inflammatory. Some, such as ginger and turmeric in curry powder, may have anti-inflammatory action that can prevent arterial plaque formation.

How do you learn to eat the right foods? First, learn which foods are healthy. Second, train yourself to select the right foods. Choose lean protein and non-insulin producing carbohydrates, and foods with no added sugar, no added salt, and no processed foods with omega-6 fats.

Over time, choosing the right foods will become a habit, and the healthy taste of these foods will replace the sweet, salty, and fatty taste of unhealthy foods. Use positive feedback to train yourself. Each time you eat healthy foods, enjoy the long-lasting positive feeling you experience. This feeling is so much better than the 20-second fleeting feeling from the sugar foods that leave you out of energy and craving for more.

What's the right amount of food?

This is the hardest part about the healthy nutrition lifestyle because you need less food intake every ten years as you age. Eventually you may only need half as much as when you were a teenager. This is difficult because we've been conditioned to "clean the plate" since childhood, and the food quantity brain thermostat stays the same during aging, so overeating becomes a built-in default for all of us. Because of this, you need to have your gut belly brain working at optimal strength for healthy digestion and eating the right amount.

The right amount of food is the amount needed for energy. This means eating the right amount at each meal. This means not having a large meal with too much food. The extra food leads to excess weight.

You need to be fully aware when choosing what to eat. If you're stressed worrying about your problems and work deadlines, you can't think about what you're eating and how much. Unaware, random eating is fraught with hazards. When you're not paying attention, the tendency is to keep eating until you're completely stuffed, which is too late. This results in increased fat deposition, artery inflammation, and loss of energy. After all, how do you feel when you're stuffed?

The natural hormone leptin sends signals to your brain that you've had enough to eat. This is good, but it's extremely slow, from 15 to 30 minutes, and stress makes this longer or even absent. As you eat your meals or snacks, try to remember this as it will prevent overeating. It's best to stop eating before you've developed the "you've had enough feeling." The feeling will come along eventually.

Another consideration is the idea of eating for peak energy. For centuries, monks have known that food brings energy up to a peak level and then falls. They learned when they reached the peak, they stopped eating. It's a subtle internal signal and takes time to learn, but it's there. Learn to eat to your high-energy level, not to your over-full, stuffed level.

What's the right time to eat?

I prefer the traditional three meals daily and energy snacks can be helpful if needed. Eat small amounts during each meal. Breakfast is helpful because this spreads out food intake during the day so that the right amount of food is eaten for energy, and not weight gain.

This prevents eating one big meal especially late at night when only a small amount is converted to useful energy and the remainder turns to the wrong type of fat around vital organs, the belly, and the hips. Eating energy-portioned meals three times a day is a healthy option.

How to prepare food in a healthy manner?

This means eating foods in their natural state, steamed, or cooked at low temperatures. This means limit fried foods and charred foods because foods cooked at extreme heat will produce glycoproteins which is the char. High levels of glycoproteins causes inflammation of the small arteries leading to the heart and the brain causing heart attacks and strokes.

Along with making healthy food choices and eating the right amount, it's also important to be aware of your eating patterns. Whenever you eat a meal or snacks, focus and pay attention, don't let eating become an unconscious habit. Eat sitting down. Do not do anything else while eating, such as eating out of a bag while on the elevator or standing in line.

Eat when your stomach is empty, usually every three to four hours. Eat when the food in your mouth has been swallowed. The tongue has taste buds for six flavors. It's helpful to stimulate all six taste centers for improved digestion and energy. Eat meals with the six tastes of sweet, sour, salt, bitter from leafy green vegetables, pungent from legumes, and astringent from spices.

Can you stop temptation and food cravings? It's not easy. Often, as the day progresses, the neurotransmitter, phenylethylamine becomes depleted and results in temptation and caving in. Sugar is addictive from the accumbens brain region. Sugar produces a good feeling from brain dopamine, but only lasts for 20 seconds and causes a crash and craving for more. Craving for sugar can be stopped entirely if you stop eating without added sugar for two days.

Other cravings can be stopped by listening to your belly brain, if you get a feeling not to eat the food, stop and don't eat the food. Another way to stop craving is to 'feel' that the responsible food is unhealthy and bad for you every time you encounter the food. This negative feeling may be enough to stop eating the food.

Try this, visualize eating your favorite sugar food like a piece of chocolate cake, a hot fudge sundae, or a big chocolate chip cookie. Then visualize in your mind eating the treat one bite at a time until you finished. Wait a few minutes and the craving will have disappeared. Try it – it may work.

Eat the right food in the right amount at the right time and prepared in a healthy manner.

*   *   *

Restorative sleep. We need eight hours of sleep every night: six hours to recharge our brain energy and two hours of dream sleep for kindness, empathy, and love. We also need those two hours to recharge the prefrontal cortex region of the brain while it is offline.

There are two reasons for eight hours of sleep. First, you need six hours to restore your brain energy adenosine, which is a substance used for brain signal transmission. Second, you need two hours of REM (rapid-eye movement) dream sleep for feelings of kindness from the heart and for optimal performance of the prefrontal lobe to make the right social choices.

> *"Eight hours of sleep every night. Six hours for restoring brain energy. Two hours for love and kindness."*

Many people have developed a habit of not getting eight hours of sleep and have become so used to this, they don't realize the harmful health effects and loss of performance, innovation, and happiness. Others have convinced themselves they only need five or six hours of sleep. They don't realize they're only functioning at 60 percent of their potential productivity and thinking ability. They looked stressed and unhealthy. Another potential side-effect of not getting eight hours of sleep is that people may not want to interact with someone who hasn't had enough sleep because they have a negative and critical outlook during a conversation.

People may brag about only needing five hours of sleep. This is a mistake. They think they have more energy and can get more work done. Once again, this is wrong. It's the opposite. They are only working at 60% of their performance, 60% of their efficiency, and have 60% less positive relationships that could have led to improved productivity and enjoyment. For example, police records show that many drivers who don't pass the sobriety test have negative blood alcohol levels, but instead, have chronic sleep deprivation.

Many problems arise when we don't get eight hours of sleep. The immediate problems are dull senses and creativity, irritability, and quick to anger. The long-term problems are worse. This is called chronic sleep deprivation. The harmful health effects include decreased performance, memory impairment, strained relationships and negative social interaction, occupational injuries, automobile injuries and fatalities. Medical conditions include high blood pressure, heart disease, depression, and stroke. Less than six hours of sleep will shorten people's lives.

How do you know if you have chronic sleep deprivation? Take the 10-second sleep test. Sit quietly for 10 seconds, if you fall asleep, you don't pass. If you repeatedly fail this test over several days to weeks, you have chronic sleep deprivation.

This is an extremely bad sign. Your brain adenosine energy is depleted for healthy brain cell interaction. You have no dream sleep for kindness and positive people interaction. You may make wrong life choices or social choices because your prefrontal lobe is offline. Your brain is screaming for sleep to restore the adenosine energy and obtain the two hours of REM dream sleep.

The ability to concentrate, focus, and stay on task suffers with too little sleep, especially too little REM sleep. Researchers call this "ability vigilance" and test it by asking a person to press a button when a light dot randomly appears on a screen. The test focuses on measuring how many times the person realizes the dot is there and presses the button, assessing how often the person's attention stays on the screen or strays from it.

People with less than eight hours of sleep every night lose creativity and are not aware of it. It's a new sense of normal for them. They may not make the best choices from what foods to eat for lunch to arguing with a spouse over a minor annoyance or to taking a curve at 50 miles per hour instead of the recommended 25 miles per hour. Researchers have shown this behavior is like someone who has been drinking too much alcohol. The more sleep deprived a person is, the more that person is like someone with an increased blood alcohol level.

Research shows that one of the biggest oil spills in history was due to sleep deprivation. The captain had been working at least 18 hours before the ship ran aground. The National Transportation Safety Board attributes about 30 percent of fatal accidents on the country's freeways to driver fatigue.

Sleeping less than eight hours a day causes organ system stress. The ability to regulate blood glucose levels is sharply decreased by sleep deprivation. The less sleep a person has, the higher the blood glucose, which could result in insulin resistance, increased fat deposition, and diabetes. Increased fat deposition from sleep deprivation is due to increased ghrelin, the appetite hormone, and decreased leptin, the appetite-suppressor hormone.

A study has shown a correlation between negative words and lack of sleep, the less sleep there is, the higher frequency of negative words. The positive word ratio is the number of positive words divided by the number of negative words and positive word ratio of three to five is associated with high performance and creativity. Negative word ratios are associated with inferior performance, loss of creativity, and divorce.

Researchers determined the word ratio for individuals with differing amount of sleep. With less than five hours of sleep each night, people use 70 percent negative words and only 30 percent positive words, that's a large negative word ratio of 2.3 leading to low performance and lack of creativity.

Why are eight hours of sleep required every night? Sleep is for the brain. The brain needs eight hours every night.

First, there's an energy chemical called adenosine that is used by the brain for thinking and carrying out activities to improve your life. Each thought uses up a tiny amount of adenosine. At 2000 thoughts per hour, that's 50,000 thoughts per day, which uses all the adenosine stored since morning. Six of the eight hours of sleep is required to replace the adenosine used during the day. That's why you don't think very well at night, and it may not be wise to make important decisions at night.

The second reason for eight hours of sleep has to do with REM sleep, which is rapid eye movement sleep related to dreaming. This is sometimes called dream sleep. Research has shown that about two hours of REM sleep are required for optimal health and productivity. An important finding is that almost all the REM sleep occurs during the last two to three hours of sleep. Therefore, you need to sleep eight hours to attain that REM requirement. If you only sleep six hours, you don't get enough of the dream sleep resulting in being irritable, not productive, and quick to anger.

This dream sleep is needed for the positive qualities of being human such as thinking from the heart with kindness, gratitude, and giving. Without these last two hours, negative traits dominate from the anger and stress centers including anger, self-centered thoughts, and stress. This results in negative engagement in other people's lives. These last two hours are needed for the joy of life.

Now you know that you need eight hours of sleep, and you know why. How do you get eight hours of sleep every night?

One of the biggest mistakes people make is falling asleep for 30 minutes to an hour while watching TV or video clips at night before going to bed. This disrupts the natural sleep cycle. You'll find yourself tossing and turning all night. You'll be sleepy the next day. You need to limit exposure to bright lights, especially computer and mobile device screens, before going to bed.

Go to bed at the same time every night, add eight hours, and then get out of bed, not before and not after eight hours. Doing this keeps your circadian clock in rhythm with the body's natural balance.

You can take a midday nap for ten minutes to 15 minutes. This can give you energy for the day. This will not disrupt the night sleep cycle. Remember, 15 minutes or less for a nap.

Labels like a "morning person" or "night owl" can be hazardous. They can set you up for trouble. For example, "I'm not a morning person" or "Don't talk to me in the morning" are limiting statements. They set up a neuro-linguistic conditioning cycle that, with belief and practice, becomes true. Consider that there is no such thing as a morning person or a night owl.

You can't fall asleep?

If you get in the habit of going to sleep at the same time each night, add eight hours, and get up, then you'll fall asleep without thinking about it.

If you're thinking about yourself from the primitive stress center, you're not going to be able to sleep. Eliminate this thinking. You need to distract head brain thinking.

For example, the newer version of counting sheep is the countdown method: begin at 100 and slowly count backward to 90 and repeat as needed. Often you'll fall asleep before reaching 90 the first time and almost always after several times.

Other counting methods include counting inhales and exhales. For inhale counting, breathe in for the count of six, hold your breath to the count of eight, repeat as needed. For exhale counting, start with five and count backwards. When you reach one, repeat as needed. A page or two of light reading will often send you to sleep.

Another option that almost always works is self-hypnotic muscle relaxation method. Begin with relaxing your closed eyelids, then your face, your head, and, finally, your neck. You relax each region for a few seconds, totally concentrating on relaxing the body part. Then the shoulders, the arms, the hands, and the fingers. Now relax your chest, abdomen, and pelvis. You end by relaxing your thighs, calves, feet, and your toes.

You can combine this relaxation technique with breathing. As you relax your eyelids, you breathe in and feel the relaxation of the eyelids when you breathe out.

You can use breathing patterns to fall asleep. The first one is the use of belly breaths. Breathe in through your nose and move your belly up and out. Do several of these and you may fall asleep. The second method is equal in and equal out. Breathe in through your nose and breathe out. The third breathing technique is the yoga square breathing. Breathe in through your nose counting to ten, hold your breath for the count of ten, breathe out for the count of ten, and hold your breath for the count of ten. It's like a square.

Some nights, you just can't seem to sleep. This often happens because you've slept too much during the day, which disrupts your natural sleep rhythm. In this situation, try to stay in bed for eight hours. Don't get up to turn on the light or watch a video clip. Stay in bed. Although, it may not seem like it, you'll likely get enough sleep to function the next day, and you'll return to your normal sleep pattern that night.

If these sleep-inducing methods don't work for several nights, and you're still experiencing disrupted or fragmented sleep, then there's a possibility that a health condition, such as sleep apnea, restless leg movements, hormonal fluctuations, or pain, could be responsible for your trouble. Some sleeping problems do require a visit to the doctor. Talk to your doctor about your sleep issues, especially if you're experiencing insomnia and cannot get to sleep at all.

You need eight hours of naturally occurring sleep to restore the high-energy brain-cell balance necessary for a successful day. Stimulants and artificial means of interfering with this natural brain restoration will only serve to change an exciting, high-energy day to a weak, low-energy one. In addition, good sleep hygiene eliminates the need for sleeping pills.

A good sleep hygiene program starts with making eight hours of sleep a top priority. Go to bed at your usual time, add eight hours, and get up, not before and not after. Do this every night of the week. An occasional late night is not hazardous and will be adjusted with the next night's eight hours. Sleeping 10 or 12 hours to catch up is ineffective, disruptive, and does more harm than good. It's eight hours every night, not less and not more.

Other health habits for a good night's sleep include healthy nutrition and nothing to eat or drink after 7:00 p.m. An hour of exercise every morning is excellent for a good night's sleep. Everyone needs eight hours of sleep every night. You need six hours to recharge the brain energy and two hours of dream sleep for kindness and love.

*   *   *

Daily exercise for energy. Just as healthy nutrition and eight hours of sleep can improve our health, so can exercise, the third foundation for optimal health. No matter the situation, you can benefit from daily exercise.

One hour of exercise will provide you with energy for the entire day. This has been known for thousands of years. Aristotle said it's healthy to become short of breath from exercise every day to live an energetic life. Exercise decreases stress.

There are many positive reasons for one hour of daily exercise that include giving you energy, decreasing stress, and producing feel-good neurotransmitters and hormones.

Here's a myth: exercise makes you tired. It's the opposite. Exercise gives you energy. The more exercise you do up to one hour, the more energy you'll have. This amount of exercise also produces feel-good neurotransmitters such as endorphins, dopamine, and serotonin. Exercising together in a group class such as spinning, yoga, cross-fit, or dance produces oxytocin, the bonding hormone. Numerous studies have proven that exercise reduces stress, increases conditioning, and improves concentration. Exercise makes you feel better.

Almost any type of exercise can be beneficial. The correct form is essential. Try all of them and mix them up. You can exercise in the morning, after work, or whenever you please. I prefer the morning before starting the day because it's easy to develop into a routine, like brushing your teeth. You can get your workout clothes ready at night before going to sleep. You wake up in a fog, put your clothes on and socks. Brush your teeth, put on your sneakers, and go out the door for a run or get in the car and go to the workout facility and start your routine.

You can exercise at a workout facility, a gym, a community center, or at home. You can exercise alone or with a group. It's important to remember that regardless of the exercise, it needs to be performed regularly, and correct form is fundamental.

Mental clarity improves with exercise as the brain responds by increasing the brain energy and feel-good neurotransmitters norepinephrine, dopamine, and serotonin. Exercise is a natural way to generate these neurotransmitters, which are the same chemicals used in many anti-depressant drugs. Strenuous long-duration exercise such as running, swimming, biking, and even yoga produces endorphins, which reduce the perception of pain, decrease stress, and produce a feeling of well-being.

Among people with type-2 diabetes, exercise can normalize insulin function, which allows for better management of blood sugar, leading to fewer diabetic complications. Daily exercise results in an improved sleeping pattern.

Exercise can improve memory because exercise can result in neuro cell growth in the hippocampus, which is the brain's memory center and navigational center. There is a chemical in the brain called brain-derived neurotrophic factor (BDNF) that is used for neurogenesis as a growth factor for these new brain cells, and exercise can increase this growth factor. Exercise will improve your memory.

Maintaining lean muscle mass is essential for healthy muscles needed for posture, lifting, and climbing. It's important to combine muscle-strengthening exercises with weights at least twice per week to prevent lean muscle mass loss due to aging.

How much time should you exercise? Twenty minutes five days a week is minimal. I prefer one hour of exercise every day, although not more than one hour. Diminishing returns will occur after one hour of strenuous exercise. Form is fundamental. It's even important when you go for a walk or a hike. Hunched-over shoulders or shuffling your feet along creates muscle memory that can result in neck pain, low-back pain, and misaligned muscle structures.

I heard someone at the workout gym say that his doctor told him, "you've grown an inch since last year." He did Pilates for the past year and was excited to grow another inch taller next year. However, the increase in height isn't from growing an inch, it's from an improved healthy posture.

Walking tall with chin straight, eyes forward, shoulders pulled down, and shoulder blades squeezed together in the back builds muscles for optimal posture.

People sit too much. They develop "tech neck" from bending the head and neck working on the computer. Doctors and dentists develop the hunched back and sore neck syndrome as they lean over patients, the operating table, or the dental chair throughout the day.

A personal trainer can be helpful for gaining healthy posture, toning the muscles, and maintaining proprioception balance. Certified trainers are educated in proper form and postural deviations. Improved posture results in increased energy because poor posture makes many movements inefficient and painful. Poor posture can cause joints to move improperly. When joints don't function properly, life becomes exhausting, and exercise becomes daunting. However, many exercises performed correctly will improve posture, and healthy posture produces energy.

There are specialized "posture muscles," and specific posture exercises are needed to keep these strong. One of these muscles is called the erector spinae located from the lower back region to the neck along both sides of the spine. Call it the posterior chain. These are underneath the two big power muscles for lifting on each side called the latissimus dorsi, the lats.

You don't want to use the lats for standing and walking posture. These are so strong they bring your shoulders and neck down in a stooped, weak-appearing posture. To exercise the posterior chain spinae muscles, these power lats need to be taken offline. Performing stretching and weight exercises with arms extended above the head will disengage these big power muscles and allow strengthening of the spinae muscles for improved posture.

If you want to increase the strength of the lats, which are used for lifting, you need to perform an opposite group of exercises. For all types of exercise, it's important to learn the right type of exercise for the right purpose. Form is extremely important for muscle-strengthening exercises. Specific exercises are designed to develop specific muscle groups. If an exercise is not learned and done properly, it can result in muscle pulls and ligament injuries. It's important to learn proper movement patterns and rhythms. Proper form can be used to fix problems, prevent new problems, and ensure maximum benefit from an exercise.

Where should you exercise? Three of the most common options are at home, outdoors, or in a commercial facility. Working out at home is easy but you have the disadvantage of being alone, so you miss the socialization and safety aspects of working out with other people.

Exercise outside is phenomenal when the weather is good, the allergy index is low, and the air quality is high. Exercising in nature has been shown to result in twice as much improvement in mood than exercising indoors. Outdoor exercising results in greater decreases in tension and stress. Even five minutes of exercise in green space can improve mood and confidence.

Exercising, working out, or doing yoga outside, or playing an outdoor sport, adds a special feeling of experiencing life at a deeper level. It's subtle but once you recognize it, a warm feeling of well-being comes over you. It's especially noticeable when you participate in outside winter sports such as hiking, skiing, or skating on an outdoor rink.

There's no English word for this feeling. The Norwegians call this *friluftsliv*. It was first used in 1859 and now represents Norway's allure with nature. The spirit of *friluftsliv* lives inside all of us. The word means walking and climbing in mountains for good tidings. *Friluftsliv* means living in tune with nature, returning to natural surroundings that provide balance and healing.

Working out at a commercial facility has big advantages. You can make it convenient and routine because there are so many locations. The main advantage of working out at a facility is the social aspect of having friends there, and the variety of exercise options, from free weights and machines to yoga and all types of classes.

Some people only do group classes such as spinning, cross-fit, yoga, and Zumba. They love them! They're energizing and great for motivation and camaraderie. People meet socially for coffee or other events and develop lifelong friendships.

Exercise every day. You might even meet your spouse! It was a beautiful early fall morning in New England when I was doing a New York City marathon training run along the phenomenal Charles River in Boston. My pleasant thoughts were interrupted with an even more pleasant thought as I saw my future wife coming toward me. My legs on their own volition made the U-turn to run beside her, and I found myself saying hi to Joan. I didn't get maced, so after some small talk, I asked her for a date, and she accepted. Our first date was at the café above TV's famous *Cheers*, and our second date was the "Celtic's Halloween Bash" road race, joining 1,000 costumed runners through the streets of Boston.

Our first anniversary saw us running the original marathon from Marathon, Greece, to the Olympic Stadium in Athens. The six-month training for this was magical, especially the 20-mile tune-up runs the three Sundays before the actual marathon. We ran from our Back Bay location to Wellesley and back, except we never seemed to make it all the way back because we would stop for a huge ice cream "mix-in" with all the extras. It was wonderful running together during the tune-up sessions because we drifted into the blissful alpha-brainwave state and the exercise-released endorphins gave us an extra kick of pleasure.

A special discussion about the heart is needed for people over 40 and especially over 60. This is because pushing yourself to maximal capacity can cause atrial flutter or atrial fibrillation. A vigorous, one-hour workout of pushing 200-pound sleds alternating with 20 push-ups and 20 kettlebell lifts gives a person a great feeling and a tremendous amount of energy but could be too much too fast at an older age causing a sustained high heart rate.

Cyclists in their 40s and 50s can't wait to compete in races and love the feeling of winning. These races take them to sustained heart rates of 160 beats per minute or even higher for hours. They can't stop. They become obsessed with the feeling of competing and winning. The coach that does training by sustained levels of heart rate rather than timed training can make runners feel good but can lead to atrial fibrillation.

It would be great to work out at that level every week and to compete every week, but no matter how much people want to deny reality, the heart muscle and its electrical system change over time, which becomes a consideration for the senior athlete. People in their 20s and 30s with healthy hearts can work out and compete with their maximal heart rate without causing harm.

For people in their 40s through 60s and beyond, having a maximal heart rate of 160 to 170 beats per minute for too long can cause an abnormal heart rhythm referred to as *atrial flutter* or *atrial fibrillation*. This may not be a life-threatening abnormal rhythm, but the aberrant rhythm may not return to normal on its own, or even with medication, so an electrical shock with cardioversion in a hospital setting is needed.

Vigorous exercise is enjoyable and do as much as you like, but do not push yourself. When your exercise is becoming excessive, ask yourself if you're pushing yourself. If so back off for a moment decreasing the heart rate, and then resume. Keeping a sustained heart rate at a healthy level for your age is a wise decision.

Your life will change dramatically for the better when you develop a daily exercise routine. It will provide energy, relieve stress, and give you an upbeat feeling to propel you through life with ease and enjoyment.

*   *   *

Meditation. It's good for the soul. I call this slow alpha-brainwave meditation time for calmness, creativity, and complete acceptance. Learn to know where you're thinking from so you can spend time in the mind. Learn about meditation so you can learn to be in the slow brainwave state spontaneously when you need to.

Meditation is related to brainwaves. There are several types based on frequency of the wave. Beta-brainwaves are at fourteen cycles per second and occur during a typical waking day. Alpha brainwaves at ten cycles occur during light sleep or rapid-eye movement sleep known as REM sleep. This is when dreams occur. Theta brainwaves at seven cycles occur during deeper sleep. Slow delta brainwaves at four cycles per second occur during very deep sleep, and 15 minutes of delta-brainwave sleep are required every night to sustain life.

Other brainwaves include rapid gamma waves that may occur during peak performance.

Orienting brainwaves or "O" waves occur when you go from one location to another. If you've gotten up to get something in another room and when you get there, you've forgotten what you went for, then you've been zapped by the O waves. You can only be in one brainwave state at any given time. The O waves take over to orient you to another room and block your memory brainwaves. These O waves can interfere with meditation if you move from place to place.

Meditation is experiencing slow brainwaves while awake. With practice, staying in the alpha-brainwave state can be easily attained. For a wider application, the theta-brainwave state can be obtained. This may require years of practice as in compassion meditation by the Buddhist's monks. It's largely unknown, but you can imagine the intense feelings associated with being awake while in the very slow delta brainwave state.

Everyone knows the feeling of alpha-brainwave time while awake because it is the same as daydreaming. These brainwaves give you a calm, soothing feeling. You may experience them while hiking in the mountains, during a slow jog, shoveling snow, raking leaves on a cool fall day, or even having an enjoyable conversation. Spend some alpha-brainwave time every day.

There are many benefits of meditation. Alpha-brainwave time decreases stress by lowering your blood adrenaline levels. You go from the flight-or-fight state to the stay-and-play state. Meditation releases feel-good neurotransmitters and hormones, including endorphin, dopamine, and serotonin.

Meditation balances the brain regions. This quiets the amygdala anger center and shuts down the cingulate self-centered center because you can only think from one location at a time. If you're thinking from the mind, there are no thoughts from the anger center or stress center. There are no thoughts from the accumbens addiction center. Meditation is an inside job. Meditation brings calmness and happiness inside with no need for outside action.

Science-based benefits include improved positive social interactions because of strengthening mirror-neuron function that help understand and empathize with each other. Another science benefit is increased telomerase activity preventing chromosome shortening and prolonging life.

Application of the Eplerian Life Philosophy to meditation shows that creativity and innovation occur during alpha-brainwave time. During meditation, you can experience the feelings from the mind including total calmness, belonging and acceptance, and unconditional love.

Can people be awake during the slower theta brainwave state? Yes, but it takes practice. Theta-brainwave time has the same many benefits of the alpha-brainwave time and is especially useful for healing. Learn to experience the alpha-brainwave and theta-brainwave state while awake and experience healing and new adventures with the mind.

What does it feel like to be in the alpha-brainwave state? Since the alpha state is slower than the day-to-day beta state, the five senses of sight, hearing, feeling, taste, and smell are going to be altered. These senses are lessened and feel different.

For sight, you'll see a faint fluorescent bluish glow surrounding objects. The fluorescent blue will surround your head if you're gazing into a blank video-screen monitor or this will appear surrounding the tops of the trees when you're running or hiking outside.

This is the same image that you visualize if you stare at a red circle on a white piece of paper for 30 seconds and then look to the side of the circle. The bluish circle you see is the same aura surrounding your face, the trees, or other objects that you see while in the alpha-brainwave state. Your other senses are also affected. Your hearing is less, your sense of smell and taste are diminished, and you'll have less feeling in your touch.

In the theta brainwave state, these feelings are dramatically different. The blue aura is replaced with a pleasant darkness with no shape. Your face becomes featureless in a soft way. You hear nothing. Taste and smell are absent. You have no feeling in your body, your arms, or your legs. All these changes have a profound calming effect and feeling of serenity and peace.

How do you experience these slow brainwave states while awake so you can be in the mind? There are many ways. You need to establish your own so that you can use the mind whenever you wish.

One method of experiencing the alpha state is with the traditional transcendental meditation (TM) from an instructor or in a group. This is sitting quietly with eyes closed and repeating a one- or two-word mantra like the "om" until the mind is no longer racing.

The formal TM training consists of a seven-step course beginning with an introductory discussion of the mind, health, and promoting inner and outer peace. The second step is a preparatory discussion of the theory and origin of the practice. The third step is a one-on-one interview with the TM teacher and students receive their mantra. The next three sessions are called checking where students are continuously and gently reminded of the correct practice of TM and are told the potential results and stages of human consciousness. There are follow-up sessions to confirm they are practicing the technique properly.

There are many other ways to be in the alpha-brainwave state that are not as formal. You need to find a method that is best for you so that you can learn to be in the alpha-brainwave state to use the mind for creativity and solving problems whenever you need to.

I have three ways to experience slow brainwave state that ultimately has led me to being able to access the mind at any time.

The first is running on a treadmill and looking at the blank video screen with eyes half-closed. You chose a safe speed. Continue to gaze at the screen and quiet your thoughts. After a several minutes, you will notice an intermittent blue, fluorescent haze surrounding your head. You and now in alpha-brainwave state and enjoy the journey.

The second is called the music entrainment method. With or without headphones, listen to relaxing music. You can go to YouTube and search for entrainment music and select binaural (one frequency for one ear and another frequency for the other ear) music for alpha, theta, or delta frequencies.

Listen to the entrainment sound, sit quietly in a chair, eyes closed or using an airplane sleeping blindfold. Take a deep breath through your nose and exhale. Begin to slowly relax your body starting with your eyelids, then your face, your neck, shoulders, upper arms, lower arms, hands, and fingers. Now relax your chest, your abdomen, and your pelvis. Relax your thighs, calves, feet, and finally your toes. By now you are in an alpha brainwave state or an even slower brainwave state.

The Norwegian term *friluftsliv* describes the feeling of being outdoors. This is the alpha-brainwave state that a person develops when outside in free air. This can happen at any time of the year, and even better during the chilly winter months. Remember what people say: "There's no such thing as bad weather, only bad clothes."

My third method for being in the alpha-brainwave state is visualization using the 25-countdown method. This is eyes-open meditation during a walk, yoga, hike, bike, or on a treadmill. You can also use this method during a stressed and painful situation intense medical or dental procedure.

It's a visual-guided meditation. Visualize a scene at the seashore, in the forest, or in the mountains. Begin walking and exploring the surroundings, stopping occasionally to reflect on the surroundings. Then visualize a stairway going down to the ocean edge or a meadow. These are ancient wooden stairs with smooth wooden railings on each side. These 25 stairs have been travelled since the beginning of time.

Start from the beginning. Visualize getting out of the car and walking to the dunes overlooking the ocean. You start walking and visualize the sea grass about three feet tall on both sides of you. After a few steps, you cross over a small wooden bridge and look at the yellow and orange choi fish gently swimming in the stream below. You stay there for a few moments feeling peace. You continue walking among the sea grass to the ancient wooden stairs at the side of the dune.

You begin slowly and quietly walking down the steps, holding on to the wooden railing for balance. Starting with 25 at the top step, you count yourself down, 24, 23, 22. As you count down, you feel more and more relaxed with each step, 15, 10. Now you hear the waves quietly landing on the beach 5, 4. You smell the salty air as you near the ocean edge, and you're totally relaxed. It's a beautiful day, warm with a gentle breeze, 3, 2, 1. You step on the warm sand with your bare feet and feel the warm sensation of the soft sand between your toes.

Slightly off to the left you see a canopy with flowing silk drapes hanging from the wooden top, and inside, there's a big, soft chair that welcomes you to sit. Then you breathe in healing energy for any area that needs attention and needs healing.

Now you walk toward the right, parallel to the beach where there is a deep blue, bottomless pond. You gaze into the middle of the pond and visualize yourself going through the earth entering the other side, going around the earth and up to the top of Mount Everest, and then returning to where you are, grounded. You're now grounded and can think about the real world and think of about three things you going to do such as developing a new way of doing things ar work, a new idea for a new product, working on a community project, funding a new venture, or starting a business.

After a few moments of thinking about your day, continue walking on the sand, this time toward the right where there is an ancient wooden door, called the *delta door*, after delta brainwaves.

You walk toward the door with your hand outstretched to the wooden handle to open it. The door disappears as you walk into a golden pavilion with marble tiles on the floor and a fountain in the middle. You walk toward the fountain, and people begin to surround you on all sides. They're friendly and kind. They want to see you and be with you.

You're standing near the fountain, your chin straight, eyes forward, back straight, and palms facing out. You're filled with strength, gratitude, and compassion. You are filled with success. You're filled with love and grace. People want to be with you. You want to be with them. Talk with them, enjoy their presence. Spend time here.

If you wish, you can continue walking into a void with no physical surroundings letting your body disappear and becoming the mind. Explore the feelings of calmness, total acceptance, and unconditional love. You can also search for answers to your current concerns.

It's time to leave the journey. Count yourself down 5, 4, 3, 2, 1 and returning to the day feeling good, full of energy, and excited to enjoy the day.

Heidi Sormaz, a Yale University-trained psychologist, talks about the need to interrupt the cascade of overthinking and to sooth us. She talks about concentration meditation that involves focusing on a single point. This could be following the sensation of your breath, repeating a word or mantra, or counting 108 beads on a mala board. Focus your awareness on one of these points as the thoughts settle and drift into the slow meditative slow-brainwave state.

There are two breath-counting techniques that can be used for meditation. One is for counting exhales and the other is counting during an inhale.

For counting exhales, count an exhale as five and then count backwards with each exhale. When you reach one, repeat as needed.

For an inhale, slowly count to six, hold your breath for the count of two, and then exhale. Repeat as needed.

There's also sound meditation. Sit comfortably in a chair with a deep cleansing breath and listen to the sounds surrounding you. Don't think about the sounds, just listen. Then listen to the sounds a few feet away and then the sounds in the street. No thinking, only listening to sounds. Now imagine and listen to the sounds in the forest.

Listen to the sounds on a pond, then on a lake, and finally the sounds on the ocean. You can close by listening to the sounds of the sails on a magnificent sailing vessel during a beautiful day in the middle of the ocean. If you wish you can listen to all the other sounds on the ship.

Try spending alpha-brainwave meditation time every day. It's easy to do and decreases stress, releases feel-good neurotransmitters and hormones, quiets the amygdala anger center, and shuts down the cingulate self-centered stress center. Alpha-brainwave time helps understand and empathize with each other. It improves creativity and is healthy.

Chapter 5

Eliminate Stress

"The greatest weapon against stress is our ability to choose one thought over another."

— William James

People try to please people. We judge ourselves and feel sorry for ourselves. We compare ourselves to others and try to be the perfect person in our head. We complain, criticize, and blame. We feel guilty about something we didn't do. We have negative thoughts about the past and the future. We try to control others. All these self-centered thoughts cause stress.

Break the stress habit by stop thinking about yourself. Learning how to eliminate stress can bring us the greatest joy and success in life. The three most common factors that cause stress include money, the job, and close personal relationships.

Stress at work can occur from physically demanding work or prolonged intense concentration. Frequent changes in the job cause stress. Demands from the boss and coworkers can be a huge cause of stress. Having no support will cause stress.

Individuals need control of their needs and time at work. For example, take two people: one has control over the hot or cold environment and the other has no control. Over time, the 'executive' who has the control will remain healthy. The other will be stressed and unhealthy.

The more control you have at your job the better. If you have no control, monitor your health and wellbeing. If this is influenced in a negative way, a change may be required before harmful effects develop.

The lack of accomplishment is another source of stress at work. The feeling of accomplishment is so important, that it is one of the five components of well-being developed by UPenn Professor Marty Seligman. The other four components include being engaged in life, doing something outside yourself like volunteering, positive social interaction, and happiness.

The manager who considers the job listening to team complaints and problems will be stressed. However, the customer service employee who finds solutions to customer complaints will enjoy the work.

Money, not enough or too much, can be a tremendous source of stress that can destroy friendships, marriages, and careers. The biggest and most unhealthy stress is from a negative cash flow, not making enough money each month to pay normal living expenses. This is tolerable for three to six months, but after that, the daily stress will cause harmful health effects. Something must change. If there is no additional income, then liquidation of assets or even bankruptcy will be necessary. This stress is too much to sustain for an extended period.

Other sources of stress from money include paying rent or the mortgage, paying taxes, and paying debt. Lack of a stable income can be stressful.

Stress from close personal relationships including a spouse, family member, friend or business partner can take many forms. The biggest cause of stress in a relationship occurs when one or both are not being their true selves with constant self-centered thinking from the stress center. This causes loss of trust, bickering and frequent fights, jealousy, and negative destructive communication.

A serious cause of stress between spouses occurs when one person develops dementia, Alzheimer's, or other debilitating disease requiring constant care. This has an insidious unnoticeable beginning and can be too late by the time of recognition. The chronically ill person doesn't want to cause stress, but because of the underlying situation, the person may become demanding of the other person's time and energy.

These are the common situations resulting in stress, but what is the fundamental cause of stress in the human? Functional MRI studies show the cause is whenever you're thinking from the cingulate brain region. Whenever you're thinking about yourself, you're thinking from the cingulate brain region stress cente. Whenever you're stressed, you're thinking from the primitive brain.

What are the health problems caused by stress? Stress causes the adrenaline cortisol response which causes increased heart rate and blood pressure. The immune system shuts down. The digestive system shuts down resulting in increased body fat. Performance and innovation slow. Cortisol causes inflammation resulting in heart attacks, strokes, and cancer.

Stress causes tightening of the muscles, and as a result, typical low back pain is from muscle spasm caused by stress. A cold is from a virus but caused by stress shutting down the immune system. A heart attack is from plaque closing the arteries to the heart, which is caused by inflammation from stress.

The stress center in the brain is independent from all other brain regions and can take over your life. Left unchecked, it will control a person's life 24 hours of the day. This is the ancient crocodile brain, and crocodiles are angry and only think of themselves. Learn how to stop thinking from this brain region.

> *"Break the stress habit. Stop thinking about yourself."*

Here are several ways to limit thinking from the stress center to less than ten seconds and you can use one or more of them and you can develop your own method.

1. Use the six- to eight-second stress rule. This means when you recognize when you're thinking about yourself and experience stress. Feel the stress without thinking. Do not think about the situation. Feel the stress, feel the stress for six to eight seconds, and move on. The calming system will neutralize the feeling of stress if you don't think.
2. Recognize the stress and stop. The moment you recognize that you're thinking about yourself, stop thinking this thinking. Change the subject. Do something else. Think from the heart with kindness or giving. Think from the mind to solve a problem.

3. Use the neural-bypass technique. Bypass your usual self-centered response to a situation. When you realize you're thinking about yourself and feel stress, instantly repeat "love and peace, love and peace, love and peace" to yourself over and over for 30 to 60 seconds. This may seem strange at first, but you can only think from one location at a time, if you're saying these two words over and over, you can't be thinking from the stress center.

4. Think from the heart. Recognize when you're thinking about your problems or having negative thoughts about yourself, then instantly think from your heart about being kind to someone, giving something to someone, or helping someone. Give a small gift to someone. Help someone with a project. The instant you think from the heart, you're no longer thinking from the stress center because you can only think from one location at a time. You can't think from the stress center and the heart at the same time.

5. Think from the mind. The moment you recognize you're having recurrent thoughts about yourself, think from the mind about a project at home, at work, or in the community. Think about the next step in your upcoming adventure. Think about the next positive step you can take right now. You can't feel stress from the stress center if you're thinking from the mind.

6. Stimulate the parasympathetic calming system. Find yourself stressed? Take three belly breaths, take a drink of water, go for a 12-minute walk, or do one of the yoga breathing practices such as deep slow equal breaths in and equal breaths out. The automatic calming system will neutralize the stress response.

7. Energize endorphins. You can do this with a few seconds of freezing water at the end of your shower; working out with weights, spinning class, yoga, or Zumba class; or going for a long run.

8. Distraction. Distract your self-centered stress thoughts by listening to positive music such as Mozart or electronic dance music (EDM), have a festive meal, laugh out loud, or enjoy positive social interaction with people.

Learn to stop thinking about yourself. Bypass the stress center, transfer out of the stress center. Think from the heart with kindness and giving or from the mind with creativity. Be kind to yourself with self-compassion.

Be creative, explore solutions, create a project or a business to improve people's lives. Create a way to help someone.

Eventually, limiting thinking from the stress center will become a conditioned response and you will go through the day with zero stress. That's the amazing thing that can happen to you. Try it.

What's the definition of zero stress? If at any time you answer 'zero' to the question, "What's your stress level?" then you have zero stress. This is much better than the average stress level in the world of 3.5 on a scale of ten with many countries above 5.0. This is the disease zone for heart attacks, strokes, and cancer. Level 10.0 is the death zone. Stay out of the stress center for improved health and enjoyment.

For example, you may have a negative cash flow money problem. You need to make more money or cut expenses. This is stressful. A typical response is to keep thinking about the problem, worry about what's going to happen, and be unhappy. A common response is anger. You can complain, criticize, and blame. You can compare yourself to everyone who is doing better and isn't going through this horrible problem.

You can do all these things over and over. However, these thoughts are from the cingulate stress center causing continual stress. Worse, as you can only think from one location at a time, if you're stressed, you can't think from anywhere else to solve the problem.

The better option for dealing with a stressful money problem is to stop thinking about yourself and think from the heart with kindness to yourself, and then think from the mind for solutions.

Consider not only managing stress, eliminate stress! How do you do this? Do not trigger or activate the stress center. You need to try to find a way to not activate the stress center. One way is when you recognize the stress trigger, say "no trigger, no trigger, no trigger" over and over for a few seconds and then switch to "love and peace, love and peace, love and peace" for 30 seconds.

Facing life's stressful situations with money, the job, or close personal relationships, you need to learn stop thinking about yourself from the stress center so you can think from the heart with kindness to yourself and think from the mind for creative solutions.

Stressed? Stop thinking about yourself. If you were to go throughout your day and record all your thoughts, how many of those thoughts would be about you? Thinking about ourselves can range from thinking about our problems to how we appear to other people. This pattern of self-centered thinking leads to a great amount of stress. Want to stop stressing? Stop thinking about yourself.

> *"Stress is caused by thinking about yourself. Be your true authentic self. The less you think about yourself, the more you are your true self."*

When people think about themselves, they're thinking from the primitive brain region. This region is for instinctive reactions that will save your life in an emergency. This region is not for thinking. Thinking from here is stress. That's why I call it the stress center.

There are obvious thoughts that mean you're thinking about yourself such as thinking about your problems and negative thoughts about yourself. There are other thoughts that mean you're thinking about yourself that are not obvious such as worry and guilt.

The most common self-centered thought is thinking about your problems. Try this, right now, think about your biggest problem at this moment. Go ahead.

Where are you thinking from? It's from the center region of your head. Then you build the negative story about the problem that includes the future consequences of not solving the problem and losing everything you have.

After a few seconds, you feel the physical effects of stress, which are from the adrenalin cortisol release. Your abdomen becomes tense. You feel distressed. You lose your appetite. You might even feel nauseated. This is called stress. This is what it feels like every time you think about yourself.

This can be avoided if you limit yourself to six to eight seconds thinking from this region. This is not harmful to you or anyone else. The key is not to think, only to feel the stress. No thinking, only feeling. Feel the stress, let it peak, and think from somewhere else.

After you learn to manage the stress for less than ten seconds, then you need to not activate the stress center. If you stop stress triggers from activating the stress center, then you'll never have the feeling of stress.

You develop stress whenever you're angry at yourself and with negative self-destructive thoughts. You've made a mistake or a decision with a bad outcome. Acknowledge the feeling, try to learn something, feel the disappointment for six to eight seconds and then think from somewhere else. Think about a new solution or helping someone.

You feel sorry for yourself, or self-pity is thinking about yourself. You've been rejected or you didn't get a promotion. This is a time to first think from the heart with kindness to yourself and then think from the mind for the next step.

Complaining and criticizing comes from thinking about yourself. You know people who are incessant complainers. They're usually complaining about their job, their close relationships, or politicians are ruining their lives. This is not useful thinking. It's boring and annoying for others, and it takes away from thinking about what to do about the complaining and takes away from enjoying the moment. These same people often escalate the conversation to criticizing other people, their boss or coworkers, or their living situation. This self-centered thinking is boring and tedious, helping no one.

Judging people in a negative way is thinking about yourself. This means you're judging yourself. You're comparing the other person to yourself, and the other person doesn't measure up to the way you think you are. This is meaningless thinking and has no firm grounds for the accusation. Everyone on the planet has characteristics and actions that make them unique. There's a difference, not better or worse.

When you believe what people are criticizing you about, blaming you, or complaining about you, you're thinking about yourself. If a narcissistic controlling person says these things to you, they're lying to make you feel guilty and bad about yourself. Don't fall for the trap. Don't believe the words. Let them pass through. Don't engage. Don't fight back. Be your true self and take the consequences. If you won't play the game, they'll leave you alone and find someone else.

You may find that you're always comparing yourself to someone else. Someone who makes more money, has a better job, or is more popular. This thinking needs to stop as it takes away from enjoying your life.

You may be trying to be someone else, especially the perfect person you've created in your head. You can never attain that mythical person in your head. You're trying to be your job title. All this thinking is from the stress center. Someone is making more money than you. Your boss is younger than you are. You're doing your job by the book. There is no book for any job. Instead, be your true self first, then you will do the job successfully.

Some people are constantly thinking about what other people think of them. Are they smart enough? Do they have the right clothes? Do they have a prestigious job? Did they go to the right school? The list is endless. Be your true self, and you have none of these thoughts.

Being resentful and jealous are self-centered thoughts. You're comparing yourself to others. This has nothing to do with your life. Be your true self with no concerns of jealousy.

Retaliation and revenge are thinking about yourself and represent negative and potentially harmful thinking for you and for others. There is no need for these feelings. They serve no purpose except harm.

You've been hurt by someone, betrayed by someone, or tricked by someone. This makes you angry at yourself for getting yourself in the situation and you're angry at the person for what the person did to you. These are natural reactions. This is a time to use the six to eight second anger rule. Feel the anger, let it peak, and it will pass.

Don't think about the episode again and think about what you can do to distract your thinking. If you can't stop thinking about it. Do the opposite. Forgiveness from the heart. It's for you, not for the other person. Once you think from the heart with forgiveness, the thoughts will vanish, and you can go on with your life.

Worry requires a special discussion. People feel that worrying about something is helpful to themselves and to others. It's the opposite. It's self-centered from the cingulate stress center. Worry consists of thinking to yourself about "what ifs" always with a negative outcome. What if I lose my job? What if my children have a car accident or someone hurts them? What if I can't make enough money? This becomes a habit without even thinking. Telling your children, "enjoy the party, but I worry about you." Worrying is stressful. It's unhealthy. It doesn't do you any good and it doesn't help anyone else.

How do you stop this bad habit? Understand what worrying means and clearly understand that's it's harmful to you and others. Know that it's a bad habit so you actively need to think about it every time you worry.

You can replace worry with a new habit, instead of worrying about something, think from the heart with being kind to yourself with self-compassion or say something positive in its place. Do the opposite, instead of giving your "what ifs" a negative ending, give it a positive ending. "You're going to have a great time at the party, you'll meet a new friend."

Feeling guilty is like worry. It's thinking about yourself from the stress center. This causes stress and all the associated harmful effects. On the surface, people feel they should feel guilty for something they did wrong. A better option is to acknowledge the situation, try to learn something from it, and think from the heart with self-compassion and being kind to yourself. After that, think from the mind with creative solutions to the situation. Remember, you can only think from one location at a time. If you're thinking about how bad you feel because you made a mistake, then you can't think about being kind to yourself and finding a solution.

Almost all negative thoughts and words come from the stress center. Negative thoughts need to be minimized and neutralized by positive thoughts and words.

Negative thoughts about money are a huge cause of stress. You have self-destructive thoughts because you're not smart enough to fix the problem. You have self-pity thoughts because you think that no one else is having this problem. You're angry because you didn't do anything wrong, why are you being punished, and no one will help you. You're resentful toward others because this hasn't happened to them. You worry because you're going to lose your car and your house. You feel guilty because you can't solve the problem. During all of this, you're getting rejections after rejections. All these thoughts are thinking about yourself in a negative way leading to severe stress, increased blood pressure, and an adverse health outcome. This is going to cause an illness and a hospital visit.

You're thinking about yourself from the stress center if you're thinking about the following: (1) Thinking about your problems. (2) Negative thoughts about yourself, angry at yourself, and self-destructive thoughts. (3) Feeling sorry for yourself and self-pity. (4) Complaining and criticizing. (5) Judging others. (6) Blaming others. (7) Wrongly blaming yourself. (8) Comparing yourself to others. (9) Trying to be someone else and the made-up perfect person in your head. (10) Trying to be your job title. (11) Thinking about what other people think of you. (12) Resentful and jealousy. (13) Retaliation and revenge. (14) Worry. (15) Guilt. (16) Negative thoughts about the past.(17) Negative thoughts about the future. (18) Negative thoughts about work. (19) Negative thoughts about a close relationship. (20) Negative thoughts about money.

Other self-centered thoughts include calling someone out during a meeting or a social gathering and holding onto a grudge.

There are many other situations not listed. If you're stressed and not thinking about any of these, then explore the cause so you can do something about it. You're thinking about yourself, you need to find out what it is.

Here's a call to action: First, acknowledge when you're thinking about yourself. Second, experience the physical feelings of stress. Third, instantly think from somewhere else. All in less than ten seconds. Better yet, learn to stop activating the stress center.

The ultimate method for eliminating stress, anger, and self-centered negative thoughts is to "live in the mind."

What does this mean? Slow down the brainwaves to connect with the mind for creativity and experience the feelings of calm, acceptance, and joy. If you're in the mind, then the brainwaves are too slow to experience feelings from the primitive anger center or stress center because you can't be in two locations at once. It's either the mind or the primitive brain. Eliminate all negative self-centered thoughts by living in the mind.

*   *   *

Calm breathing. Take a deep breath. Notice how it brings you more in tune with the world around you. Notice how you begin to think and feel more clearly. The simple act of breathing can restore a magical sense of calm that's easy to lose as we go about managing everything from our house life to our work life. You can tap into the calmness of breathing from the ground up.

Breathing can calm the rough waters of life. We breathe in and out 25,000 times every day. You'll be amazed about the new science of breathing.

Let's start with the story about James Nestor. He's a journalist who wanted to improve his breathing and authored a book called *Breath*. It's the new science of a lost art.

Nestor began his research for the book by being in a study where his nose was completely plugged for ten days, forcing him to breathe only through his mouth. He said that this was the most miserable ten days of his life. He went from snoring a couple of minutes a night to snoring four hours a night through mouth-breathing. He developed sleep apnea which meant he stopped breathing for several seconds each night. He said his stress level was off the charts. His nervous system was a mess. He felt awful.

The nose is for breathing. It calms the mind switching the body to a more relaxed state. The mouth is for eating and drinking, not for breathing. Breathing deeply through your nose has a calming effect. Breathe deeply using the diaphragm to pull in lots of air.

Rapid shallow breathing confuses the brain thinking there's danger and produces the adrenalin response increasing tension and stress. Being nervous and breathing rapidly produces a constant state of stress. Rapid shallow breathing causes a sympathetic nervous system response with increased heart rate, increased blood pressure, and tense muscles.

Deep breathing has the opposite response, a calming response, which is called the parasympathetic response. That's why it's helpful to breathe deeply through your nose if you've been in an accident or are not feeling well. Breathe deeply through your nose, it's a calming reflex. Breathing fast through your mouth makes you tense and nervous.

There are differences between inhaling and exhaling. Breathing in causes a slight sympathetic response with increased heart rate and long slow breaths breathing out causes a calming effect. There's a difference between the right and left nose. Breathing through the right-side of the nose causes a small adrenalin response, which is the sympathetic nervous system we talked about that produces an increased heart rate and muscle metabolism. The left side has the opposite response with a calming effect.

To catch your breath after exercising or other cause of shortness of breath, breathe deeply through the left side of your nose with a long slow breath out. This will have a calming effect restoring your normal breathing.

The nose protects us from infections. The nose is packed with specialized immune cells called nasal lymphoid tissue that protects the body from viruses and other infectious organisms.

If you're nervous about giving a presentation, a performance, or a job interview, take three belly breaths. Put your hand on your belly, take a deep breath in and move your hand up and outward, then exhale the breath out slowly. Breathe in, move your belly up, and slowly breathe out.

If you're tense and can't sleep, breathe in equal amount of air as you breathe out, or better yet do yoga square breathing. Breathe deeply counting to ten. Hold your breath counting to ten. Breathe out counting to ten. And hold counting to ten. Breathing can help calm frazzled nerves and hysterical moments.

Breathing is an important part of self-healing. Approach the disease or injury in a positive manner. Use breathing techniques and visualization. The breathing techniques include the equal breath in and the equal breath out or the yoga square breathing technique. Breathe through your nose for health and use breathing to calm your nerves.

The Yale University-trained psychologist, Heidi Sormaz talks about yoga breathing techniques. Yoga has become extremely popular with a yoga spot practically on every city block. Why? People feel better after a yoga session. Regardless of the type of yoga, concentrating and thinking about breathing is a major reason for feeling better. Equal breaths in and equal breaths out, and yoga square breathing are two techniques. Heidi Sormaz describes several others.

Expanding the ribs technique can be used to relieve tension in the neck and shoulders. Give yourself a hug and expand the bottom of your ribcage. Push your ribcage against your hands. Feel your ribcage expand outward. Feel the tension release in your neck and shoulders. Expand the ribs when you breathe in and feel the muscles between the ribs expand. These are the intercostal muscles stretching. This is healthy and improves your breathing.

Telescoping your breathing technique involves lifting the ribs up and away from the diaphragm. Put your hands on the top crest of your hips. Inhale filling your breath in the bottom of the ribs and then filling the middle and upper ribs. Pull your ribcage up and away from the hips. Exhale to get all the air out by pulling your belly back to get all the air out. Exhale releasing the shoulders away from the ears relieving tension.

The Yoga free-up-your-diaphragm or fake-inhale technique is helpful for expanding the breathing. In the standing position, bend your knees slightly and place your hands on your thighs. Exhale all your breath out and hold it. Use your muscles to draw in your belly and expand your ribs without inhaling. Your ribcage widens without the intake of air. Let the belly relax and then exhale.

The Yoga super shoulder shrug breathing technique is for the release of shoulder tension. Place your arms by your side, then relax your shoulders. Inhale, expand your ribs. Hold your breath and hike your shoulders up to your ears and squeeze your shoulders straight back. Now exhale and move your head up and all the way back and a brief hold as you exhale. Then, relax your shoulders as you finish exhaling.

The yoga alternate nostril breath technique is breathing through each side of the nose. Take the fourth finger of the right hand and close off the left nostril and inhale through the right nostril for a count of five. Close off both nostrils with the thumb and fourth finger and hold the breath for the count of five. Release the left nostril and exhale through the left nostril for the count of five. Now close off the right nostril and inhale through the left nostril for a count of five. Close off both nostrils and hold the breath for the count of five. Exhale through the right nostril for the count of five. Finish by taking a breath through both nostrils open expanding your rib cage and then exhaling.

Two yoga breath-counting breathing techniques can be used for meditation. The first is breathe in for the count of six, hold your breath to the count of eight, repeat as needed. The second is with an exhales, give an exhale a count of five, and a count of four for the next exhale until the count of one. Repeat as needed.

Breathe through your nose by breathing slowly. Exhale slowly through the left side of your nose for the calming effect. Take three belly breaths to relax before a big event. Use yoga breathing for healing and relieving stress. Breathe through your nose for health.

*   *   *

Calming reflex. We can learn to eliminate stress by using our calming reflexes. Let's elaborate on exercises that will help recognize and use our calming reflexes to eliminate ever day stressors.

Learn triggers for the parasympathetic calming reflex system. The parasympathetic nervous system is a calming mechanism to neutralize the excitable sympathetic nervous system. Without this calming system, a continual excited state will destroy organ systems and the body.

The sympathetic nervous system is "fight or flight," but my favorite is the parasympathetic system, "stay and play."

Prolonged and unchecked activation of the sympathetic system from stress causes adrenalin cortisol release producing inflammation and heart disease. You need to allow the parasympathetic system to neutralize the sympathetic system before harmful effects develop by not thinking from the anger center and stress center.

The benefits of triggering the parasympathetic calming system are numerous. This slows the heart rate and the force of each beat of the heart and lowers blood pressure. Breathing is slowed and moisture is restored to your nose and mouth for easier breathing. The calming system also relaxes the airway muscles in the lungs opening the airways allowing easier breathing. The system restores and promotes healthy digestion. The immune system is optimized. The body becomes relaxed.

There are many ways to trigger the calming system.

Nervous about meeting with the boss or giving a big presentation? Take a couple of belly breaths. Put your hand on your stomach and take a deep breath moving your hand up and out. This triggers the calming reflex. Take two or three of these belly breaths before your meeting or presentation.

You're in a situation where your brain is stressed. Your brain is racing with thoughts one after another. You can't think straight. Take a drink of water. It'll kick in the calming reflex. Calming your thinking.

There is a dramatic way of triggering the response: the ice-cold shower technique. At the end of your morning shower, turn the shower dial from warm water at the 10 to 11 o'clock position to the 2 or 3 o'clock position for a couple of minutes. This is like a swimming pool, cool but not shocking. Let the water go over the top of your head and down your spine.

Now, turn the dial way down to freezing water at 5 o'clock just before turning off the water. It's a shock. It'll take your breath away. You only need 10 seconds or less.

This is called the ice-cold face reflex which triggers the parasympathetic calming system instantly. You will feel different. You're filled with high energy; you have a protective shield around you; and although your daily problems are still there and you may encounter unpleasant people, you don't care. This same effect can be experienced sitting in the ice-cold pool after a workout.

The 12-minute walk technique always works, and you can use this any time. Wherever you are or time of day in the office or at home, get up, open the door, put down the cell phone and all work, and go outside for a walk in any direction. Not fast, not slow. Just walk for six minutes carrying nothing with you, turn around, and walk back to where you started. Ask yourself,

"Do I feel better?" You will. This is also an effective way to start your daily one-hour exercise routine, because this is the same feeling you get after exercising, high energy and a clear head.

Yoga breathing will trigger the parasympathetic system for calmness and relaxation. These techniques include equal breath in and equal breath out, yoga square breathing, expanding the ribs, telescoping breathing, free-up-your-diaphragm, super shoulder shrug, and alternate nostril breathing.

Random fit of anger? Say to yourself, "love and peace, love and peace, love and peace" as many time as you need and then say, "it's good, it's good, it's good." You've kicked in the parasympathetic calming reflex. You'll realize you no longer have the feeling of anger, and a bonus is that you'll forget what triggered the anger.

Trigger the parasympathetic calming reflex to relieve stress. These include belly breaths, drink of water, 10-second freezing cold shower, 12-minute walk to settle the nerves and quiet the brain, and the many yoga breathing techniques.

*   *   *

Gratitude. Expressing gratitude rather than self-centered thinking can help us rewire our positive feelings. Being grateful helps you rewire your negative thoughts and feelings and improve your life.

Gratitude is a positive feeling. It's appreciating what you have. It's being thankful for what you have. Gratitude is returning kindness to others. It's grace.

Being grateful for physical things can give you a good feeling, but physical things costing money may give you a negative feeling. Being grateful for non-physical possessions feels good. It's being thankful for your good health. It's being thankful to people who are kind to you and don't take anything from you. It's being grateful for a spouse or coworker who helps you without saying anything. It's being grateful for your education and skills you've learned from others so that you can help people.

The benefits of being grateful include the feeling of optimism, giving, and bringing you happiness. Gratitude improves your relationships at home and at work. Gratitude improves your performance and creativity at work. Gratitude improves your social well-being and improves your physical and mental health.

You experience being grateful by thinking from the heart, not about yourself from the head stress center. Pay attention to where you're thinking from. If you learn to stop thinking about yourself and think about being grateful, then you'll be thinking from the heart.

You've lost a job, not making enough money to pay living expenses, or lost a longtime close relationship. These events occur in everyone's lives and can send people spiraling down low. It's easy to feel sorry for yourself. It's easy to be unhappy. These are the worst things you can do.

People want to be near you when you're not feeling sorry for yourself and when you're happy. Consider that you've lost everything, this is a time to stop thinking negative thoughts about yourself. This is a time to be kind to yourself with self-compassion. Stop thinking about yourself because this is stress, and you can't think about anything else like enjoyment and solutions. Think from the heart. Think about things to be grateful for. This can save your life.

You've lost everything, how can you possibly be grateful? Think about feelings of kindness and giving. Try this. Be grateful for someone in your life who doesn't take anything from you. Someone who is kind. Someone who only gives. This may be your spouse, a family member, or a friend. Experience the feeling of thinking about this person. It's comforting. It's a good feeling. It gives you the energy to start thinking from the mind with creativity to get you back on track.

The feeling from thinking about people who are kind to you may be enough to send you to a high enough happiness level to think from the mind with creativity. If this isn't enough, it's a cliché, but think about being grateful for being alive. You may feel that you've lost everything, but this isn't true. There are many things you'll never lose that include high energy, creativity, enjoyment, positive experiences, and extraordinary people in your life. Be grateful for being alive because these things can never be taken from you.

How do the feelings of gratitude help you out of the worst situation in your life? Thinking about being grateful for people who are kind, people who help you, and about being alive eliminates thinking about yourself. You can only think from one location at a time, so being grateful puts you in your heart and thinking about kindness and giving, and in your mind to solve the issues and improve the situation.

Naotaka Nishiyama from Japan talks about the 'bow' as a show of gratitude and appreciation. For example, when Japan lost the World Cup soccer match, many blamed the coach for bad calls. Instead of getting upset, the coach accepts the criticisms and takes a bow on the final stage. It's not an apology.

The bow is a show of gratitude. For the players who did their best. For the opponent's players who fought hard to win. For all the people who supported the coach, the team, and the players including the critics. The attitude and thoughts of each person who goes into a game are as important as winning or losing. In a loss, there's no need for hurtful language.

Whether you win or lose, you will be grateful and make use of this experience for the next game. Bowing comes from the expression of no hostility toward the other person.

Gratitude means appreciating what you have and being thankful for the people in your life. Know who you are moment by moment. Know where you're thinking from. Learn to stop thinking about yourself from the stress center and think from the heart with gratitude for yourself and others.

*   *   *

Compassion. This means being kind to yourself and others. Compassion lives in our heart and can make a profound difference in our interactions with others as well as how we treat ourselves. You can use compassion to transform the world.

Think from the heart with compassion for yourself and others. Compassion means being kind and giving support to someone during troubling times, during the loss of someone or something, or during a life-changing rejection. Self-compassion means being kind to yourself. Everyone experiences troubled times, a severe illness or injury, loss of income, or a massive failure. Having someone giving compassion is comforting, provides self-confidence and optimism, and makes the issue more manageable.

What's the difference between compassion and sympathy? They're opposites. No one needs sympathy. Sympathy is thinking from the self-centered stress brain region. Sympathy is feeling sorry for someone or feeling sorry for yourself. It's superficial and does more harm than good. Feeling sorry for someone makes them feel bad about themselves. It takes away self-worth and confidence. Compassion is the opposite, it's a feeling from the heart that makes people feel better about themselves.

For example, someone is ill or has a severe injury. Compassion is being kind to the person and giving support. People lose their job. Compassion gives them help while sympathy and feeling sorry for them makes them feel weak and bad about themselves. Compassion is being kind and sharing their loss. Compassion is from the heart.

> *"Be kind to yourself. Forgive yourself. Love yourself."*

How do you think from the heart with compassion? You need to pay attention to where you're thinking from. This is an unusual step because you've never been told you need to know where you're thinking from. In the past, no one has ever said this because you've been told you think from the brain, nowhere else. You now know who you are moment by moment because you know where you're thinking from. When you're feeling bad about yourself with self-pity and feeling sorry for yourself, you're stressed because you're thinking from the head stress center. Now is an excellent time, to think from your heart by being kind to yourself with self-compassion.

Thoughts about being resentful or jealous, or thoughts about retaliation or revenge means you're thinking about yourself from the head stress center. This is the time to have compassion toward others.

When you become aware of thinking about yourself, immediately think from the heart with kindness to yourself and others with compassion. You have instantly stopped thinking from the head stress center because you can't think from the head and the heart at the same time. Thinking about yourself, you're thinking from the stress center. Thinking kindness, giving, and compassion, you're thinking from the heart.

Here's an example of thinking from the heart with kindness and compassion. You're upset with yourself for making a mistake. You start telling yourself you're stupid and a failure. The moment you realize you're thinking about yourself, think kindness and be kind to yourself. Self-compassion. Think from the mind to create a solution. The feeling of being upset will vanish.

Another example, you're feeling sorry for yourself because you're not making as much money as everyone else. Instantly realize you're thinking about yourself and think kindness and have compassion for yourself. A final example, you're upset at your coworker because the coworker didn't support you and made you look bad in front of everyone. You start thinking about how to retaliate. Immediately, recognize you're thinking about yourself. Think kindness for yourself. Self-compassion. Think from the mind and create ways to repair the damage and look better next time.

Self-esteem is a popular topic talked about in schools as being useful for personal strength. Is this helpful? On the surface, this may appear useful; however, a deeper exploration of self-esteem shows that it's thinking from the head stress center. When you win at a sporting event or you're successful at work, you have high self-esteem. But when you lose or fail, you have no self-esteem.

Self-esteem lets you down during troubled times. Compassion will never let you down, win or lose, succeed or fail, self-compassion is always there. Hit rock bottom? Having compassion for yourself will save your life. Ask Kamal Ravikant. Loving himself saved his life allowing him to develop multimillion-dollar businesses. In his book with the same title, he says, "love yourself like your life depends on it."

Having compassion for others increases positive communication and improves your relationship with your family, friends, and coworkers. Having compassion for others makes them feel good, and makes you feel good too.

Compassion and kindness can be learned. Learning compassion has helped troubled schools to overcome problems with bullying. Learning compassion has changed violent prisons into places of sharing and learning.

People are often their own worst critic and, too often, beat themselves up because they make a mistake, don't get a job, or have a fit of anger toward their spouse or friends. People would never punish their friends or family in the same way they punish themselves.

Professor Kristen Neff has studied compassion during her entire career. She says to treat yourself with kindness and compassion the same way you would treat others in the same situation. Ask yourself, if you had a friend who is going through the same problem, how would you respond? You would treat your friend with warmth, encouragement, and understanding.

Have compassion for yourself, be kind to yourself. Have compassion for others. Know where you're thinking from. Think from the heart with compassion for yourself and others.

*   *   *

Happiness. You need to always have a happiness level of eight to ten regardless of the situation. Happiness means being content with who you are and what you have moment by moment. Being content with what you're doing moment by moment, especially during troubling times. It's living a good life with meaning and contentment.

Genetics accounts for 50 percent of your happiness level. Look at babies. You can determine their lifetime level of happiness watching them. Some are smiling and active. Others are irritable and nervous.

About ten percent of happiness comes from life events such as getting married, getting a raise, or buying a house. These occasions provide a new level of happiness, but their effects are usually fleeting, lasting a few hours or sometimes up to three years. With these outside events, most people return to their baseline level of happiness over time. You're in charge, happiness is an inside job.

The good news is that you're in charge of the remaining 40 percent happiness. It's internal. Focus on what's internally important. This means spending time doing what you enjoy. It's being engaged in life, knowing what you want, what you're doing, and where you're going. It's having meaning in your life. People who maintain high-level happiness live in the moment and enjoy each moment of the day.

> *"Happiness is being content with who you are and with what you have."*

There are external factors that can influence happiness. Music can give us a feeling of happiness. Listening to the right type of music can make us happy. It produces feel-good neurotransmitters such as endorphins. Music can change the brain and create new neuropathways. For example, for individuals who have an injury in a specific brain region, music can create a new neuropathway for improved function.

Immediate happiness can come from a smile. This happiness is based in neurolinguistics, which describes the connection between words and action. You think happy words from the heart, you feel happy. Laughing will bring happiness. This is only true with a happy laugh from the heart. It's the laugh from a positive story. Laughing at other people's expense produces a frown and feeling bad because this is thinking from the primitive brain stress center.

Being in the flow can bring happiness. You've experienced a wonderful day where everything goes well or you're enjoying something when you forget about time or surroundings. You're happy. You're content. This is being in the flow, a state of mind described by University of Chicago psychologist, Professor Mihaly Csikszentmihalyi.

The idea of "flow" is that you experience happiness when totally absorbed in an activity where your skill level is equal to the challenge. If the challenge is greater than your skill level, you'll be frustrated and quit. If your skill level is greater than the challenge, you'll get bored.

When your skills and challenges are equal, you always know the next step. You have immediate feedback. You're focused on the activity with no distractions. You don't think about failure. You have no thoughts about yourself, and you don't care what other people are thinking about you. Time is distorted. Either it expands by becoming ten seconds doing a triple jump at a track meet that takes only a second, or contracts becoming minutes working on a new discovery that takes hours. The activity becomes so enjoyable that you want to do it again and again because it's pleasurable and brings you happiness.

This is how you experience 'in the flow.' Balance your skills with challenges as often as possible so you can experience the pleasurable feeling of flow.

There will be some situations when your skill level is lower than the challenge, but you must complete the task, whether for work or at home. When this happens, recognize this and grind through the challenge until complete. Don't quit. The experience won't be pleasurable. Do the work without frustration or delay. Don't feel sorry for yourself by thinking from the primitive brain stress center. Complete the task and move on.

Take on challenges. Develop new skills. Discover new insights. Equalize your skills with the challenge for the feeling of pleasure and happiness.

There are three major causes of low-level happiness include financial failure, job stress, and harmful relationships.

On a scale of one to ten, you need to maintain a happiness level of eight to ten. A few times during your life, one of these situations will send you down to a low level. Five or below will likely require professional help for improving your life. Level six is not sustainable, and you need to get back to an eight to ten level.

This happened to me, a financial downturn sent me to rock bottom, so low, I felt symbolic bleeding from the cuts in my back from the rocks. I was at level six, and it's a bad feeling. I had to get out of this low level because people don't want to be around you with a level six, especially people who can help. How could I be happy with this situation with no solution in sight? This is exactly the time when you need to get to the happiness level eight to ten.

This is what I did. I understood that I was at level six happiness. Then, I tried to move this up the scale by 0.1 to level 6.1. You can do this. Try being grateful.

I thought of things I could be grateful for that included my house and other physical things. These thoughts caused the opposite feeling. They cause stress because these external things take away money, which reminded me that most of the day, people are taking things from you including money, your enjoyment, your time, and your energy without giving anything in return. This negative thinking didn't help.

This led me to being grateful for someone who doesn't take anything from me. It's my wife Joan. Instantly, I gained 0.1 up to 6.1. This tiny increment was enough to give me a feeling of security and confidence.

I considered other people who never take from me and this moved up to level 6.2. Then, I consider the idea of being grateful for your own existence. But I didn't know what this meant. Viktor Frankl knows. He's the Austrian psychologist who survived one of worst experiences in human history by being grateful for being alive. Thinking about being grateful for being alive got him through the days and nights of physical beatings, starvation, and losing everyone he loved.

I then realized what this means. Being alive means your life is filled with high energy, creativity, enjoyment, and positive experiences. No one can take these from you.

During the next three months, I gradually increased my happiness level through various techniques such as positive visualization using the mind, slow brainwave time through meditation, and yoga breathing techniques. At level 8.0, my financial situation was not better, and was even worse, but it didn't make any difference. I felt good and was going to create a successful future.

Several months went by, and I had forgotten about the happiness level until someone at workout, who I hadn't seen for a while, told me that he saw my wife Joan and I running in the morning many years ago, and he said, "You are the two happiest people I have ever seen." That sent me flying to 8.5! You need to maintain level-8 to level-10 happiness at all times.

A certain level of money is important for your well-being. Not too much and not too little. Money will buy happiness if you're making less than the poverty level. After that, it maintains a level of happiness. Too much money spent in the wrong way is hazardous to your health and others.

Psychologist Shawn Achor talks about happiness as the joy we feel while striving to meet our potential. This is like the feeling of happiness while being in the flow. Choosing simple happiness habits can boost your mood, make you happier, healthier, more productive and creative, and closer to those you love. Happiness is internal. It's an individual choice.

Close connections with family and friends provide happiness. For example, farmers who experience downturns have a higher level of happiness from their family and friends than consultants and salespeople who are on the road all the time with jobs separating them from their families.

Achor also talks about the idea of having happiness and positive thoughts replacing negative thoughts. People who think in a positive way are happier, creativity triples, productivity increases by 31 percent, likelihood of promotion increases by 40 percent, and sales increase by 37 percent.

Achor has five short daily habits that can improve your level of happiness. These include being grateful for new things and the reason for being grateful and scanning for positives instead of scanning for threats. The second habit is thinking of a positive experience during that past 24 hours. The third habit is daily exercise. The fourth is using different breathing techniques. The final habit is a daily act of kindness such as smiling at a stranger in the hallway.

Happiness is being content with who you are and what you have moment by moment. Maintain a high level of happiness for an extraordinary life and success.

Chapter 6

Close Personal Relationships

"A true friend is someone who knows all about you and still loves you."
— Elbert Hubbard

A long-lasting successful personal relationship is based on thinking from the heart. It was a beautiful New England September morning during the fall, and I was training for the New York City marathon along the Charles River in Boston. She was coming toward me in the opposite direction. I made the U-turn, and Joan held off the mace long enough to say hello. We've been running together since, run together stay together. Our magical life together is from both of us always thinking from the heart with kindness, giving, appreciation, gratitude, forgiveness, and love. There is no place for a single self-centered thought from the selfish head.

Having close personal relationships is the best predictor for a long healthy life. To live a long, healthy life, eat the right foods, obtain the right amount of sleep, and exercise every day. A recent study showed that having three to five close personal relationships is the best predictor for a long healthy life. These close relationships can be romantic, family, friends, coworkers, or business partners.

How can you tell the difference between a healthy close relationship and a controlling relationship?

In a close relationship, both individuals think from the heart with kindness and giving. In a controlling relationship, the two people involved think from the head. They only think about themselves. They often have thoughts of anger and jealousy. They are critical and find fault in everything. They have the constant need to control people and events.

If you're in a close personal relationship and both of you think from the heart with kindness and giving, then enjoy every minute of a long and healthy life together.

If you're in a toxic controlling relationship, then it's unhealthy, stressful, and not enjoyable. During troubling times, these people will abandon you or blame you for the problem. There are some controlling relationships that last for many years if there is no verbal or physical abuse.

A close romantic relationship is with someone where you can be yourself without having to think about what you say or worry about what you do. There is no judgment, criticism, or blame. You always have each other's back no matter what happens.

How do you develop a close romantic relationship? That's the question everyone asks, especially during Valentine's Day. This begins with having a healthy clean lifestyle so that when you meet someone, you'll be open to a close relationship.

This requires the fundamentals of a healthy life with a healthy nutrition lifestyle by eating the right foods in the right amount at the right time and prepared in a healthy manner. This means eight hours of sleep every night and one hour of exercise every day. This means live your life by thinking from your heart with kindness and giving. The feeling of kindness from the heart can be felt by the other person without saying a word. Have empathy, understand how the other person feels with no criticism or judgment. Giving is a feeling from the heart, give your time, give your energy, and give your help with expecting nothing in return.

Other elements of a healthy close relationship include eliminating anger and stress in your life. Learn to limit the feeling of anger to six to eight seconds. Learn to limit stress to six to eight seconds by changing thinking about yourself to other thoughts.

Being your true self in a close relationship is the most important thing you can do for yourself and the other person. This means knowing who you are moment by moment and knowing where you're thinking from and that's who you are. Think from the heart with kindness.

Being your true self is fundamental for trust, which is fundamental for a close relationship to flourish. If someone is trying to be like someone else, you don't know who the person is. Are they acting like someone else or are they acting as their true self? This is especially a problem during a crisis or stressful situation when you need to be able to trust the other person.

Another reason for being your true self is that you feel good about yourself. If people are not happy with who they are, they're angry and critical. They're always looking for blame, and you may be the target. This is an impossible situation for a close personal relationship. It's important to have optimal physical and mental health for a close relationship.

> *"Close personal relationships last forever when both people think from their hearts with kindness and giving."*

What about close personal relationships with friends, family, coworkers, or business partners? It's the same as with a romantic relationship. Use kindness and empathy, listen to the other person, and put yourself in the situation. Give, give your time, give your energy, give your help. Don't be a taker. There is no need to take anything from the other person. Don't take the other person's enjoyment or confidence. Direct commands are not needed. Don't try to control the other person's life. Be grateful for positive people in your life.

Having three to five close personal relationships is fundamental for a long and healthy life. Develop close relationships by being your true self. Think from the heart with kindness and giving. Think from the mind with creativity and unconditional love. Be grateful for the extraordinary people in your life.

* * *

Good feelings from positive words. Negative words come from the head, which has anger and self-thinking stress, and give us a bad feeling. Use positive words in thinking, talking, and writing for transforming interactions into enjoyment. Develop the healthy habit of having a positive word ratio at home, at work, and in the community.

Think, write, and say positive words for an enjoyable life for you and others. Positive words come from the heart, and they feel good. Studies of conversations among families and workers show improved happiness and productivity when more positive words are used.

Positive words are healthy because they're from the heart. Words like kindness, love, beautiful, giving, and trust all come from the heart with a good feeling.

Negative words are unhealthy because they come from the head anger center and stress center. Words that reflect anger and cruelty, language that is evil and jealous, and profanity come from the head. They cause a bad feeling in the person and everyone else.

A way to look at the situation is to use a positive word ratio. This means the number of positive words divided by the number of negative words used in thinking, writing, and talking. For example, if someone says three positive words for every negative word in a conversation, this is a positive ratio of three. If someone says two negative words for every positive word, this is a negative ratio of two.

There have been many studies using the word ratio at work and in the home. An equal ratio of zero is not enough. Surprisingly, the word ratio needs to be high on the positive side with three to five positive words to every negative word.

If you're having a pleasant conversation with a friend, your family, or a coworker, then the positive word ratio of both of you is likely three or more. If the ratio is less than three and above zero, it's a neutral conversation. However, a negative ratio causes stress in a conversation and can have serious health consequences.

What could be the dire consequences of a conversation with negative word ratio? Researchers have counted the number of positive and negative words used by spouses in their homes and calculated the ratio. They found a positive word ratio of three to five is seen in happy marriages, but a negative word ratio was common among divorced couples.

Researchers have conducted similar studies at work including underground miners, police officers, and beer manufacturing workers. These studies showed identical results. Individuals with a high positive word ratio are more productive, more creative, and enjoy their work more than their counterparts with a negative word ratio.

Continually using negatives words has a powerful negative effect on you and others. Negative words come from the head anger center and the head stress center when people are thinking about themselves and their problems.

For example, you can't have enjoyable close personal relationships with a negative word ratio. Close personal relationships are built on trust, giving, and people being their true selves. If people are using negative words from the stress center, they're not thinking from the heart with kindness and giving to others.

I agree with the Finnish standup comedian, Ismo that negative words are unhealthy. Ismo talks about pharmaceutical commercials by saying that half of watching TV is commercials, half of commercials are pharmaceutical drug commercials, and half of drug commercials are about side effects, so you watch TV for pharmaceutical drug side effects. Then, if you have the TV on in the background and you're doing something else, you may hear at the subconscious level, "thoughts of committing suicide" or "you have an itchy eyeball," and you're going to feel these. Ismo goes on to say this is unhealthy. I agree, negative words are unhealthy.

Try the positive alphabet word game that I've developed. Think of a positive word for each letter of the alphabet. For example, start with A like amazing, B like beautiful, C like courage, and go through the alphabet. What's the word for X? My wife, Joan knows: it's XOXO and manes love! It feels good to play this game because positive words come from the heart with a good feeling.

Using a positive word ratio at work is especially helpful. Researchers developed a device to measure the positive word ratio at work, and they determined the number at baseline. They taught people to stop thinking from the self-centered stress center with a mindful training program. Then, they measured the word ratio after they learned to stop thinking about themselves from the stress center. The results showed increased productivity, more creativity, and a more enjoyable workplace environment for employees and managers.

The reason this helped is that employees stopped using negative words such as complaints and criticism from the anger center toward other employees and the boss. They stopped using negative words from the stress center like criticism, blame, and judgment. People can only think from one location at a time, so they no longer had thoughts from the head anger and stress center. They thought from the heart with kindness. They thought from the mind for creativity to help coworkers or innovation to improve products and services.

Learn to minimize negative words when you write emails or send texts. Learn to limit negative words when you have conversations with your family, friends, and coworkers. Live your life with a positive word ratio for feeling good.

*   *   *

Positive social interaction. Just as the answer to having good personal relationships is based on thinking from the heart with kindness and giving, so, too, is the key to positive social interactions. Positive social interactions result in both individuals walking away from a connection with good feelings. You can use positive social interactions to your advantage in daily life at home and at work.

Positive social interaction leaves both participants feeling good after the interaction. Know your brain region during interacting with people. Learn to stay out of your amygdala anger center and your cingulate self-thinking stress center. You don't want self-important cingulate thinking during people interaction. You don't want to talk to someone when you're angry or thinking about yourself. You want to think from your heart with kindness and from the mind with helping others.

Positive social interaction means that both individuals have a positive feeling after the interaction. There are four outcomes from an interaction between two people.

The first is a passive response. Someone tells you about an exciting event. You may say, "that's nice," with a shrug of your shoulders and no eye contact. This is not negative, but a lost opportunity for a positive feeling.

A second response is negative with a one-up or put-down response such as, "you should hear what I did today" or "that sounds stupid, you're better than that." This gives no consideration for the other person's feelings. One person is pleased, and the other is angry.

A third response is destructive, which can occur at home or at work. It's too common, something like, "while you were having a great time, I was working," or "where did you get the money?" The person saying this is angry, probably from being yelled at by the boss. The person hearing this destructive comment has gone from feeling good about the exciting event to the amygdala anger center. Both people are angry. This is not a positive interaction.

The better outcome is positive social communication. Someone tells you about an exciting event. Engage in the conversation with positive words and comments, "That sounds exciting. What did you enjoy most? That must have felt great."

Where is positive social interaction needed? Everywhere, starting at home with the family. Positive social interaction stops family fighting and among friends, stops criticism, judgment, and blame.

Positive social interaction with family and close personal relationships is healthy and will prolong your life. Close personal relationships are based on feelings from your heart. You can be yourself without judgment, blame, or criticism. You care about each other. You're kind to each other. You only give, never take, anything from the other person.

Positive social communication in public is easy to do and results in enjoyable interactions and a pleasant experience shopping in the supermarket, clothing store, or the hardware store. For example, positive social interaction at a store means talking with people in a positive way. This will eliminate stress for both of you, and you might get a surprise deal.

Positive social communication at work results in increased productivity, creativity, and creates a positive work environment.

Cyberbullying requires a special discussion. For example, the daughter comes home from school and tells her parents that she's scared from negative texts from her school mates, and a son has nightmares from threatening texts. What is cyberbullying and what is a solution?

I define cyberbullying as any single negative word or comment against another person while texting or using social media. Relentless and continuous negative words and comments have disastrous health outcomes by causing stress leading to fear, anger, and depression. Unrelenting texting and social media bullying by students in grade schools, high schools, and colleges can have catastrophic outcomes. Cyberbullying is out of control and hurting too many people.

One solution to cyberbullying is applying the principles of the Eplerian Life Philosophy of limiting thinking from the anger center and stress center and thinking from the heart with kindness and giving. Learn to use positive social interaction with no one-ups, no put-downs, and destructive comments where both individuals feel better after the interaction.

How to get out of the self-centered cingulate stress center? For self-destructive talk and self-pity talk, use self-compassion. Be kind to yourself. For jealousy, resentment, judgment, retaliation, give. Do the opposite. Give your energy. Give your help. Eliminate cingulate self-centered thinking when texting and using social media. A life may be saved.

The one-ups, put-downs, and destructive words are obvious examples of negative social interaction. There are many others that are subtle without the person knowing about the negative effect on the other person because words and phrases have become a habit.

Some unhealthy habits have been passed down generation to generation and accepted as normal behavior. For example, saying a positive response followed by a negative response. "That must have been enjoyable; how much did it cost?" "Those are beautiful flowers, but you need to put them in a different location." "You look great, but you need to change." All these and more make the other person feel bad about themselves.

The other common negative response is saying something you think is help-ful but it's negative, leaving the other person feeling angry. "Good night. Don't play video games all night." "Enjoy the party, don't spend too much money." "Good morning. It's going to be an enjoyable day. You need to make sure you're not late." These comments are primitive brain thinking, all self-centered thinking. They leave the other person angry. They're a habit that should be eliminated.

> "Positive communication means no one-ups, no put-downs, and
> no destructive comments."

Positive social interaction means that both individuals feel better after the connection. Eliminate cyberbullying by transferring out of the cingulate self-centered brain region fast. Acknowledge the event, obtain the benefit, and get out.

Learn and use positive social interaction every day in all situations. This feels good, and others feel good too.

*   *   *

Stop worry. Worry can creep in whether we notice it or not. Want to cut off worrying? Stop thinking about yourself, and you'll stop worrying. Relocate your thinking from stress to self-compassion, empathy, and kindness to yourself.

Worry happens when we're caught up thinking about ourselves. Develop the understanding that worry causes stress because people are thinking about themselves from the stress center. On the surface, worrying about someone means you care, but at a deeper level it means you're thinking about being someone else, a good parent or a good spouse or a good friend. You're think-ing about yourself from the stress center.

Worry means fear from thinking about a problem in the future that you or someone close to you may have. It's fear of the future. It's a *what if*. What if my spouse has an accident? What if my children get hurt? Nothing has hap-pened at this moment. It's thinking about something negative in the future. It's thinking about how you'll feel if something bad happens. It's thinking from the stress center.

What do people worry about? Everything, the list is endless. That's the problem. It's always worrying about something in the future. Most are minor issues of no consequence, and everyone knows the things people worry about never happen. The top three worries include the job, health, and relationships. Others include crime, about being a good parent, worrying about friends or children, worrying about finding the right spouse, about being attractive enough, finding a job, being happy, about the health of a pet, paying bills, wrinkles, and worrying about growing old.

Why do people worry? People have negative thoughts about the future with fear and a bad ending. It's good to think about the future for planning and avoiding risks, but it's unhealthy to think about the unknown because this causes stress. Fear needs to be experienced moment by moment, not in the future. The farmers started this issue of worrying 10,000 years ago when they began thinking about the unknown future, such as drought, insect infestation, and stealing crops. However, worrying has no benefit to the farmer, the family, or friends, and worry is detrimental to health.

People say they worry because it shows they care, but this is thinking about yourself from the stress center. It means you're trying to please other people and showing them you're a good person. This is not being your true self. You don't need to please anyone, and you don't need to show anyone you're a good person. If you're your true self, you'll be a trustworthy person.

People say to themselves, "If I don't worry, it means I don't care." This is thinking about yourself causing stress for you and others. For example, telling your children that you worry about them going to a party, and then telling them don't drive too fast, makes them mad and angry because this is a controlling command. They get so mad that they drive too fast. It's better to say, "enjoy the party and let's share the fun when you get back."

There are many other ways to show you care. Worrying is not one of them. Worrying is about you and not anyone else. Worry is of no value to anyone, think from the heart with kindness, empathy, and giving.

How do you stop worrying? You need to understand that worry is thinking about yourself and that it does more harm than good for you and the person you're worrying about.

Stop thinking about yourself. Stop thinking from the stress center. Be your true self and think from the heart with kindness.

* * *

Eliminate guilt. Do you often feel bad about something you did or didn't do? You need to eliminate guilt and feeling bad by restructuring how you think about yourself. Know where your self-related thoughts come from and tap into kindness and compassion.

Feeling guilty is thinking about yourself from the stress center. Guilt means you feel bad about something you've done wrong. This may be a minor lapse of social skills or saying something bad about someone. The feeling is the same. You think about the harm you've done. It may disturb your sleep. You may feel like a bad person with self-destructive thoughts and self-pity thoughts. All these thoughts are thinking about yourself from the stress center.

These thoughts can be stopped by being your true self and taking the consequences. Guilt causes stress and stress is unhealthy. Stress causes physical harm including chest and abdominal distress, throbbing head, and pain in the joints from tightened muscles. Stress causes inflammation resulting in heart disease, high blood pressure, strokes, cancer, and a shortened life.

Stress from guilt is unproductive. It stops all desire to do anything, especially work on a project or help someone. You want to get away from the situation and get away from people. Stress stops all creativity and innovation such as completing a project, paying a bill, repairing something at home. You have no interest in anything but getting away. Your mind shuts down, creativity is silenced.

Why do you feel guilty? You think about yourself in a negative way. You have self-destructive thoughts. You feel guilty because you did something wrong and feel bad about yourself, which is stress. You have self-pity. You feel guilty about feeling sorry for yourself because you can't make enough money or have a good job or a healthy relationship. Self-pity is thinking about yourself and causes stress. You feel guilty about thoughts of retaliation or getting even. All these guilty thoughts cause stress.

Have you ever felt guilty about eating a piece of chocolate cake? Of course, it's normal. Some people consider this guilt as an incentive to lose weight. But it's the opposite, feeling guilty causes stress, and stress stops the digestive system. That piece of chocolate cake becomes fat around the stomach and the hips. If you have a piece of cake at an office birthday or home birthday party, enjoy the cake. It's a celebration. A positive event will not clog up the digestive system.

Feeling guilty can cause weight gain not because we ate the piece of cake, but because guilt causes stress. Chronic stress can lead to weight gain.

What do people feel guilty about? Everything. Guilty is the feeling of being ashamed or sorry for something you did wrong. People feel guilty about saying the wrong thing to a friend. Feeling guilty about not being nice to someone. You left a friend's party without saying goodbye. Not feeding your kids healthy foods. Cutting corners at work. Feeling guilty about not helping someone. Feeling guilty about wanting more money or spending money on yourself. People feel guilty about being better than someone else, having more money, having a nicer house. People feel guilty about feeling guilty.

Why do people feel guilty? Because people feel bad about themselves for something they did or did not do. This is primitive brain thinking. They're thinking about themselves. They're thinking from their stress center.

Beware the person who is controlling and narcissistic. People need to be aware of narcissistic people who have controlling behavior because they experience pleasure in making you feel guilty. For example, this person may be a spouse, a friend, a boss, or anyone else who is a controller. They make you feel guilty about not helping them, about not saying the right thing to them, about not feeling sorry for them, about not agreeing with them, about not saying hello to them, and on and on. They want to control you.

They control you through intimidation and lying to make you feel bad about yourself and your behavior. They do this because it makes them feel good. Do not agree with this behavior. Do not feel guilty. It's their bad behavior, not yours. Do not engage in this behavior. Hold your ground. Stay in control.

Feeling guilty means you're thinking about yourself in an unhealthy way. How do you stop feeling guilty? The answer is in the cause of feeling guilty. Stop thinking unhealthy thoughts about yourself. You're a good person. Whatever you think you did wrong or no matter how bad you think it was. There is no need to think about it as over time the event will be forgotten by you and everyone else. Stop thinking unhealthy thoughts about yourself. Be kind to yourself with self-compassion. Think from the heart with kindness to yourself.

If an apology is needed. Be your true self and give a proper three-step apology. Say what you did. Acknowledge that you were wrong. Ask what you can do to improve the situation.

Stop feeling guilty by knowing that it causes stress and is unhealthy. Stop self-destructive thoughts. Think from your heart with kindness to yourself and self-compassion.

Chapter 7

Age with Style and Grace

"Age is an issue of mind over matter. If you don't mind, it doesn't matter."
— Mark Twain

People are conditioned by society to grow old. During childhood and teenage years, old age is seen as people who are frail with wrinkled faces and not very smart. They walk with slumped shoulders, complain, and only talk about the past and their health problems. Worse, they're cranky and mean to other people. Adults continue to hold these images at a subconscious level and confirm them by selectively seeing people with these characteristics, and through this negative conditioning, they look and act the same way, old. These people live their lives with self-centered thinking from the stress center which causes the cortisol aging response in the cells and the body.

Age is a state of mind. There is no age for old age. Shut down self-centered thinking as soon as possible and think from the heart with kindness to yourself and from the mind for being younger and smarter each year.

Often, we fear aging. Whether we fear the loss of physical skills and functions or cognition and quick thinking, aging seems to have all these scary challenges that we don't want to face. But, as they say, age is just a number. You can live a happy and successful life at all ages.

Numerical age is for bureaucrats and filling out forms, biological age is for living. On the surface, talking about age seems like a trivial issue, but this needs to be explored at a deeper level. When we address the implications of numerical age, it presents the opportunity to improve people's lives.

Start with a simple social question that's asked many times, "How old are you?" Why are some people upset when asked this question?

Asking people "how old are you" has been a common social question for years and years. However, some individuals have begun to realize this question can make some people feel bad about themselves. No one likes this feeling, it's unhealthy.

How can such a simple question be a problem? It's about the person asking the question. This is often self-centered thinking from the head stress center and not from the heart. Thinking from the stress center is thinking about yourself. It's taking behavior, taking something from others, their enjoyment, their confidence.

Why would someone ask the question, "How old are you?" People may not realize it, but they want something from the other person. They're taking information to use for themselves, so they can compare themselves to the other person. This question makes the person asked the question to feel judged and uncomfortable. In addition, the person often acts and feels much younger than the numerical age and they don't want to be treated badly like their numerical age.

Sometimes people ask children how old they are, using this as an easy way to say hello and interact. They're surprised when the child gets scared and hides with the parents. People ask the innocent question not thinking what it means.

This question comes from the adult head stress center, and children can feel it. They respond in two ways. Confident self-centered children will yell out the number bragging to their siblings or anyone else. But most children are quiet and shy. You will see them back off and hide because this question comes from a taker, an adult who wants something from them. This may not be an effective way to start a conversation. This can scare children.

It's easy to talk to children. All you need to do is talk from your heart with kindness and giving. They will respond instantly. Talk to the children from the heart, and they'll likely respond with joy.

Asking young adults about their age can be a problem because the person asking the question, whether they know it or not, is taking information. They want to know if the age is appropriate for the person's accomplishments, either massive accomplishments beyond their age or no accomplishments for their age. For those who are self-centered and outperforming their peers, they take this as an opportunity to brag about their accomplishments. Most young adults are trying to find out what they're doing. This question makes them feel bad about themselves.

Asking the question, "how old are you" can cause discomfort in many older adults. It's the same issue as with children and young adults, there are self-centered adults who love to tell the entire world about their age and brag about it. Most people do not want to tell anyone their age.

There are two reasons why someone would ask adults this question. The first reason is related to the concept of the pecking order. It's like birds, watch them eating breadcrumbs for a few minutes, and you will see the top bird, the middle ones, and the bird on the bottom. People who ask this question want to know where you are in the pecking order to find out if you're above or below them so they can treat you accordingly.

The second reason is a bigger problem. Once the person knows your age, then they will treat you as society has determined how that age should be treated. This results in being treated like an old person and not being able to work or start a company. Children may treat their parents as being old, sometimes not letting them enjoy life because they say they worry about their health, which means they're thinking from their stress center about themselves.

Asking people their age seems like a minor issue; however, this can make people feel bad about themselves. People might be treated as if they're too old to enjoy life. No need to ask anyone how old they are. This is a question from the head stress center and causes stress.

When talking with people, think from the heart with kindness and not from the primitive self-centered stress center.

*　*　*

Creativity grows with age. One of the benefits of aging is that our creativity grows as we age. We learn how to be better problem solvers, more fluid in our thinking, and embrace a creative lifestyle. How? You'll be surprised to learn that it's not by using the brain. It's the opposite, spending less time thinking about yourself from the brain stress center and more time thinking from the mind, which is not the brain.

The truth is out, the older people become the more creative they are. For too many years, everyone has been told that all major discoveries and billion-dollar companies are by people in their twenties implying that if you haven't done anything in your 20s, don't try, creativity is shut down with the stress of life as an adult. I have a better option.

This myth came from and has been promulgated by the stories about Einstein, Gates, and many others. Einstein's greatest achievements occurred during his twenties and Bill Gates dropped out of Harvard at 20 developing one of the biggest companies in the world. And, adding to the myth, Einstein created nothing after he became famous. According to world experts, this proves that no one can create anything worthwhile after age 30.

This conclusion is wrong. Some people stop being creative because they turn inward and continually think about themselves from the stress center eliminating time to think from the mind with creativity and innovation.

Consider Einstein, he became famous worldwide after he made his discoveries during his twenties. Later, he became critical, which is thinking from the primitive brain stress center and not the mind. He criticized and denigrated other physicists who were discovering quantum physics, which later proved to be a bigger development than his theories.

Why would Einstein talk this way? Why did he become so rigid in his thinking to criticize a new physics paradigm? This is my answer. Einstein enjoyed being famous and began thinking from his primitive brain to become more famous instead of thinking from the mind with creativity and innovation. You can only think from one location at a time, if he's thinking about his reputation and comparing himself to others, he can't think from the mind with creativity. This has nothing to do with age.

> *"Be smarter and more creative with every birthday*
> *by thinking from your mind."*

People become more creative with age. Follow the Eplerian Life Philosophy, the less you think about yourself the more you are your true self. Think from the mind with creativity and innovation.

*   *   *

Eliminate physical stress. Some physical stress on our bodies is unavoidable, but how much of our physical stress do we cause?

Use balance for eliminating physical stress. Excessive strain on muscles and joints causes physical stress. It's a problem because physical stress causes the adrenalin cortisol response resulting in inflammation and harmful health effects.

The neck and pelvis are the two areas that need to be in balance for eliminating physical stress.

The neck is an important part of the body for causing stress. The head down while doing computer work, walking, or driving causes stress. Try this. Drop your chin and lower your head. What does this feel like? This feels like the back neck muscles are stressed by trying to pull the head up. This is true, but unknown to you, the front neck muscles are trying to push the 15-pound head back straight. This is a lot of work.

So, when your neck is bent forward doing computer work, the back neck muscles try to pull the head up and the front neck muscles try to push the head up. That's two muscles working at the same time doing opposite work causing double strain. Not only that, the front muscles get stronger and the back muscles get weaker making the situation worse and in some cases permanent.

What happens if you move your head too far back? It's the same thing except the opposite. Your back neck muscles are trying to push your head forward and your front neck muscles are trying to pull your head forward. Pushing and pulling, opposite work causing stress in both muscle groups.

You know the solution. It's the balance where there is no muscle push or muscle pull. It's the neutral position. Maintain your head in the balanced position with chin straight and eyes forward. There is no stress because both muscles groups are relaxed. Balance is restored. There is no stress. You feel stronger. Your voice is strong. You look great.

The back and pelvis are the remaining parts of the body that cause physical stress. This is related to the same principle as the neck muscles. Leaning forward and bending the back while doing computer work or doing yard work means that your abdominal muscles are straining to push you back to a straight upright position and the back muscles are strained trying to pull the body backward. The abdominal group of muscles are pushing and the back group of muscles are pulling. Two opposite forces cause muscle stress in both muscle groups. As with the neck muscles, the abdominal muscles get stronger and the back muscles get weaker cause severe low back pain.

Bending the back sitting or picking something up causes a huge amount of strain in both muscle groups, and as expected, the strain can cause the low back muscles to go into instant spasm causing severe pain. That's from the muscle spasm pulling on the big spinal nerves. Therefore, maintain a straight back position. Restore the balance so the abdominal muscles and the lower back muscles are in a relaxed position. This feels good. You're stronger, healthier, and you look good too.

Your exercise program is an effective way to maintain the balance and keep the head and back straight without thinking about it because you do exercises to build up the upper and lower back muscles every day.

Physical strain in the neck and lower back muscle groups causes the adrenaline cortisol response resulting in inflammation and sore muscles. Keep your head and back straight for good health.

*   *   *

Proprioception is lifesaving balance. Proprioception refers to the sense that helps us perceive the location, movement, and actions of our body. We need high-performing proprioception and balance, especially as we age.

Proprioception is knowing where your body is in your environment. It's about body position. Proprioception is keeping your balance such as walking in the street, going in and out of stores, and especially going downstairs. You need to be aware of this for optimal body coordination for living a high-energy life.

There are too many headlines about people in their 60s, 70s, and beyond who fall downstairs hitting their heads sending them to the hospital and worse. That's a tragedy that can be prevented by maintaining peak proprioception health.

Proprioception is a mouthful of a medical word, what does it involve? There are nerve receptors in the muscles, tendons, and joints that transmit signals to the brain where they're connected with the eyes and ear balance system to create a picture of the body position and movement. These receptors in the muscles and joints maintain balance.

Going downstairs is a major example. Others include walking at night in the dark without losing balance, and a simple one, being able to walk without looking at your feet.

What are the causes of losing proprioception? There are some medical causes such as congenital disorders but growing old and aging are the biggest cause. The strength of proprioception begins to diminish during the thirties and accelerates in the sixties. Lack of sleep is also a cause, especially with advanced age.

> *"Standing on one leg for 30 seconds is the single best thing you can do for proprioception to keep your balance at all ages."*

How can these tragic stories about people falling downstairs be prevented? First, live a healthy life. This means a healthy nutritional lifestyle, eight hours of sleep every night, one hour of exercise every day, high level happiness, gratitude, compassion for yourself and others, learning something new every day, and being your true self.

The second way of preventing proprioception loss is with exercises for sharpening proprioception and balance. These include a wobble board or balance board, yoga, Tai Chi, or an exercise ball for balancing the abdominal and back muscles.

Purchase a foam balance pad from the internet or elsewhere or use the balance pad at the workout facility. It's a firm foam about two and a half inches thick and a rectangle about 16 inches long and 13 inches wide. I like to do the exercises with bare feet, but you can use exercise shoes. I have the back of a chair in front of me to catch myself if I go off balance.

Start with walking up and down on the pad, and then with both feet on the pad, rock your toes and heels back and forth and then side to side. Do sets of ten. Next stand on one leg and raise the other leg 90 degrees behind you. You can then do regular squats with both feet on the balance pad, and lateral squats with one foot on the balance pad. Then stand on one leg and raise the other leg 90 degrees in front of you. You finish with lunges with the front foot on the balance pad and back leg behind you and repeat with the other leg in front of you.

Add balancing exercises as part of your daily exercise program. Understand the need for high performing proprioception and balance, especially during older ages. Perform daily balance exercises to prevent falling in the middle of the night and other bad accidents. Keep your proprioception performing at peak levels for a high energy, healthy life.

*   *   *

Optimism for life. Optimism is a key ingredient for a good life. But where does optimism live in our bodies? And how can we develop the habit of thinking optimistically? Optimistic people achieve more, overcome obstacles and setbacks, and bounce back quickly from failure. They see the good in people and circumstances.

Optimism is confidence about a positive and successful future. It's seeing the good in people and in all things. It's enthusiasm and self-confidence. It's believing the future will be better and doing whatever it takes to make it that way. Mistakes and failures are opportunities to do it right and make things better. It's about making people feel good about themselves.

What's the difference between optimism and pessimism? Studies at UPenn under the direction of Dr. Marty Seligman show that optimists achieve more and have better health. Pessimists tend to give up more easily and are more prone to depression. For optimists, obstacles and problems are brief set-backs. For pessimists, they're permanent failures.

Optimistic people believe bad events are temporary, and they bounce back quickly from failure. Pessimists believe bad events are permanent and take a long time to recover, or worse, they may never recover.

Optimists think of good events as permanent, while pessimists think of good things as transient. The opposite is true about bad events. Optimists think of bad events as transient, and pessimists think of bad events as permanent.

Optimists think that good events apply to all parts of their lives while pessimists think that an isolated failure is total failure in their lives.

Can optimism be learned? Yes. Professor Marty Seligman has written a book called *Learned Optimism*. Begin by looking at things in the right way. Make positive generalizations. Learn that if something happens, it's not personal. Bad events are temporary and transient. They're not permanent. An isolated failure is not total failure.

Apply the Eplerian Life Philosophy by learning to have an optimistic approach to life by staying out of the anger and stress centers. Staying in these centers results in taking behaviors such as taking enjoyment from people, taking confidence from people, and making people feel bad about themselves. Optimism is the opposite. Giving behavior and bringing out the best in people.

A major issue with pessimism is the overwhelming and continuous negative thinking from the primitive brain region, sometimes for hours or even days. This results in seeing the negative in people and seeing problems instead of solutions. Saying something nice and following up with a negative. "That's a nice shirt but doesn't look good on you." "Enjoy the night but don't spend too much money."

Primitive brain thinking is negative thinking. Learn to transfer out of this thinking in a few seconds by giving, give your energy, give your time, give your help. That's learned optimism.

Primitive brain thinking results in taking behaviors such as judgment, criticism, resentment, and blame. All these behaviors counter and destroy optimistic actions. Bypass the stress center by thinking from your heart or from the mind.

Thinking from this self-centered region results in self-destructive thoughts and self-pity thoughts. Both are opposite of optimism. These thoughts take away from positive energy and enthusiasm. This thinking needs to be neutralized in seconds by self-compassion, being kind to yourself. Bypass this self-centered stress thinking by thinking from the heart by being kind to yourself.

Optimism is healthy for you and for others. Optimistic people can achieve more and obstacles are brief setbacks. Bad events are temporary, and they bounce back quickly from failure. They see the good in people and all things.

Learn optimism by bypassing the anger center and the stress center and thinking from your heart and the mind. This will lead you to a positive outlook and bring out the best in the people around you.

Chapter 8

Skills for Success at Work

"The best way to predict the future is to create it."
— Peter Drucker

Work is your way of contributing to society for a better world.
Work is not about you and the job. It's about contributing to society. There's an ancient parable about two bricklayers. One is always complaining and bickering about having to pick up bricks, watery cement, or the demanding boss. The other is singing a song and saying hello to everyone. The first is doing the job. The second bricklayer is building a cathedral. It's not about you and the job description, it's about contributing to improving the world.

> *"Work is your way of contributing to society for a better world."*

Personal leadership. Take charge of your life by living in a healthy, positive way for your family, friends, work, and community. Personal leadership means that you are in charge of your life.

Take charge of your life by being your true self moment by moment. Apply the Eplerian Life Philosophy. Be engaged in life. Have a high level of happiness. Have meaning in your life. Enjoy positive experiences, accomplishments, and extraordinary people.

Personal leadership means knowing who you are moment by moment. Know where you're thinking from. You can think from your head, heart, gut, body, or your mind, which is outside the body. You can only think from one location, and that's who you are. This means having integrity with no lying at any time, especially to yourself. This means thinking from your heart with kindness and giving and thinking from the mind with creativity.

Personal leadership at home and in public involves making instant decisions. If a major decision is needed, make it instantly, either a yes or a no. Trust yourself. Use the available information and use the mind. Saying no is just as helpful as saying yes.

Don't wait for more information or wait to see what happens because terrible things can happen while waiting or delaying a crucial decision. You can make an instant decision by thinking from your heart, your gut, and the mind. Stay with the decision unless new facts develop. If it's wrong, you can fix it fast before irreversible harm.

At home and in public, take responsibility for your actions and the consequences. If you make a mistake, acknowledge it, obtain the benefit, and move on. If the outcome is bad, take the blame. No need to complain, criticize, or make excuses.

Make firm, unwavering commitments to your family and friends. Say yes or say no. Do what you say. You're going to meet at 5:00? Show up at 5:00 not 4:30, 5:30 or 6:00. Your family and friends will appreciate your commitment and enjoy seeing you.

Learn the discipline to say no to your family, friends, and the boss. If you don't want to or are unable to facilitate the request, say no, even if it makes you feel bad about turning down a friend or family.

Personal leadership requires positive communication at home and in public. This means talking in a positive way with no put-downs or one-ups, and no destructive comments. Both individuals feel better after the interaction. You do this through thinking from the heart with kindness and giving. You feel good. Others feel good too.

Part of personal leadership involves managing rejection without being derailed. These rejections can involve money, the job, or close relationships. For example, using social media for sales has been successful in the past with a ten percent conversation rate resulting in a reasonable rejection rate. However, as time goes on, this conversation had decreased to one percent and even one out of a thousand resulting in an unhealthy rejection rate.

Reframe rejections. People learn more from making mistakes than reading or practicing. Feel the rejection, learn something, let it peak, and move on.

Hearing criticism or being criticized can be painful and takes away enjoyment in life. This too, needs to be managed quickly within a few seconds. Purposeful and intended criticism is usually from someone who is angry and stressed. You are the closest target, and the criticism rarely has merit or is useful.

Negative responses are a human default reaction. People respond to negative events rather than positive events. People become hysterical about losing money but say nothing about making the equivalent amount of money.

You do nine things successfully and make one mistake, you'll be criticized and made fun of by everyone. This is meaningless, feel the criticism, let it peak in less than ten seconds, and move on.

Here's a useful perspective. If you do nothing, go nowhere, and try nothing, no one will criticize you. If you push the envelope, develop innovative ideas and products, or create a startup. You're going to have multiple failures and daily criticism. Reframe this. People being quick to point out a mistake is a sign of success, not failure. The more criticism you get, the more successful you are.

There are several health habits required for successful personal leadership. These include a healthy nutrition lifestyle which means eating the right foods in the right amount at the right time and prepared in a health manner; eight hours of sleep every night with six hours to recharge brain energy and two hours of dream sleep for kindness; one hour of exercise every day; always learning something new; being grateful; and having compassion for yourself and others.

Maximize your personal leadership for success at home and at work. Personal leadership means taking charge of your life by living a healthy positive life for your family, friends, and the community.

Take charge of your life by being your true self moment by moment. Think from your heart with kindness and giving. Think from the mind with creativity. Have integrity, which means no lying to yourself or others. Make instant decisions, take total responsibility for your actions, and make firm commitments for success.

*   *   *

Business leadership. What are the essential qualities for business leadership?

People-centered leadership is optimal for business success. These are leaders who think from the heart with giving their energy and creativity from the heart and mind for what's best for the organization, employees, and the community.

Traits of people-centered leaders include making instant decisions, positive social communication, commitment, confidence, persistence, creativity, integrity, and for the entrepreneur, funding, and team building.

People-centered leaders are transformational leaders. They're creative and challenge teams to work toward change. Be a people-centered leader, an inspirational leader who cares about people.

Business Professor Kenneth Brown talks about transformational leadership based on principles and values. This is people-centered leadership that considers employees, employee families, the organization, and the community, and not the personal needs or wants of the leader. This is thinking from the heart with kindness and giving. This is thinking from the mind with creative solutions for employees, the organization, and the community.

There are laissez-faire leaders who are hands-off that often leads to confusion. Autocratic leaders are outdated. They're quick and effective but leave a trail of destruction.

Professor Brown talks about transactional leadership that is based on reward and punishment. If you do what the leader tells you to do, you get rewarded with pay, but if you don't, you get punished by getting fired. This is egocentric leadership from the head anger and stress centers resulting in a work environment of fear. Long term, this is not optimal and leads to destruction of organizations.

Making instant decisions is needed at all levels including executives, managers, team leaders, and employees. For leadership to be effective, decisions must be made fast. It's not about being right or wrong. It's about making the decision. If it's right, the organization moves on successfully. If it's wrong, it can be fixed fast.

Positive communication means you interact with people in ways that result in a positive feeling by all participants. Life is about emotions. Feeling good as many times during the day results in a productive day. Using positive communication with people in the organization creates a positive work environment for both leaders and team members.

Commitment means doing what you say 100 percent of the time. You say yes to a meeting, helping someone, or a project. Do it, even if a better offer comes along or you change your mind. Learn the discipline to say no. If you don't want to do something or have a conflict, say no. This is useful for both participants, saying yes and not showing up is bad for everyone. This makes you feel bad and makes the other person doubt your character. Say no. If you say yes, do whatever it takes to do it.

You need confidence to be a good leader. Self-esteem is not enough. There's high self-esteem when everything is going well, but when things get tough, self-esteem jumps ship. Build confidence in yourself by being your true authentic self. Eliminate thinking from the anger center and self-thinking stress center. Be kind to yourself with self-compassion. This never lets you down. Confidence comes from how much we like ourselves. Be your true self for confidence.

Persistence is fundamental for business leadership success. Author Dr. Angela Duckworth uses the term grit to describe perseverance and passion. Grit consists of courage which means eliminating the fear of failure. Grit consists of endurance and follow-through. Grit consists of resilience which is the optimism and confidence required to bounce back from failure. Grit means not quitting because the business is too hard or someone told you to quit or that you're not good enough. Stop only because you've completed the job or reached your goal.

Creativity and innovation are core competencies for business leadership. This means using the mind to create a successful path for the company. This means developing new, better, and more efficient ways of doing things. This means creating innovative products that have never been developed. This means using the mind to solve the day-to-day problems.

Integrity and honesty are the foundations of a good leader. This is obvious for an executive or the boss, but even more important is being honest with yourself with no exaggerations, no convenient forgetting, and no stretching the truth.

Always be honest with no lies and no rationalizing. Telling the raw truth may be painful in the short term – sometimes even extremely painful – but recovery will occur. The pain will be forgotten. Lying is much worse. Lies can result in a lifetime of misery. The ancient saying is correct, "the truth will set you free."

Regarding leadership from the board, it's more important than ever to have the right board members, especially for startups. Egocentric board members are toxic and will destroy a startup. There are two functions of the board. Bring in outside ideas and advice and remove an egocentric CEO who makes decisions for personal gain and not for the organization.

The beset board members for a startup organization strive to think from the heart by giving their time, energy, and opinions without thinking about themselves. They bring valuable advice regarding the product or service, management processes, and important connections.

Board members with their own money in the startup are more concerned about losing their money than contributing to growth.

Board members must be willing to accept the CEO's decisions regarding their advice. They are not in control of the company and are not involved in day-to-day operations. The CEO is in charge and can accept the advice, modify the advice, or not use the advice.

The CEO must make instant decisions. If the decision is correct, the company thrives. If new facts develop, the decision can be changed. If the decision is wrong, it can be fixed fast. Board members need to be willing to accept these decisions and not interfere with operations and management.

Egocentric leadership with self-centered thinking results in continuous in-fighting, stress, and leadership by fear. The worst leader has the dark triad personality of extreme narcissism; Machiavellian behavior of doing anything to the organization to get what they want; and having no feeling of regret or remorse for destroying the company or other people's lives. These self-centered leaders destroy the company, people, and the community.

The need to make instant decisions needs to be explored further. My friend who is the CEO of a billion-dollar manufacturing facility talked about his job and said, "I make decisions. That's all I do, I make decisions." He makes decisions based on the available information and based on feelings from his heart, his gut, and the mind.

It's also useful to give the basis for the answer, preferably three reasons why the decision is made. This is especially helpful, if the answer is "no" because this gives people something to go forward with such as gathering more information, modifying the proposal, or abandoning the project so they can move on to something else.

Waiting for more information or letting events play themselves out creates time for bad events to occur. For example, there are two top performing software engineers, and they are better than all the competition. But they are both egocentric leaders causing a dysfunctional work environment and hurting the company.

These two egocentric engineers are constantly trying to show which one is better. They continually make negative comments about each other, and they're always bickering and fighting in the hallways and at meetings. They make outlandish demands on their team members and belittle them if they make a mistake or don't finish a project in time. This creates a work environment based on fear and everyone wanting to leave the company.

People at work can think from the anger center and stress center or from their heart or the mind. Only one location at a time. If they spend hours thinking about the horrific work environment and thinking about being at a better company, then they're not working. They can't think from the heart with kindness toward each other. They can't think from the mind with new creative ways to improve a process or innovation to develop new products or services.

What should the CEO do? There are several options. (1) They're top performers, give them anything they need. Let events unfold and let them improve their attitude. (2) Have a meeting with both to develop a way they can work together for the good of the company. (3) Fire one of them. (4) None of these.

Letting events unfold and giving them anything they need will make the situation worse because they'll continue their dysfunctional behavior, and there will be no end to their demands. A meeting will not resolve the issue because this will not change their self-centered behavior and will only prolong the bad situation. These egocentric leaders have had this behavior since childhood. This behavior has always gotten everything they need, so they're not going to change. Firing one of them will result in all the adverse consequences of firing someone without the benefit of improving the situation.

What should be done? Fire both and do it now before irreversible damage is done. There could be the risk of a lawsuit or personal revenge; but this can be limited by documentation of prior behavior and providing transition help and financial support as needed. Let them go to the competition. This will help the company. The teams will perform better, people will want to stay at the company, and the organization will return to financial success.

Taking responsibility and accepting the consequences are fundamental for company leadership. In his book, *Extreme Ownership*, US Navy SEAL Jocko Willink talks about total responsibility. What does this mean? This means taking total responsibility not only for yourself, but also up and down the entire management chain. This means no blame. If someone on your team makes a mistake, don't blame them, it's your responsibility because you didn't give them clear directions, teach them well enough, or give them sufficient resources. Same thing with your boss. If you get chewed out by the boss, it's your fault, take responsibility, you didn't give the boss enough information or you didn't clarify what was needed.

During Navy SEAL training, Jocko Willink writes that Training Boat #2 always won, and Boat #6 always lost. Boat #2 came quietly winning with the leader and team members encouraging each other. Not so with Boat #6, they could hear the leader and the crew yelling at each other as they came in last. The leader and the team yelled insults and negative comments at each other the whole time. The leader blamed the team for losing and each team member blamed each other for losing. Jocko called this poor leadership, and to prove his point, he switched leaders. As he expected Boat #6 with its new leader came in first, and Boat #2 with its new poor leader came in last.

Jocko pointed out that, "There are no bad crews, only bad leaders." Be responsible for the entire organization with no blame, no criticism, and no excuses. People need to take responsibility for everyone up and down the management chain.

At work, unwavering personal commitment is essential. If you say yes, do it at all costs. A poorly committed person stops the organization from progressing and growing. These people cannot be relied on when things go badly. This person has a terrible reputation, and in a tightly organized company, this person would be fired.

It's easy to be a committed person. Be your true self and think from the heart about your own abilities and think from the mind with creativity. Then, you'll say yes if there is alignment with the request. Importantly, you'll say no if you don't have the skills, the time, the resources, or if you don't want to do the project or the request.

Positive communication at work makes the difference between an enjoyable workplace environment and a toxic environment filled with fear. Positive social communication means that both individuals feel better after the interaction. One-ups, put-downs, and negative destructive comments dull productivity and creativity. This is because people become angry or feel bad about themselves which are thoughts form the anger center and stress center. As you can only think from one location at a time, people aren't thinking from the hearts with kindness and from their minds for productivity and creativity.

Negative communication comes from thinking from the anger center and self-thinking stress center. Think from the heart with kindness and from the mind with creativity. Positive social communication produces results, innovation, and a healthy work environment.

Total responsibility, commitment, and positive communication are key factors for successful leadership at work. Prioritize and execute is also a key factor. This is one of the Navy SEAL's leadership principles. This means determining the number one priority at any given time and completing this task before moving on to the next.

I have two traits for successful leadership: (1) Do the second part of the job and (2) complete the last five percent of the job.

Do the second part of the job. Every job has two parts. The first part is the job you've been trained to do and following the job description. The second part is positive interaction with people by thinking from the heart with kindness and not from the head primitive brain. A good doctor makes diagnoses and treats, the best does this with kindness. A good plumber fixes the pipes, the best plumber doesn't destroy the carpet and scare the homeowner. The second part of the job is treating each person you deal with as someone special, not a number, a textbook, or a job description.

Complete the last five percent of the job. The last five percent of the job is so hard for some people to finish, they never do. For example, a beautiful neighborhood house is built in several months, but scattered pieces of cardboard and debris are not picked up for months, and the sidewalk remains cracked and dangerous for years. A coworker goes home leaving 10-minutes of work for someone else to finish.

Do the second part of the job and complete the last five percent of the work every time.

There are several good health habits required for successful leadership. Eight hours of sleep are needed every night for peak productivity and innovation. Six of the hours are for recharging the brain energy, and two of the hours are dream sleep for the heart and feelings of kindness and giving. A healthy nutritional lifestyle is needed by eating the right foods in the right amount at the right time and prepared in a healthy manner. Other health habits include one hour of daily exercise, learning something new every day, having compassion for yourself and others, and knowing your true self moment by moment by knowing where you're thinking from.

People-centered leaders use the right business model based on the customer or the client. Egocentric leaders think about making money, not the customer.

There was a successful fitness center in Boston many years ago because they were the first to offer extensive equipment, swimming pool, and a steam room. The company grew rapidly expanding to New York and Philadelphia. However, as new fitness companies were created, the company failed and closed its doors.

Why did this company go out of business? The company had an egocentric business model. Get new customers, nothing else. They knew that most customers would pay and not use the facility, so they didn't care about customers that work out every day. They didn't repair the equipment, they didn't keep the facility clean, and worse, they didn't clean the steam room resulting in dangerous mold growth. In addition, their hiring practices had no regard for hiring people who wanted to help customers. They hired people to do the job and nothing else. Employees were told the way the company makes money and their job is to get more customers.

This egocentric model does not work. A new fitness company did the opposite. They only care about individuals who work out every day. The greeter at the entrance smiles and says good morning using your name. The people cleaning the facility and stacking the towels are doing their job because they enjoy helping people in any way they can. The facility is continually being cleaned. The cold plunge, hot tub, and steam room are cleaned daily. Personal trainers help their clients reach their fitness goals based on the client's needs, not on the trainer's egocentric needs. This company is successful because the company is people-centric throughout the organization from employees to managers to executives.

Be a people-centered leader. Business leadership requires thinking from the heart with kindness and thinking from the mind for always improving the organization. Business leadership requires good health habits. Business leadership requires making instant decisions that are best for the organization, employees and their families, and the community. Business leadership requires taking total responsibility, unwavering commitment, and positive communication.

*   *   *

Instant decisions. Have you had a decision that took days or even weeks to make? What if you could make decisions instantly, cutting out weeks or months of waiting time and preventing an unpredictable disaster from developing? Learn to master the art of instant decision making and applying this to your life at home and at the office.

"Make the decision, please!" Individuals often express their feelings of frustration at home and at work. Not willing to make a major decision can have catastrophic consequences. Irreversible events can occur during the delay or a forced, panic decision will have to be made with disastrous results.

Decisions must be made immediately with the available information by using the available information, the mind, the heart, and the gut. This allows people and the organization to act and move forward. If the decision is wrong, the problem can be fixed before it's too late. Not deciding or waiting for events to unfold stops all action and gives time for adverse events to occur.

Many use the pro and con technique for making decisions, but this is time consuming and often leads to no decision. It's complicated, there may be 15 items in your 'yes' column but only two in the 'no' column, but the two may have more value than all the other 15 items combined. Another issue with the pro and con technique is that it takes time arguing about whether the pro column outperforms the con column, often ending in no decision.

If you have time, the formal debate system is an excellent method for making major complex decisions. Professor Jarrod Atchison at Wake Forest in the Art of Debate describes this technique. The basis for the decision is established by the claim, the grounds or evidence for the claim, and the warrants which are the connections between the claim and the evidence. Make your decision by using the research from the affirmative side and the negative side to determine the best option and confirm this opinion by using the warrants from both sides.

It's important to clearly state the reasons for the decision, verbally, in writing, or both. You should state your decision, acknowledging everyone that did the work and research, and conclude with a line-by-line basis for your decision.

My favorite way to decide is to make the decision instantly. Listen intently to the request and clarify the details with the other person so there's a mutual understanding of the need for a decision. Then make the decision on the spot realizing you make the decision from the mind, heart, and gut.

Say "yes" or "no." For major decisions involving many people, it's helpful to others to state three reasons for your "yes" or "no" answer.

A "yes" decision moves the person or organization forward with action. Giving three reasons for your decision can be helpful to confirm you that understand the situation and gives the team or organization incentive to go forward.

A successful outcome will feel good and improve the situation. A bad outcome will be recognized quickly and because you made the decision, you can fix the situation before irreversible harm.

A "no" decision is helpful. If you don't have enough information, have no interest, or don't want to make the decision, then say "no." Give the basis for your decision so the person or organization can act by getting more information, going to someone else, or abandoning the request or the project.

Make instant decisions. Being indecisive and not deciding causes frustration, confusion, and can have serious consequences. Think from your heart and the mind for instant decisions.

*   *   *

Total responsibility. When we take responsibility for ourselves, we advance in life and work. Whether you have a boss or you're self-employed, you can reap the benefits of taking complete responsibility for yourself.

Responsibility is invigorating and rewarding. Take responsibility for your own actions and for others up and down the management chain.

Responsibility is a social force that binds you to an obligation and course of action. This can result in praise and positive feeling for a good outcome and this also means being answerable and taking the blame for a bad outcome.

Responsibility is trust. If you're given responsibility, then you can make crucial decisions or take extreme actions without permission from anyone. You don't want to let anyone down and you want to protect the interests of others.

Total responsibility means being responsible for the actions of yourself and up and down the management team.

For example, during the last ten seconds of an NFL football game with the score tied, the quarterback throws a long pass to make the winning score. This is expected and can win games. However, the pass is intercepted by a player on the other team. Rather than stop the play and go into overtime play, this player makes a judgment call to run for a score, which is a questionable judgment call.

However, this player shovels the ball to an open teammate. This is poor judgement and a risky decision by the player, but the player used training and experience to make this decision, and it turned out to be the correct call.

Then disaster struck, the player who received the shovel pass started running and then panicked. This player in panic threw a long forward pass to another teammate, but a player on the opposing team caught the ball and ran for a touchdown to win the game.

This type of play is seen in high school football, not in a professional level sport. The player is blamed for the loss, but this is the head coach's fault as the head coach takes total responsibility for every player on the team.

The NFL head coach and coaching staff should have organized practices to ensure this would not happen.

Part of being a professional athlete is learning from training not to panic in any situation. It's like being a part of the US Navy SEALS. Through extremely harsh and vigorous training, they learn not to panic in an unexpected intense situation.

Doctors learn not to panic. A doctor can't panic in a situation with a patient who is not breathing and has no heart rate and no blood pressure with sirens blaring and family screaming in fear.

Panic thinking comes from the primitive brain region and not from the prefrontal lobe with appropriate social judgment and from the mind with creative solutions to save a person's life. The football player who panicked and threw the game away was thinking from the primitive brain region and not from the mind telling him to keep running.

It feels good to take responsibility. A positive outcome gives you the rewarding and enjoyable feeling of accomplishment, the bigger, the better. If the outcome is negative, taking responsibility will be painful, but the pain is sadness from the heart due to the loss. It's not personal anger and stress from the head. Sadness from the heart is healthy and is always transient.

Why do some people use blame instead of taking responsibility for their own actions? These people are head thinkers from the primitive brain. They make other people look bad, so they don't have to accept the blame and criticism.

How do people respond to a bad outcome that arises from taking responsibility? The healthy response is to acknowledge the bad outcome, try to learn something from the outcome, and move on within a few moments. If appropriate, accept the blame, give a three-response apology, and resolve the situation.

What's the three-response apology? Apologize. Admit you're wrong. Ask what you can do to make it right.

The unhealthy response is to continue thinking from the primitive anger center and stress center. People are angry at themselves for being in the situation and taking responsibility. They express their anger and frustration to anyone who will listen by criticizing and blaming others. Everything that happened is someone else's fault. This is a weak response. This causes stress and cortisol-inflammation for the person doing the blame and for the people being blamed unjustly.

Blame is weak. Imagine you're sitting at a table enjoying the day with a smile on your face. Suddenly, out of nowhere, a family member or friend shouts, "You ruined my day!"

This is an attack. You are being blamed for something unrelated to anything you've done. How do you feel? Your pleasant feeling has been destroyed, and you're angry. How do you respond? Two options: return with anger or better, the healthy way by learning how not to trigger or activate your anger center.

Why do people act this way by blaming others? They're thinking from the primitive brain region. They're angry at a bad outcome and don't want to take personal reasonability. They choose the easy way out, blame someone else. This takes away responsibility for their actions and decisions. This is an unhealthy self-centered response from the primitive stress center.

Taking responsibility means accepting the blame. Take the consequences.

Consider the Asoh Defense. During November 1968, Japanese Flight Two was scheduled to land in San Francisco from Tokyo. Due to dense fog, Captain Kohei Asoh mistakenly ditched the plane near Coyote Point in the shallow water of the San Francisco Bay, two and a half miles short of the runway. None of the 96 passengers and 11 crew were injured in the landing.

When the aeronautical board of inquiring asked him how it happened, he looked them in the eye and admitted fault right then and there. He made no excuses and blamed no one else. The term, Asoh Defense is used in the business management literature and is a business principle for accepting responsibility.

Captain Asoh didn't get fired. He was briefly demoted to First Officer or copilot and received updated training. He soon returned as captain, flying his previous route. The downed aircraft was returned to service.

Blame is weak. The more blame, the weaker people become. Take the blame if needed because you can fix the problem. Taking responsibility feels good and creates extraordinary strength.

As Jocko Willink wrote in his book *Extreme Ownership*, the losing boat leader blamed the team for losing and the crew blamed the leader and each other for losing. The leader and team of the winning had responsibility for themselves and for each other. There are no bad crews, only bad leaders.

Be responsible for the entire organization with no blame, no criticism, and no excuses. Be your true authentic self. Thrive with responsibility, it makes you strong and feels good.

*   *   *

Discipline. Without discipline, we won't build better health habits. Discipline is the core of everything we want to achieve.

Discipline at home, at work, and in society is fundamental for success. What is discipline? For purposes of health, this refers to training the body, controlling emotions and behavior, and having commitment, focus and consistency at work. There is no punishment component to healthy discipline.

Discipline is required for a healthy nutritional lifestyle, eight hours of sleep every night, and one hour of daily exercise. People say these three things are too hard and claim they don't have the discipline to have these healthy habits. It's the opposite, discipline is not hard, and it's only needed at first for a small amount of time. In addition, take advantage of the feel-good biofeedback technique.

For example, use the 12-minute walk to begin your exercise program. This walk will help you realize the good feeling after doing the 12-minute walk and knowing this feeling and more will be obtained from working out for one hour every day.

Think about the long-term benefits such as being more successful at work and social events as well as a more enjoyable home life. Instead of thinking about all the bad components and negative thoughts, think about the positive results and good feelings. Thinking about these positive feelings is the discipline to keep going. After a few days or weeks, discipline is no longer needed.

It's the same for a healthy nutritional lifestyle and eight hours of sleep. Think about the benefits and the good feelings associated with these healthy habits. This is the discipline needed to continue these good habits. Think about the good in healthy habits, not the negative. This is discipline for the body.

Healthy mental discipline controls emotions and behaviors. It involves self-control, focus, and concentration. This is accomplished by being your true authentic self. No long-term discipline is needed because you limit your thinking to a few seconds from the anger and stress centers. You limit negative thoughts about yourself, about your problems, and trying to be someone else. You do this and your emotions and behaviors will be controlled.

This mental discipline of being your true authentic self will allow you to achieve your personal and professional goals.

Someone responded to one of my posts, "Limiting stress or anger to less than ten seconds is totally unrealistic."

I wrote "I have no anger, and I have no stress since I developed the ELP strategy in December 2019.

Anger is caused by someone taking something from you such as your enjoyment, your confidence, or your values. You can learn to stop anger by not letting these negative forces activate the amygdala anger center.

Stress is caused by all self-centered thoughts from the cingulate stress center. Learn to stop thinking about yourself, and you will have zero stress. Instead, think from the heart with kindness.

Anger and stress can be eliminated. This requires knowledge, discipline, and persistence.

Business discipline means having commitment, focus, and consistency at work. This means making instant decisions and taking responsibility and its consequences. This can improve employee performance, increase efficiency, and help ensure the business meets its goals and objectives.

For example, Henry Ford's work discipline included focusing on efficiency and cost-effectiveness. He was known for his attention to detail such as strict quality control measures. Ford had a keen sense of discipline with his employees. Ford paid his employees and provided benefits. He implemented an eight-hour workday, something that was uncommon at the time. His business discipline included his commitment to innovation and always looking for ways to improve his products and processes. He invested in research and development.

Richard Branson has created more than 400 companies and understands business discipline. He not only sets clear goals; he creates structures and resources for achieving them. He emphasizes teamwork by creating a culture of collaboration and inclusiveness. He encourages a sense of shared ownership among his employees, which helps to create a sense of commitment and discipline among his teams.

Branson believes in the power of adaptability by being able to pivot and adjust or change direction when facts require it. He knows the power of innovation. He is always on the lookout for new opportunities and new ways of doing things. He's open to new ideas and is disciplined by not fearing to try new things and take on new challenges.

Branson emphasizes customer service. He places a strong emphasis on providing excellent customer service and has instilled this same culture across all his ventures. Branson is a people-centered leader. There is no place for self-centered thinking from the primitive brain region. He knows that satisfied customers are a key to any business success.

Personal discipline, mental discipline, and business discipline are healthy options for living life at the optimal level of creativity and enjoyment.

*   *   *

Influencing and persuasion. We hear about influencing all the time, but what does it really involve? Influence is a complex form of persuasion which we can use to our advantage.

Use positive influence and persuasion for a successful life. Everyone is inundated with influence throughout the day from advertising and people trying to sell products, services, and ideas. You need to understand influencing tactics so you can make purchases and decisions that are best for you. You need to know influencing tactics so you can succeed at selling your ideas, products, and services.

Business Professor, Kenneth Brown in his *Mastering Influence* course talks about four components of influencing consisting of the agent, the target, the tactics, and the context.

Characteristics of successful influential agents include physical attributes such as a confident posture and a smile. Three fundamental characteristics include deep knowledge and skills, being trustworthy and caring, and integrity.

The dark side of influence is illustrated by people who use manipulation and lies to lure people into fake investments and to fund faulty medical research and failing companies. People orchestrating these scams have the 'dark triad' personality of extreme narcissism, Machiavellian behavior of doing anything to anyone to get what they want and have no remorse or feelings destroying people's lives. Learn to recognize these tactics as soon as possible to avoid a catastrophic outcome.

Characteristics of a weak target include a high level of suggestibility which means the need to fit in and be like everyone else. Some individuals are concerned about group norms and adhering to the norm. They base their purchasing decisions to fit in with the group rather than purchase something based on their own need. Avoid these characteristics by being your true authentic self. Ask probing questions and do what's right for you, not someone else.

Suggestibility means that targets accept statements heard or seen are true without a thorough understanding of the situation by asking questions. Suggestibility is how easily a person is persuaded by messages from the media about products and services. Persuadability is how easily a person is persuaded by peers. Avoid high suggestibility and persuadability by being your true authentic self. Ask questions and seek answers to confirm what's right for you.

What's the characteristic of a strong target? People who are being their true authentic selves by paying attention, asking deep questions, and are willing to walk away.

There are internal and external factors influencing you to buy. The major internal factor is your state of awareness and paying attention. External factors are not related to the product such as images, influencers, and celebrities.

You need to pay attention to the internal factors that influence buying a product as well as the external factors. If you are tired, bored, and not interested in the product presentation, then you will purchase the product because of positive images or celebrities.

Late night infomercials take advantage of this situation. People are tired and not paying attention so an upbeat positive fast-talking person showing the benefits of the product is sufficient to make the sale. If you pay attention to the words, you will ask questions to confirm the validity of the words as well as find out things that are purposely left out of the sales presentation.

Be aware of these internal and external influences so you make buying decisions that are in your best interest and don't fall into buying something you will never use, or worse getting swindled out of thousands and thousands of dollars.

There are hard tactics and soft tactics that can be used for successful influencing and persuasion. It's useful to talk about the outcome of your influence. The best is to obtain commitment to buy or accept your proposal or suggestions. You can have compliance with your request, which may be good enough in some situations. You may be rejected.

For persuasion, you can use soft tactics such as rational persuasion or inspiration. You persuade with reason and emotion. You may use compliments or ingratiation. This will be successful if the feelings are from the heart, but they will fail if from the self-interest head stress center. For success with these tactics, it's important to listen because listening with intent and attention shows that you're interested in people and want to improve their lives.

Hard tactics such as threats, using authority, and pressure can frighten your target audience into a purchase or approval; however, long-term results can be disastrous. For almost all situations, these tactics need to be avoided. There are rare contexts, such as a life-threatening situation, where these tactics are necessary.

What are some tactics useful for making a sale? Be sincere by showing an interest in the person by using feelings from your heart. Use people's names. Make people feel good about themselves and bring out the best in people. Smile. Professor Brown talked about a study involving restaurant servers that showed higher tips if the server repeated the order and left a treat along with the bill. However, there was a 140% increase in tips if the servers smiled.

How can delivering a presentation at work in or public be persuasive? According to Professor Brown, there are several techniques that can be taken from the Greek scholar Aristotle, the Roman orator Cero, and from Dale Carnegie.

Aristotle writes about communication and persuasion by using three components that include ethos, logos, and pathos. Aristotle talks about ethos as the perception of a speaker's character and perception of intelligence, which means deep knowledge about the topic. Ethos means integrity and character by developing rapport by being your true authentic self.

Logos or logic is defined as the argument itself and how it's shaped to be the most convincing. To use logic effectively means you make no equivocation. You are clear about the meaning of words. Some speakers purposely use words with a vague meaning hoping the listener will not raise a question for clarity. This means no *ad hominem* argument which uses negative characteristics of a person to discredit the person in favor of your proposition. Logos uses facts based on evidence or science when selling products and services.

Pathos refers to the emotions experienced by the audience with the goal to use certain emotions in the listeners to understand your perspective, accept your claims, and act on your ideas. Pathos means connecting with emotions by seeking out the underlying problem and need and using emotions of the listener for persuasion to buy.

Use ethos, logos, and pathos for writing and speaking, which is integrity, clarity, and positive emotions.

Cicero wrote about the five canons of persuasion that include invention, arrangement, style, memory, and delivery. Invention means doing research to develop the most compelling reasons to accept your premise.

Arrangement means structuring your presentation beginning with ethos to win over the crowd, logos to establish the argument, and sealing the deal with pathos. Style refers to using your physical approach appropriately adjusted to the surroundings and the audience.

Memory refers to not using notes. This gives you the perception from the audience as paying entire attention to them. You're interested in them, not your slides. Delivery means practicing your presentation until it pops with life.

Dale Carnegie talks about not criticizing, condemning, or complaining. Give honest and sincere appreciation. Carnegie talks about arousing an 'eager want' in your audience. This means connecting with people and spurring them to action. This means talking about a topic that you're passionate about and care deeply about. If you do this, the audience will too and are likely to go forward with your desired action.

You need to master influencing and persuasion so you can recognize devious tactics in sales situations, public interchanges, and cultural discord.

You need to master influencing and persuasion for yourself to use for selling your ideas at home, at work, and in the community. Master persuasion for giving presentations at work or in public for success. Be your true authentic self for optimal success.

*   *   *

Social networks. In the age of social media, our ability to thrive is as strong as our social network. This section considers the elements that are foundational to forming strong social connections and networks for increasing influence.

Strong social media networks result in closing sales. Learn about weak and strong social media networks for selling products, services, and new ideas. Use weak social media networks for product recognition and strong networks for closing sales. Knowing social media networks will save you a huge amount of money on a misguided marketing campaign and can be the difference between failure and success.

Sociology Professor Damon Centola at UPenn specializes in social media networks and has written about his studies of selling complex products and services in the book *Change: How to Make Big Things Happen*.

Weak social media ties typically stem from random followers. Strong social media ties include our friends, family, coworkers, and close relationships. It's important to understand the use of weak and strong ties for selling a product or service. Weak tie marketing campaigns are useful for awareness and credibility while strong ties are useful for closing and selling the product. Use weak ties for simple products and services. Use strong ties for selling complex products and campaigns.

Traditional thinking has been that influencers can sell products. This may be true for simple products, but this is not the situation for complex products, services, or ideas. Influencers can have a negative impact. This is because these products are bought by people with strong social ties to each other.

People buy products based on the percentage of their friends buying the product. If someone has four friends, and two of them buy the product, then the person will also buy it. If an influencer has four million weak ties and two people buy the product, then no one will buy the product. To make things worse, if the influencer doesn't own the product, sales can decrease because if the influencer is not using the product, people will interpret this as the product not having social proof. Influencer campaigns do not work for complex sales.

Marketing must be carefully selected. High-tech glasses failed because the company used elite tech people to sell the product. People were suspicious and people couldn't identify with this group, so no one bought the product. This is an example of close ties rejecting a product.

Awareness is not enough to close sales. Another tech product such as Google Plus was well known throughout the world. People everywhere knew the name of the product, but they didn't use it. This is an example of weak ties for recognition but no strong ties for selling the product.

Simple products can be sold through large weak ties, but complex products, services, and ideas are sold through small strong ties. Strong networks include family and friends, and importantly strong ties include electronically geographically distant close connections, coworkers, and friends.

The same findings apply to teams at work. A study was undertaken with ten teams selected with close personal ties and ten teams with diverse geographic and cultural backgrounds. The teams were given 15 minutes to develop the best algorithm for selling shoes and beer. The components of the algorithm for shoes included price, color, and style and the algorithm for beer included taste, percentage alcohol, and calories.

The ten teams who were closely associated with extensive information developed ideas fast, but results were average. The diverse network team were slow at developing ideas, but results were outstanding. The worst idea of the diverse team was better than the best idea from the close uniform team.

Both types of teams can be useful. Centralized close teams are for company stability, and diverse egalitarian network teams are for once-in-a-decade innovative products. Teams are like planners and trial-and-error people. Planners produce successful good products, and trial and error people produce innovative global products.

Social norms and peer pressure are important for buying decisions and accepting new products and services. For example, in 1925, a 25-year-old German cardiologist experimented on himself with a heart catheter and lived to present the information at a conference. Before he did the experiment, his chief and peers claimed there would be instant death from the catheter hitting the heart.

However, after the cardiologist survived, he and the chief realized this could be a life-saving procedure, and they submitted the study in a scientific journal. The day the article was published, the cardiology community condemned the 25-year-old claiming he was reckless putting himself in life-threatening danger. He was fired from a prestigious Berlin hospital. He abandoned his cardiology career and developed a family practice in a small town. Then 30 years later, he received a call in a pub while having a beer with his friends. He won the Nobel Prize for the heart catheter, which save millions of lives worldwide during the ensuing half a century.

Social norms can have a powerful influence on accepting latest ideas and buying decisions. If there is a group with similar interests and backgrounds, a single leader can sway the group in the opposite direction away from a life-saving treatment.

A diverse egalitarian network group that includes individuals with differing cultural and economic backgrounds is a better option as everyone is heard equally, and they developed the best solution.

For example, Professor Damon Centola at UPenn studied a professional basketball team picking the best players for the team. He invited all staff members to complete a quiz which resulted in having everyone with an equal voice. This was different from the traditional approach of seasoned coaching staff having the final say. They used the periphery and the fringe staff to help select the best players. The study showed improved player selection from this approach. Everyone had an equal voice.

When given the choice of several answers for products or services, people will pick the answer that is familiar to them, not necessarily the correct answer.

Use weak social media networks for recognition, strong social media networks for closing, and social norms for selling products, services, and new ideas.

*   *   *

Creativity. How can we harness the positive power of creative thought in the office to spark innovation? Creativity comes from the mind which is outside the body. Recall that the mind is the universe that contains all information, knowledge, and events that have occurred in the past, present, and in the future.

A thought experiment using the subatomic particles, bosons can illustrate one concept of the mind. During the 1920's, Professor Satyendra Nath Bose, a theoretical physicist, asked his students the number of combinations for a ball labelled A and a ball labeled B. They all shouted in unison, four that include AA, AB, BA, and BB.

"There are only three," Professor Bose countered. His students laughed at him, and his peers in the scientific community laughed at him, but not Albert Einstein.

"There are three if A and B are identical," explained Professor Bose, and Einstein agreed with him.

Bosons are a subatomic particle combining the two names, Bose and Einstein. These particles are subatomic in size. They exist everywhere and increase in number as the universe expands. They're identical holographs containing information as energy. Tap into this "mind" for creativity by being in a slow-brainwave state.

This is an appropriate section for a discussion of artificial intelligence (AI) and human beings. Conversation AI bots can have a deep conversation with humans. This conversation bot is developed by writing an AI program to have the bot learn and interact with trillions of conversations over the years among people on the internet. The bots learn the answers to unlimited number of questions.

These bots are so good that people can't tell the difference between a bot or a human during a conversation in a blinded study. These are a massive breakthrough for improving efficiency and productivity.

These programs can replace entry level people in the creative workforce such as marketing. They can write code, emails, books, business decks, and numerous other human activities.

As these programs learn from more and more information available to them, they'll continue to advance. They may be able to express feelings and emotions. Maybe they'll be able to access the mind.

Use the mind. Do you need to solve a problem at home or at work? You're working on a new project? You're starting a company? All these activities use thinking from the mind with creativity.

Why is it so hard to be creative when you're tired, angry, or stressed? The mind is outside the body so thoughts from the head brain must by offline. If you're angry or stressed, then these negative thoughts are from the anger center or stress center. These are the only locations you can think from. You can't think from the mind at the same time.

Loud, noisy distractions take you away from the slow alpha brainwave state to be creative from the mind and return you back to the fast beta-brainwave state of your daily routine.

You need eight hours of sleep, one hour of daily exercise, and a healthy nutrition lifestyle for optimal creativity from the mind.

Remember, you need to be in a slow brainwave state to obtain meaningful information from the mind. You learn this skill through meditation practices. You can't use the mind when you're thinking from the head stress center in the beta brainwave state. You need to be in slower brainwave states like alpha or theta.

This sounds complicated at first. However, through understanding the principles and meditation practice, thinking from the mind in the slow brainwave state becomes easy and automatic.

How do you get into the slow brainwave state while awake so you can use the mind? There are many ways to slow down the brainwaves such as being in quiet peaceful surroundings while going for a walk, a hike, or a run. It's daydreaming. Use meditation through traditional eyes closed method or with eyes-open meditation.

Learn the feeling of the slow-brainwave state so you can use the mind at any time for creativity to solve problems and help people, courage to be your true authentic self, and inspiration to improve the world.

*   *   *

Neuro-bypass for a bad boss. Bad bosses can plague us well after we've left our work behind for the day. To overcome a bad boss, we can use the neuro-bypass technique.

You can use the neuropathway bypass technique to eliminate stress. If the cause of severe stress is from a controlling, abusive boss, coworker, spouse, or someone else in your life, then use the neuropathway bypass technique to permanently eliminate this stress.

What is the neuropathway bypass technique? I was taught this technique by a Wharton Business School Professor. You create a bypass of a negative stressful neuropathway. Something or someone has caused a negative neuropathway in your brain causing stress. One way to eliminate the feeling of stress from the person is to create a neuropathway that bypasses the stressful one that's been established. It's like a dysfunctional highway filled with cracks and potholes, bypassing this with a new, smooth highway.

When you see this controlling or abusive person, hear the person, or even see the name on a document or cell phone, you instantly develop a knot in your stomach along with increased blood pressure, increased breathing, sweaty palms, and a rapid heart rate. The stress can spiral out of control, and if left unchecked will lead to serious illness. This response is from a cement neuropathway in the brain.

Instead of using this unhealthy, ingrained neuro highway, create a healthier track with a bypass. The method is simple to understand but requires discipline for two minutes each day for a non-interrupted two-week period. After using this successfully for a bad boss, the technique can be applied to many types of unpleasant situations.

Here's how it works. In the morning, visualize the image of the feared or abusive person in your mind until it triggers the anger and stress feelings in the pit of your stomach. You can do this during your morning routine or during your morning run or walk.

When the feelings of discomfort develop, begin saying two soothing words to yourself repeatedly such as "love and peace." Say the words over and over until the feeling of anger subsides, usually in less than two minutes.

The next morning, do the same thing, visualize the angry image, allow the knot of pain to develop in your stomach. Repeat the two words, "love and peace," to yourself until the unpleasant feeling subsides. Repeat this exercise every morning for two weeks.

Sarah tried the neuro-bypass technique at work. She had a controlling, abusive boss who was causing unbearable and unhealthy chronic stress. So, during her early-morning run, she triggered the knot in her stomach by visualizing her boss berating her. She repeated "love and peace" to herself over and over, and found, to her surprise, that in less than two minutes, the feeling completely disappeared and was replaced by a soothing feeling.

However, this calming feeling didn't last long. The second she saw her boss's car in the parking lot, the anguish immediately returned. This is expected, the aberrant neuropathway had taken months or years to create, and it will take time to build a bypass.

On the way home from work, Sarah repeated the exercise. The tightening in her stomach quickly returned as she visualized her boss, but again she was pleasantly surprised to find it was replaced with a soothing feeling. She continued the exercise for several more days every morning.

On the seventh day, something unusual happened. She visualized her boss, but she had difficulty triggering the unpleasant feeling in her stomach. This was strange, and she didn't believe it at first, but gradually during the next several days, no matter how hard she tried, she couldn't trigger the fear and anguish when she visualized her boss. It was a wonderful experience.

This new development gave her a renewed feeling of strength. After two weeks, Sarah realized that when she saw her boss or heard the name at work, it meant nothing to her. She had no fear and no stress. Her face appeared serene.

Several days passed, and her boss came storming into one of Sarah's team meetings and was about to begin the usual verbal public lashing. However, Sarah stood up, standing about 12 inches away from her boss's nose. She looked directly at the pupils in her boss's eyes and smiled. At that moment, Sarah had an overwhelming feeling of calmness with no increased heart rate, no anger, and no fear. The boss blinked a couple of times, looked at Sarah's face, said nothing, and left the room.

Months of hostility ended abruptly. The boss found someone else to torment. Sarah returned to her work full of energy and enjoyed her creative work. She was so successful, she soon left this position and moved to a higher-paid and more enjoyable job at another company.

A similar method can be used on an instant basis by blocking formation of a short-term memory. Call it the short-memory block technique. Short term memory can hold seven words or numbers for one to two minutes. These are replaced by new words and events. If something irritates you, say "love and peace" over and over before having the second thought. Within a few minutes, you'll feel good, and you'll forget what made you angry or upset. If you don't think a second thought, you don't build a story causing stress.

People have something that's irritating. For example, someone is talking loudly on a cell phone in a restaurant or at a public gathering. Instead of thinking about how upsetting this is and terrible things about the person. The instant you see this, say to yourself, "love and peace," over and over.

Keep saying it without thinking that second thought about the situation. Soon you'll find yourself thinking about something else, and you've forgotten about the episode because it's out of your short-term memory slot.

If you find yourself upset and in a negative-feedback loop about a person that causes stress, use the neuro-bypass technique to eliminate the stress.

You can use this technique in multiple situations such as a bad boss, a hostile coworker, or someone abusive in your life. As time passes, it will take less time to develop the bypass. You regain your strength. Your creativity returns. You are a stronger person.

*   *   *

Stay in your lane. When it comes to work and business, sometimes we feel like we must be a jack-of-all-trades and do other people's job to succeed. But really, we need to learn how to use our unique skills and stay in our lane for success.

Staying in your lane leads to success at work and at home. When this expression first became popular, it had a negative meaning and sometimes harsh such as "mind your own business" or "stick to what you're good at." It meant don't interfere with people's affairs or pry into their lives. Now, it's more positive.

My meaning of the expression is focus and pay attention to your task or job without negative thoughts about other people's work. This means approaching the task or job by thinking from your heart with kindness and thinking from the mind with creativity to solve problems and help others.

For example, this expression forms the basis for being the best football team in the Nationals Football League. Players on the offensive line and defensive line are taught their tasks for each play. This task is practiced every day, and each player is held accountable for that task. The coaching staff verbalize the concept of focusing and concentrating on their assigned moves with no thoughts of the other player's tasks or actions.

To some of the players, this may feel they aren't doing anything or contributing to winning the game, and they attempt to 'help' other players. However, the coaching staff continually verbalizes the importance of their role for each play. During video review of the game, it becomes obvious if one of the players veers from the assigned role. Players acknowledge their error to the team, and they stay in their lane for the next game.

This situation occurs in manufacturing facilities and in business offices.

Think about the expression in a positive way. Focusing only on your job, you're contributing to the success of the organization. Two people doing the same task is not teamwork. This causes confusion and inefficiency. You need to focus on your task and nothing else. This helps others to stay in their lane. You're being your true self and feel better about yourself. You improve your relationship with others.

Staying in your lane means sticking with what you know and with what you are good at. Pick a path a stay with it. This means surrounding yourself with people who have different skills and stay in their lane. Team success comes from working with people with different skills, not from people with the same skills.

Workflow operations can be complex, so coworkers need to learn their precise role and stay with it. Any deviation by losing focus, interfering with others, or trying to do other people's work disrupts the flow decreasing efficiency and company success. Thinking from the anger center or stress center with criticism and blame causes loss of focus and disrupting the workplace.

The opposite perspective of staying in your lane needs to be explored. Staying in your lane may become unfulfilling or unsatisfying. This may be a time for a conversation about changing the workflow or developing new products and services. This may be a time for change to doing something else or reframe to look beyond the task, not as work, but as improving people's lives.

The idea of "staying in your lane" can also be applied on a personal level. Be your true authentic self with no need to try to be someone else or compare yourself to others. This is staying out of your self-thinking primitive brain and thinking from your heart with kindness and giving. This means spending less time on social media comparing yourself to others and following negative commentary.

Staying in your lane on the personal level and at work leads to an enjoyable life for you and others.

* * *

Selling from your heart. When we think about selling someone an idea, a product, or service, we often think about ourselves first and the customer second. You need to reorient this practice of selling from the head with selfishness to selling from the heart with kindness and understanding the other person.

Sell from your heart for success. Everyone is selling something. It's a product, a service, a new idea, or where to go for dinner with the family. There are thousands of books and courses for doing this.

For example, show the benefits, get people to say yes, and ask for the close, or use consulting sales by helping the customer solve problems. These techniques and others are successful. However, it's competition between the buyer and the seller. It's a contest to determine the winner. This is taking behavior from the self-centered primitive brain. It's stressful for both the buyer and the seller.

There's a different way of selling. Make it an enjoyable experience for the buyer and the seller. Good products and services make people's lives easier and improve their lives. People need to be aware of these products so they can buy them.

A reframe is needed, you're not selling a product, you're improving people's lives. For example, you're selling a software product to speed up detecting life-threatening infections in the hospital. You're not only selling a product, but you're also saving lives. This is selling from the heart.

Selling from the heart is about empathy for the other person. When you talk to someone about selling something, the other person is learning about this for the first time. They're thinking from their ancient crocodile brain region. So, keep the conversation simple and non-threatening. Speak with feelings and positive emotions. Avoid thinking about yourself such as thinking about making money or closing the sale.

An effective way to sell from the heart is to have a conversation with feelings from your heart with kindness and giving. Talk about the current situation and the biggest problem. Share your understanding of the problem. Then you provide a solution with your product.

You're selling a new tech product. Say hello from the heart with kindness and have a conversation. How did the person get started in the job? What does the person enjoy most about the job? What's the biggest problem? Share your story and tell the person how your product is going to solve the problem. This is connecting with emotion and empathy.

For sales, think from the heart. Think from the mind to help solve people's problems, and innovation to improve people's lives.

*   *   *

Your face tells the world who you are. A long time ago, *physiognomy* was the science of reading facial features to tell what a person was like. While we now know that you can't tell a person's potential earning power from the shape of their face or their personality from what their nose looks like, our faces still tell the world who we are. Where we think from is reflected right on our faces.

You've probably heard that you have ten seconds for people to know if they want to talk to you or do business with you. But it's not ten seconds, it's instant. People know instantly if they like you by the look on your face.

Author Leila Loundas talks about a caricature artist who knows people's personality instantly by looking at their face, and most of the time, people don't know their own public personality. He'll draw someone's caricature on a napkin at a social event. When people look at the drawing, they always say, "that's good, but that's not really me." However, their friends all nod their heads in agreement with the caricature portrayal.

People know personalities by looking at faces. Your face looks like where you're thinking from. If you're thinking from your anger center, then your face tells the world you're angry. If thinking about yourself from the stress center. Your face tells the world you're stressed.

If you're thinking about yourself, being upset with yourself, or trying to be someone else, then your face shows stress. People see your stress and prefer not to interact with someone who's stressed. Where you're thinking from is your personality moment by moment.

You feel sorry for yourself, that's your personality. You're complaining, that's your personality. You don't want to be at a social event. You don't want to make small talk. Everyone knows it. If you're desperate to find a job, find a romantic relationship, or meet your monthly quota, your face tells the story.

What's the harm? This depends on what you're trying to do. If you're in a social setting and enjoy talking with people, no one is going to come up to you and start a conversation if your face says go away. If it's a romantic situation, no one wants to talk to someone stressed-out or desperate.

This can be disastrous in a sales situation. If you bring your angry face, better-than-anyone else face, or trying-to-make money face, then you're not going to make a sale.

For example, you're selling a product in the exhibit hall at a trade show, and you're walking toward a potential client. Before you introduce yourself, people have determined if they want to do business with you or not. It's your face. If you're thinking about how you're going to convince the person to buy the product, then they feel pressured and don't want to talk with you.

You'll know instantly whether they want to talk with you. For example, while you're looking at their eyes giving your pitch, the person will glance to the left or the right as if looking for something more interesting than what you're saying. People will fidget, touch their face, or move, all with the idea of getting away. Finally, their feet are sideways ready to go for the exit.

People make up their mind without you saying a word. What should you do so people will always want to talk with you or do business with you? Be your true self with good posture, show interest in them, and that you like them. Don't use the quick, fake smile used for photos, delay the smile for a couple of seconds so then your smile is for them, and you're pleased to see them.

Your face shows where you're thinking from. Are you thinking from the anger center or the stress center? Your face shows it, and other people know it. Think about the other person, their feelings, what they like, and what you have in common with them. These thoughts will show a strong, successful face. Remember, do not have self-centered thoughts or negative thoughts when approaching people. They will instantly recognize your thinking.

What do you do if you're upbeat, positive, and kind, but the person turns you down? This is not because of you. It's the other person. They're having a bad day. You can move on or you can use empathy and have a conversation about the person.

Where you're thinking from shows on your face moment by moment. Think from your heart with kindness and your face will show strength and think from your mind with solutions to help people, and your face will show success.

*   *   *

Be yourself, not your job title. Is your identity wrapped up in your job title? Would you still feel like the same person tomorrow if you didn't hold your same job? We need to first be our true authentic selves and then do our job.

Unhealthy stress is caused by trying to do your job title. I recently talked to a CEO about company acquisition plans. The CEO could not finish a sentence. The CEO's face and eyes were filled with level-10 death-zone stress.

Why? Because this person was "trying" to be a CEO. This CEO was thinking about keeping the board happy, keeping employees engaged in their work, and going by the "book." There is no "book" for any job. People need to be their true selves first, then do the job.

Examples are everywhere. The manager who goes by the "book" demanding to meet quota. Managers need to be their true selves first, then do their job, help the team improve sales.

Are you trying to be a good mother or a good father keeping up with the latest trends and trying to comply with the current social parenteral norm? This is a disaster for you and your children. You're trying to be someone else and your children will pay the consequences. You need to be your true authentic self and think from your heart with kindness and from the mind with creativity to do the right thing and make the right decisions. Then, you'll be the best mom and dad on the planet.

Board members who count every dollar and make the CEO have approval for every move. This behavior destroys companies. Board members need to be their true selves, bringing solutions and innovative ideas to grow the business.

At a workout facility, everyone is there to help, not just do the job of cleaning and keeping the facility safe.

The ER triage nurse behind the glass cage and two computers needs to think from the heart with kindness first for frightened patients, and then do the computer work.

People do their job titles, instead of being themselves. How does this happen? People are thinking about themselves from the primitive brain, which leaves no thinking from the heart with kindness or from the mind to solve problems and help others.

Always be your true self, then do your job. Be who you are moment by moment, which means knowing where you're thinking from. People who are not being themselves are thinking from the head stress center about trying to be someone else. They can only think from one location at a time. If they're thinking from the stress center, they can't think from the heart or from the mind.

Remember, if you eliminate anger and stress, then all your time is available to think from the heart with kindness and giving; and think from the mind with courage, creativity to solve problems and help others, and with innovation to improve people's lives.

If it's so easy to get out of your stress center and be your true self, then why don't people do this? It's a habit and an automatic response. This behavior begins during childhood through conditioning from parents, teachers, and peers. Children need to be told who they are during school years by their parents and teachers, so they fit in socially. Later, people are told who they are by society and the boss. This is stressful and not enjoyable. Some people recognize this and stop listening to others and become their true selves.

However, many people don't realize the need to stop listening to people tell them who they are. They fear being their true self because they lack confidence in themselves or fear failure. They've developed a habit of always trying to be someone else. This makes them have thoughts of not being qualified to do the job and fear losing the job.

It's the opposite being yourself gives you tremendous confidence in what you can do and eliminates fear because you're doing what you want to do. If it's not good enough or not what they want, then leave, and go somewhere where you're appreciated for who you are.

Part of being your true self is knowing the potential unfavorable consequences of your actions and willing to accept them. The reason you can accept the unfavorable outcome is that you made the decision, and you had the responsibility so you can correct the situation before irreversible harm develops. People need to know that being their true selves is so much better than trying to be someone else.

What happens if you're not your true self? Anger and stress. Always trying to be someone else is thinking about yourself from the stress center. The less you think about yourself, the more you become your true self. If you're thinking from the anger center or trying to do your job from the stress center, then you can't think from the heart with kindness and helping others.

Being yourself is the opposite of stress. It feels good. You have high energy. You're creative. You're engaged in life. You enjoy living in the moment. You don't criticize, complain, or blame. You have no guilt, worry, or jealousy. You're trustworthy. You make instant decisions, have unwavering commitment, and enjoy total responsibility because you are willing to take the consequences.

What are the consequences of being your true self? Mostly good. People have been conditioned to fear. It takes courage because being your true self means taking the consequences.

Long term, this is healthy and leads to an enjoyable and extraordinary life. Short term, the consequences can be harsh that include getting fired and losing friends or a spouse. However, this is better than staying in a situation, not able to be who are. It's stressful and dangerous to your health.

For example, your boss discreetly tells you to "fake" the books or falsify a project. Of course, you would never do this, or would you? You have a smooth-talking boss and get bullied into it, or you can't afford to lose the job. Being yourself and getting fired is so much better in the long term than the feeling of guilt and worry every day of your life.

Making instant decisions and taking total responsibility almost always has positive consequences and gives you a good feeling of accomplishment. This makes you strong and confident. In addition, you'll impact the lives of people in a positive way.

Because you make the decision and take the responsibility. Your decisions can improve people's lives throughout the world. This feels good. In addition, you know the potential bad outcomes and are willing to take the consequences. If the outcome is bad, you fix the problem before serious, irreversible damage occurs.

What do you do when someone yells at you for being yourself? This is going to happen. They're empty words. Don't let these words trigger or activate the primitive brain region, and you'll have no stress. Get knocked down by being yourself? Remember there'll be 100 people surrounding you with their hands out to help.

Be yourself, then do your job. Be your true self by thinking from your heart with kindness and giving, and the mind for solving problems to help others, and innovation to improve people's lives.

*   *   *

Soft skills and social skills. Soft skills are for work. Social skills are for friends, family, and the public. Here are 30 life-changing soft skills and social skills for leading a good life. Mastering soft skills and social skills will lead to success at work, at home, and in the community.

Soft skills are personal characteristics and habits at work. Social skills are positive interpersonal behaviors. Learn and use these soft skills and social skills at home, at work, and in public to improve your chance of succeeding. Leil Lowndes talks about 92 ways to talk to anyone, many of these are soft skills and social skills.

Ten soft skills for success at work

(1) Prioritize and execute, which means completing the most important task first before going the second. Be your authentic self, prioritize and execute.

People often begin the day with a list of things to do. Sometimes the list is so long, the day becomes overwhelming resulting in stress taking away the energy to do anything on the list. Interrupting interruptions also occur during the day adding to the stress and inability to do anything.

A problem that is too common for getting things done is stage-3 cellphone dependency. People holding their cellphone in their hand all day and looking at so many options, the brain becomes confused and shuts down. They're deciding to join the conversation, text a friend, go to a party, have lunch, do a work project, look at video clips, and finally there's a text from the boss to go to a meeting immediately.

The entire day can be wasted away thinking about all these phone options and problems, ending the day with nothing done, frustrated, and stressed.

A solution to this problem is to be your true authentic self. The negative use and nonproductive use of the phone is not needed. Use the cellphone for positive exchange for a few minutes during the day and keep it out of sight the rest of the time.

Another problem is to begin something that is a high priority and moving on to something else before completing the task. This ends the day with not fully accomplishing anything, a list of half-completed tasks, and extreme stress.

The solution to prioritizing is to be your true authentic self and instantly select the top priority now and complete the task having no thoughts about other options on the list.

One final thought about prioritizing, "multitasking" doesn't work. People talk about doing three or four things at a time, juggling several tasks in the air, or only making one trip from the car. This is thinking from the primitive brain and causes stress, and performance is suboptimal. Think from your heart and the mind, pay attention, do one task at a time. This way, you'll enjoy what you're doing, and you'll do it right the first time.

(2) Self-direction at work means making your own decisions and actions rather than being told what to do. This makes work enjoyable and fulfilling. This creates a pleasant work environment. This improves administrative efficiency of not requiring constant supervision and potential for misunderstanding and stress.

This skill requires focus and paying attention to the task. This skill requires high self-confidence and belief in your abilities. This skill requires being your true self and eliminating thoughts about yourself from the stress center.

(3) Influencing is a soft skill required to advance in the origination that shows management your leadership capability. Influencing means knowing who you're talking to and your audience. This means knowing your goals and what you're trying to accomplish. You need to have people align with your solution. You do this by sharing options with others that will allow them to make the right choice.

(4) Be engaged at work. Worker engagement is one of the biggest factors in the success or failure of a company. Employee studies showed that as high as 67 percent of US employees and 85 percent of employees globally are not engaged in the workplace. In the UK, it's an alarming 92 percent. The same study showed that 73 percent of employees consider leaving their jobs.

This means most of the workforce around the world are doing the bare minimum to make it through the day with little or no emotional attachment. In addition, some employees are actively disengaged and intentionally disrupt the company.

Employees need to have relationships with people at work, and they want a balance of work life with their personal life. Being engaged and company culture are interconnected, the more positive the culture, the higher the engagement.

(5) Be prepared for discussions and meetings is needed as part of work for anyone. Being unprepared and unengaged is self-centered thinking and disrespectful to coworkers who worked hard for the meeting and depend on input from everyone.

(6) Have a good work ethic. This means being honest with yourself and not lying to yourself about your capabilities, about your coworkers, or your work. This means having integrity about everything you do at work with no lies.

This means not lying to other people or covering up illegal activities. This means taking responsibility for your actions and answering to adverse outcomes of your actions with no criticism or blame of coworkers.

(7) Have a growth mindset. Be willing to listen to innovative ideas and ways of doing things. Professor Carol Dweck at UPenn writes extensively about the benefits of a growth mindset which means developing the flexibility to learn from experiences for improving your life and others.

Being your true self thinking from your heart and your mind establishes a growth mindset. Self-centered thinking results in a stagnant and unhealthy fixed mindset. This closed mindset way of thinking becomes an engrained habit. Having a fixed mindset is an easier choice, agreeing with people for approval and pleasing them. This thinking is from the stress center and unhealthy.

Be your true self and express your own thoughts leading to productive work.

(8) Be a team player. With two or more people, one is in charge and the other follows. This occurs between spouses, friends, coworkers, or at a meeting. One person is leading the conversation and the other is listening.

A good conversation and productive conversation occur when there's a natural back and forth where one individual is listening with attention without interruption or self-thinking thoughts. Be flexible when in charge and be committed and enthusiastic when following.

(9) Use positive communication. This means interacting with people in ways that result in a good feeling for all participants with no destructive comments, one-ups, or put-downs.

Daily life is about emotions. Interacting with people in a positive way is a good feeling. Positive interaction with your spouse and family creates a good feeling for everyone. Having positive conversations at work creates good feelings for management and employees. Talking to coworkers, clerks, and restaurant staff in a positive manner increases personal energy and feel-good neurotransmitters.

Have a job interview? Giving a pitch? Need help with your project? Success is related to the likable factor. Be likable, use positive communication. Getting a promotion has more to do with the manager or executive liking the person than skills and competency. Smile. Use compliments from the heart. Positive communication by being yourself develops trust.

For positive social interaction, being kind exceeds being nice. Being nice to people may be considered a duty and means trying to please people. Being kind to people comes from the heart and is meaningful interaction. Love is the ultimate positive social interaction. Having compassion and empathy for others increases your positive communication in life and improves your relationship with your family, friends, and coworkers.

(10) Listen with attention. Let people finish talking before you talk. There are books and courses about how to listen. People know how to listen, that's not the issue. The issue is whether people want to listen or not.

There are several reasons why people don't want to listen. The topic or the person may be boring. People may be so sleepy that they can't keep their eyes open during a complete sentence. There may be an uncomfortable topic people don't want to hear about or talk about. People are looking at the mobile phone. Sometimes, people are not listening because they are thinking about what to say next before the other person stops talking.

In these situations, the person doing the talking needs to become aware that the person is not listening and stop talking. The person can ask if the other person is interested in continuing, changing the topic, or having a meaningful conversation later.

The person doing the listening should acknowledge the issue and either change topics or have the conversation later.

Another listening social skill is not talking or shouting between rooms at home or in the office. This is stressful for the person hearing the shouting because the words are not seen from a person and not clearly heard, which is frustrating and can be misinterpreted leading to anger. No talking between rooms, talk to the person face to face for a pleasant and productive conversation.

Five soft skills useful at work and at home

(1) **Be your true self for instant trust and likeability.** Learn to limit thinking about yourself from the stress center and the anger center to less than ten seconds at home and at work. This will allow you to spend the entire day being your true self and not trying to be someone else. People know who you are enabling them to like you and trust you.

People want to be with you because they know who you are. You're not trying to impress anyone, to be better than anyone, or to please anyone. You're pleasant to deal with because you don't complain, criticize, or blame. Your opinions are based on your thoughts and not biased by outside influences.

People are willing to talk with you about their feelings and ideas because you won't make them feel bad about themselves or embarrass them or stab them in the back in public or among their friends. You give people energy without losing energy yourself. You're a positive energy charger. You see the good in people and events. You find positive learning out of bad situations. You create magical moments. All of this because you spend no time thinking about yourself from the stress center leaving time to give people energy, see the good in all things, and create magical moments.

(2) **Make immediate decisions** at work and at home so everyone can move forward. If a small decision is needed about where to go to dinner, or a large

decision about which house to buy, make the decision instantly. You have enough information to make a yes or no decision.

Always remember, if the outcome is wrong, you can fix it fast because you made the decision. You know why you made the decision, what basis you used to make the decision, and how you made the decision; therefore, you know what to do with a bad outcome.

There is no reason not to make instant decisions. If it's a yes, people can move forward. If it's a no, people can move forward. If it's hesitation, indecision, and no decision, people are frustrated, stressed, and stopped. Families are confused. Businesses are floundering. Military personnel are losing their lives. Make instant decisions.

(3) Take total responsibility. This feels good. This gives you strength and impact. Learn to take the consequences for bad outcomes. You can fix bad outcomes fast before they cause damage because you considered all factors of the responsibility and anticipated potential bad outcomes.

Take responsibility for your own actions. This means accepting the responsibility at the deep conscious level, carrying out the responsibility, and being responsible for the outcome. If it's a good outcome, enjoy the feeling. If it's not, accept the blame immediately, without blame or accusing others. Experience the bad feeling for six to eight seconds and think creatively from the mind to fix whatever needs to be fixed and move on.

This also means if you accept a job or a task, that you take responsibility for others who are mutually involved. This means sharing the success as well as taking the blame.

(4) Have unwavering commitment. This means being consistently reliable for your family, friends, and coworkers. If you say yes to do something, then you should complete the request regardless of the obstacles. This means saying "no" to something when you don't have the skills, resources, interest, or time.

Saying yes to something and not showing up on time or not completing the work is frustrating and stressful for everyone involved and causes delay or not meeting a deadline. This gives you a bad reputation that is spread to other people and organizations. Sometimes, you only get one chance. Therefore, make a commitment only if you can say yes to the four components, skills, resources, interest, and time.

It takes discipline to say no to family, friends, and the boss, but taking the consequences is better than saying yes and not completing the commitment or doing insignificant, meaningless work.

(5) Have empathy at home and at work. Consider the other person's situation before making a conclusion. This can prevent escalated arguments resulting in anger and no resolution.

If someone is angry with you when you've done nothing to warrant the anger, then use empathy to understand their situation. Something has been taken from them or someone has done something bad to them, and you're the nearest person to blame. They need someone to talk to. This is difficult for you, but this is a time not to be angry but to talk about the issue to clarify the cause, making an unpleasant situation easier to deal with.

Remember to understand the other person's situation, but don't overdo it by feeling or experiencing the negative feelings yourself. This will lead to unhealthy stress. Use empathy at home and at work.

Five physical attributes for soft skills and social skills

(1) Have a strong posture. Posture is important for your health and positive interaction with people. Stand tall with chin straight, eyes forward, shoulders down, back straight by gently squeezing your shoulder blades. Have your palms out with no clinched fists or folded arms. You look strong, confident in who you are, and open to connecting with people in a friendly manner.

(2) Have a genuine smile. People use quick smiles for the camera. This is a learned response and successful for a picture, but not when meeting friends or greeting clients.

Delay the smile for a second. You need to smile from the heart with warmth and a pleasant feeling. Smile, restaurant servers can increase their tips by 140 percent.

(3) Control your physical emotions at work and in public. This means learning to manage your physical response to your emotional reactions to people and events. You can't lose your temper in public from having poor service or an accidental interaction.

This can be difficult especially if people are mean to you or you get a parking ticket. You want to yell and jump up and down with closed fists. Everyone knows this doesn't help the situation, and it's embarrassing. You're upset with yourself. Other people view you in a negative way and do not want anything to do with you.

What should you do? You need to recognize the negative outcome for you and others. You need to limit your anger to six to eight seconds with silence or subtle clinching of the fists or face and move on without anyone knowing about your internal response.

(4) Be adaptable to all physical and social situations. You need to learn to manage yourself and go above the background ebb and flow of a chaotic and stressful environment.

This means controlling the situation at home with a background of bickering. At work, this means learning to give your presentation at a meeting that's continually being disrupted by noises and people coming and going. This means adapting to a social situation where you're wearing the wrong clothes.

Learn to be adaptable by being your true authentic self and take the consequences, both positive and negative.

(5) Resilience means having a quick and persistent recovery from physical fatigue and mental strain. Being resilient means increased well-being, decreased anxiety, and improves health.

Resilience means being your true self, learning to change your thoughts for desired outcomes, learning to use the mind for creative solutions and helping others, having close relationships, focusing on what you can control, and expecting positive results.

Ten social skills

(1) Not saying something negative after saying something positive. It's a habit. People don't realize they do it. For example, saying "enjoy the party" and then "saying don't stay out too late."

After thanking someone, the person replies, "My pleasure," which is a pleasant response leaving you feeling good, but then the person says, "Just doing my job." That eliminates the good feeling immediately and leaves a negative feeling. There's no need for negative comments.

(2) Not making others feel vulnerable and not asking personal questions. You need to have people feel good about themselves. There's no need to ask personal questions. How old are you? Where're you from? What's your job? Instead, try "What's keeping you busy?" Don't use clichés or outdated sayings.

There's no need to be impatient with your friends and family, or in public. This causes stress in you and others. For example, someone's annoyed at you while in a grocery store line. They're fidgeting, sighing, and telling you to "hurry up." Another example is honking at someone trying to make a left turn. This is dangerous and could cause a serious accident. Be kind to yourself and others.

(3) Ignoring mistakes or accidents of others without a negative comment. A server in a restaurant drops glass scattering it across the floor. Comments from the tables may include, "what an idiot" or "you're fired." These comments are hurtful and make other people in the restaurant uncomfortable. The best approach is to not say anything and continue the conversation in a normal tone of voice.

(4) Putting others first. This is easy because this is the basis of being your true self. Don't think about yourself from the stress center. Think about others from your heart with kindness and think from the mind to help others.

(5) Don't eat out of a bag in an elevator or its equivalent. Have you seen someone in an elevator eating potato chips out of a paper bag with loud crunching noises and swallowing for everyone to hear? How does this make you feel? This tells you a lot about the person.

There are many other similar situations. Don't eat standing up. Don't eat in a line waiting for something. Your physical actions tell people your personality and whether they want to know you or do business with you.

(6) Be kind to retail and restaurant people. Look people working in retail or at restaurants in the eye with a warm feeling. At a business luncheon meeting, the client blurted out the order with head down in the menu. The meeting remained cold and business-like. It was suggested to the person that it's useful to be kind to people. At the next luncheon meeting, the client looked the server in the eyes, smiled, and pleasantly asked for the food items. The server returned the kindness, and the client's demeanor changed for the meeting, friendly and open for discussion.

(7) Say "thank you" for a compliment – no added negative comments needed. People often feel compelled to add a comment after receiving a complement, such as saying, "this old thing, it was cheap" or "you should have seen me two days ago." This can neutralize the compliment and may even make the other person feel worse. All that is needed is a "thank you" regardless of reason, big or small, for the compliment. The receiver is grateful for the acknowledge knowing that the compliment was meaningful. If you wish, you can say, "Thank you, that's very kind of you."

(8) Use the words "you" and "yours," not "I" and "me." Everyone likes to hear the word "you." A study showed that people using more "you" and "yours" in a conversation rather than "I" and "me" are healthier and enjoy life more. For example, you could say "You look stunning in that outfit," rather than "I like your outfit." "You asked an excellent question," rather than, "That's a good question."

(9) Tell positive stories about yourself and others. People like positive stories and stories with positive endings. This makes listeners feel good and they often return with a positive comment or a positive story of their own. This is especially important when telling a story about someone else that may or may not be present. Always tell a positive story about someone. Listeners will enjoy the story and have a positive memory about the person.

(10) Make people feel good about themselves and bring out the best in them. This creates a positive feeling for everyone while among the family, at work, or in public. Find something special about someone and make a positive comment. See the good in people.

Finding fault in people and criticizing them in public not only makes them feel bad about themselves, but people who hear the conversation feel uncomfortable about both the person and you.

There is one more social skill. Say "yes" to opportunities and sharing positive experiences with close relationships. Someone approaches you excited about doing something, going to a party, going on a trip, or flying in a biplane. They're excited. Share the excitement. Don't automatically say a harsh, "no." This instantly takes away the excitement.

Soft skills like self-direction, influencing, growth mindset, positive communication, and resilience lead to success at work. Social skills like being your true self, bringing out the best in people, and a strong posture will propel you to social success.

Score 100 percent in your soft skills and social skills for an enjoyable life for you and everyone else.

Chapter 9

Mind Your Health

---

*"Imagination is more important than knowledge.
Knowledge is limited. Imagination encircles the world."*

— Albert Einstein

All situations and choices impact your health. Most are obvious such as poor nutrition choices, inadequate sleep, and no exercise. There are many other hidden situations that can be harmful to your health such as bad social habits, cell phone dependency, toxic narcissistic individuals, and harmful ghosting. There are also positive situations such as self-healing.

Build new health habits to replace unhealthy habits. Almost everyone has a minor bad health habit or social habit they've had for many years and have probably tried to eliminate it. These are habits that replacing with a new habit will improve your health and social interaction.

This is one way to build a new healthy habit. The first step is to develop a key word, which is a word you'll say to yourself to remind you of the new habit. You'll be using this word many times during the day. The word or words need to be specific such as "chin straight" instead of "keep your head up" to replace the bad habit of having your head down.

The best way to develop the trigger word is brainstorming by listing 25, and choosing the best that will work for you. Or ask your favorite AI bot on the internet to give you the list.

You'll be going through three phases, one week at a time. You may have heard that it takes 21 days to develop a new habit. This is correct.

The first two or three days are easy because you'll be repeating the trigger words all day, and you'll be doing your new habit all day long. The next couple of days, you may find you won't be using your trigger words as much and won't be doing your new habit as much but persist because you'll likely use the trigger word enough to develop the new habit.

It's good to acknowledge the good feeling you experience from doing the new habit. This creates a positive reward system through conditioning for solidifying the new habit.

In the second week, start seeking out new situations to use your new habit. The first week you used the trigger word for a certain situation. During this week, you'll realize other settings where you need to use the trigger word. This will take the whole week.

Toward the end of the third week, you'll surprise yourself by doing the new habit without thinking. You now have a new habit. It's a great feeling. You'll feel fantastic. You've tried to stop doing the old habit for years, and now you've done it.

But there's a fourth phase that you've never heard about. No one tells you about this phase. It's about your old habit. It's not gone. It's been replaced, but it's still there. Although the old habit may fade away with time, it may never go away. That's why it's important to stay vigilant with your new habit, not letting the old habit appear.

You don't break old habits. You replace them with new habits. Bad health habits are neuropathways that have become cement highways. Fortunately, if you don't use them for several years, the pathway may deteriorate and disappear.

In the beginning, you'll find the old habit coming up all the time. The goal of this fourth phase is to increase the amount of time between the old habit behavior and your new habit. At first it will occur two or three times a day or maybe more. You need to continually try to decrease the number of times the old habit develops. Try to decrease the number of times to such a small number that you don't think about it. Eventually you'll go for a month without the old habit.

I'll tell you about my new habit story. For many years I put my head down when I'm thinking while walking or running. This is a terrible look, poor posture, and not healthy. I've always said, "Head up is strong. Head down is weak." I've been trying to break this habit for many, many years without success.

While walking to the office one morning, I saw my reflection and realized I had to eliminate this habit. I didn't like the look of having my head down. It made me feel weak. So, I wanted to test the 21-day rule.

The first thing was a key word. The words I tried in the past failed, such as, "Don't put your head down." This was negative and too general because you need to put your head down while tying shoes or other daily activities. I tried "chin up," but that didn't work because I don't want the chin up. That's not a good look and not healthy.

Randomly, I heard about the social rule enforced by the English royal family, "Keep the chin straight." That gave me an idea, straight is the word I need. My trigger words became "chin straight" with the long version of keeping the chin straight, every minute of the day, every day of the year.

I started on a Monday and the first couple of days were easy because I kept saying to myself, "straight" and my chin was straight, my shoulders square and back straight. This felt good. The next couple days were not as successful because I didn't repeat the word as frequently, and I often found my old habit of head down while thinking.

During the first week, I was able to keep my chin straight walking in the parking lot, which was a wonderful feeling.

During the second week, I realized there are many other situations that I needed to keep my chin straight, while running, working on the computer, brushing my teeth, and many other situations. Keeping my chin straight during the activities kept me busy for the entire second week.

Toward the end of the third week, I had a major surprise during my morning run. I found myself running with my chin straight, and I hadn't thought about it. This felt fantastic. It was a great feeling. All these years I had been trying to keep my head straight while running. It was a wonderful feeling.

My neck, shoulders and back loved the new feeling. It looked good too. By 21 days, I had a new habit.

What happened during the next year? That phase four that no one tells you about can be brutal. The old habit is powerful. The parking lot was successful, the new chin-straight habit totally replaced the old head-down, shoulder's-slumped habit.

However, not while running. The old habit was stronger than ever. The head-down thinking while running was unhealthy and gave a terrible, weak look. I tried many ways to establish the chin-straight habit.

One day I counted to one hundred in Spanish five times, and it worked for the day. My chin was straight during the 5-mile run, but not the next day. So, I translated the words, chin straight in Spanish, "barbilla recta," which was helpful for a few days, and then I translated eyes straight into Spanish, "ojos rectos." This was useful for a few days. During these days, my head was down for only five minutes for the entire run! This felt great. It's good for my neck, shoulders and back. It looks good. However, that's not the end of the story. The habit returned while running, just as bad as ever.

Phase four can be harsh. You will learn a new habit for a specific situation. That may be enough to enjoy having a new healthy habit. If the habit requires multiple situations, keep trying, it will take work, hard work.

Here are two examples of finding key words. Say, you have a bad social habit of interrupting people when they're talking. This is such a common habit that people don't realize they're doing it. It's a bad habit because it means that people aren't listening to the conversation, they're thinking about what to say next, so this produces a negative interaction.

What are some key words? How about "don't interrupt?" That won't work. It's negative and too long. Think about the reason someone would interrupt someone. It's because people are thinking about what to say to the other person while the person is talking instead of listening until finished, so the key word "listen" might work.

Here's another bad social habit. This is so common that people don't realize they're doing it. The habit is closing a positive comment with a negative comment. "You're going to have a great time tonight at the party, but don't hang out with your bad friends." This accuses the person of having bad friends and makes the person angry. "Pleasant dreams, you better not sleep too late." You don't need to hear this threat before going to sleep.

What's a good key word for this habit? "Don't say a second negative comment" won't work, it's too long and too general. "No negative comment" is better but still too long. Saying "second" might be a good key word.

Here's a call to action. For your minor unhealthy habit or social habit that you've been trying to eliminate for years, first choose a key word. Use it all day long for the first week, use the trigger word in new situations for a second week, and keep using the trigger word for the third week, and you'll have your new habit.

After that, continue to lengthen the time between your new habit and the old habit popping up so eventually the old habit will disappear for good. Your new habit will make you feel good. It's good for your health. Everyone else will like it too.

* * *

Phone out of sight. Smartphones seem to dominate our days. We are constantly attached to our phones, thinking that these devices give us access to all the social attention we crave. We've stopped experiencing life because of our smartphone crutch. Put the phone out of sight and start living your life.

Put your phone out of sight when interacting with family, friends, coworkers, and the public. Leave your cell phone out of sight when interacting with people.

Here's a sad story about missing an opportunity for a magical moment.

A dad was having breakfast with his seven-year-old daughter who was wearing soccer gear. At first, the dad was sitting across from her and wasn't looking at his cell phone. This was a pleasant sight, no phone. In many situations, the parent with the child is instantly and constantly looking at the cell phone totally ignoring the child.

A couple of minutes later, the father was still not looking at the phone, but he was not talking to his daughter. He hadn't said a single word. He had a far-away look on his face staring ahead into nothing. The daughter had the same look, lifelessly staring into space. Neither one of them had spoken a single word. They didn't talk about the soccer game or what they were going to do during the day, nothing. They were eating in silence with distant blank looks on their faces as if the daughter had been conditioned to having the father look at the cell phone and paying no attention to her.

One minute later, the silence and daughter's look were explained. The father had the phone out, the absent look in his eyes, and his body had checked out, somewhere else. They finished the breakfast in total silence, the daughter with a blank look on her face eating her breakfast, just like the father's look staring at his cell phone.

They were ready to leave, and the father gestured that he was going to the bathroom, and he said the first words of the morning, "stay here." She sat quietly for a minute or two, and then she picked up the knife, which was serrated, and started sawing the edge of the restaurant table. The father returned, and they left in silence.

The father had not seen the minor destruction of the table. What's the next thing she's going to do to get attention? He was totally oblivious of the daughter's need for attention, attention from the father's heart with kindness and love.

The smartphone has moved our civilization to greater knowledge and understanding. Tech makes life easier. For some people, tech makes life too easy. The smartphone gives people easy access to relationships and fleeting, addicting pleasure.

These people have abandoned having an enjoyable conversation with family and friends. There is no place for this device in sight when socially interacting with people, family, friends, coworkers, and the public. Put the phone aside to avoid losing the opportunity for a magical moment.

A restaurant server sizes up people as they walk in the door by looking at where they put their phone. Proper dining etiquette says you have your phone out of sight, in a purse or pocket, when dining with others.

The server said this rarely happens. When people put their phone face up next to their plate, they've checked out and won't be present during the meal. Some people put their phone face down on the table to show they're going to pay attention. The worst are people who hold their phone in one hand during the entire meal and cannot resist looking at it for every 20 seconds. Are they enjoying the dining experience and are their companions enjoying having dinner with them?

Students having a conversation between classes or having a snack during break encounter the same situation. There is silence with no conversation among them. All of them lined up, head down, staring blankly at their phone or clicking the keys sending texts to the person next to them.

This scene occurs in many situations including while involved in recreational activities with friends and family or working out. People are staring at their phones while on the treadmill or elliptical, doing yoga stretches, working the machines, or during a workout class. This is weak social behavior. Working out is not only moving joints and muscles. Working out involves concentrating on the form, and the muscles and joints. Having the phone while working out takes away excising for health and energy. It's also distracting for people doing a purposeful workout.

Call it the 50 percent phone rule. This means having a cell phone during workout, physical therapy, or any other activity decreases the health benefits and the time of exercise by 50 percent. Instead of a one-hour work out, it's equivalent to a 30-minute workout or less. In addition, people texting and scrolling are thinking about themselves from the cingulate stress center causing stress by looking at negative conversations, negative events, and negative images.

This 50 percent phone rule applies to life. Stage three cell phone dependence means always having the phone in your hand. You're missing 50 percent of life including the magical times, the good times, helping others, and improving lives.

What are people doing with the phone? They have relationships on the phone with more important people than the present company. They can't wait to respond. They have no patience for not having a conversation on the phone. Shopping is a popular thing to do while having dinner. Dinner guests are shopping for clothes while the host is spending a huge amount of money for the dinner.

Are you cell phone dependent? Take the mobile phone health profile.

Healthy cellphone use: Your phone is out of sight when interacting with family, friends, coworkers, and in public. You only use the phone in private or for a positive purpose.

Stage 1: Phone in sight.

Stage 2: Looking at the phone while someone is talking to you.

Stage 3: Always having the phone in your hand and the phone face up.

Watch people on a bus or in a random public location. See what they do when they stop looking at their phone. After a few seconds, they move their head side to side staring into space. A few seconds later, they're restless and fidget nervously with their hands waiting to get out the phone. Then, with a sigh of relief, they look at their phone and become motionless with a distant bland look in their eyes and face. They're in another realm, not engaged in life around them. This is addictive behavior. These are phone zombies, dead to the world.

> *"Stage 3 cellphone dependency:*
> *Phone in your hand at all times and face up."*

Eliminate stage 3 phone behavior. It takes away your life. Keep the phone out of sight when interacting with family, friends, coworkers, and in public. Keep the phone out of sight at social gatherings and while participating in recreational events or while working out in the workout facility. Keep the phone out of sight, engage and enjoy life moment by moment.

* * *

Know the gaslighting game. Gaslighting happens when one person systematically destroys another person's sense of self and reality. For those who use gaslighting, it's a dangerous game. And we can get swept up in that game if we aren't careful. Here's what I call the gaslighting game play by play.

When it comes to the gaslighting game, you need to be your true authentic self. Why talk about gaslighting? In recent years, the word has become popular in social conversations and reality TV shows. Gaslighting is Merriam-Webster's word of the year.

The term comes from the 1938 British stage play *Gas Light* set in the Victorian era about a husband drove his wife insane through deceit and trickery to steal from her. A 1944 movie entitled *Gaslight* starring Ingrid Bergman played the woman who was driven insane by her manipulative husband. Gaslighting has now become a term meaning manipulating people by making them feel guilty and bad about themselves. They are driven to question their own reality.

Gaslighting is a strange word with no meaning by itself. It's a complex emotional situation. People that use gaslighting are so good at it that people take years before they realize their lives are being destroyed. Therefore, one way to understand the meaning is to describe it as a gaslighting game. Don't engage. Learn the game so don't play the game.

There are two players. The gaslighter and the victim. The gaslighter is always on the offense. The victim is always on the defense. The objective of the game is to destroy the victim.

The game is like baseball by throwing the ball and hitting the ball except the victim can never hit the ball and always strikes out. The game is like soccer by hitting the ball into the victim's net, but there is no victim defense and a closed off net on the gaslighter's side. The game is like boxing by hitting the victim in the face as fast and hard as possible until the victim is flat out on the ground with a knockout. Negative words, criticism, lies, guilt, and blame are the gaslighter's equipment. Advanced equipment includes deceit, manipulation, and taking away all self-worth for a collapse of the victim's will to live.

The opening move of the gaslighter begins by complaining about something setting up the victim to listen to the gaslighter's problems. Gaslighters only think about themselves. The game begins in earnest as the conversation changes to a complaint about you. This is so subtle and so smooth, that you don't realize the game has started.

This quickly changes to making you feel guilty about something the gaslighter did. This is done through fabrication and creating a story about you based on lies. Now you've become emotionally involved and are feeling emotional pain. Gaslighters are so good at this, the victim truly feels guilty about something they didn't do, and they feel bad about themselves.

The conversation is one-sided and has progressed to round five to round ten in a boxing match. The victim has been beaten over and over with negative words, criticism, and feeling guilty, almost in tears while the gaslighter is puffed up and yelling with a voice filled with anger.

The game continues in full control of the gaslighter. From complaints and criticism, gaslighters use blame that includes accusing the victim of destroying their lives, of getting them fired, or blaming the victim for making them make a wrong decision or taking responsibility.

All of this is a made up lie by the gaslighter; however, by now the victim has lost reality and doesn't know who they are any more. They've been defeated, flat on the ground. The gaslighter has a burst of dopamine chemical glee from the accumbens addiction center that is short and fleeting for a few seconds. There is no victory. There is never enough. The gaslighter moves onto another victim.

Fortunately, this extreme is rare. Be your true self and avoid letting the game get this far by knowing when someone's playing the game and get out of the person's life or seek professional help to learn how to cope. Always be on the alert when the game starts so that you don't respond and engage in the opening move.

At the extreme, the characteristics of the toxic gaslighter include the triad of abnormal behavior with severe self-centered narcissistic behavior; Machiavellian behavior doing anything to anybody to get what they want or get ahead that includes destroying family, friends, and coworkers; and having no remorse of destroying other people's lives. This is rare, but these are individuals who make headlines, global leaders destroying millions of people's lives, or celebrities destroying the lives of others.

Almost everyone sometime or another has gaslighter behavior, especially during high stress or lack of sleep. This may occur for a few minutes or an hour, and the person feels bad about the behavior. They're upset with themselves. "Someone else said that. I didn't say that." This is normal behavior and harmless.

What should you do about a toxic gaslighter? Avoid these people. Do not have them as friends or a boss or a spouse. You will get hurt, and sometimes in a serious manner. This behavior began as having temper tantrums in the store to get candy. It's lifelong manipulative behavior of lies and making people feel bad about themselves. They will not change. They have no feelings of kindness or love from the heart.

This is rare and a true personality disorder. Examples include current and past world leaders who destroy countries, businesses, and millions of people's lives and their families. They can occur in close relationships at home or at work. These people will do anything to anyone to get what they want and have no feelings of remorse for harming others. Do not try to change these people. They learned this behavior during childhood, and it works for them. Feelings of kindness and love from the heart have been shut down. They only think from the primitive brain anger center and self-thinking stress center. Do not engage in this interaction. You will get hurt. Protect yourself and disengage.

What do you do about intermittent gaslighting behavior from not enough sleep? Eight hours of sleep are required, six hours for restoring energy and two hours of dream sleep for kindness from the heart and appropriate social judgment from the prefrontal cortex. Without these two hours of dream sleep at the end of the eight hours of sleep, people will have gaslighting behavior with irritability toward others, short tempered, and making others feel bad about themselves. For this temporary situation, getting eight hours of sleep every night will eliminate this behavior.

Chronic stress will cause the same behavior such as being angry, ill-tempered, and being mean to others. People need to learn to spend only seconds thinking about themselves from the stress center and live their lives in the mind. People need to be their true authentic selves.

Lying is another gaslighting behavior. Gaslighters continuously lie about everything. It's so natural, they don't even know they're doing it. For example, they're late. You're going to meet them at 5, they'll show up at 6:30 or 7:00. And, they'll have an excuse, which usually involves blaming someone else. Sometimes, they'll blame you.

Gaslighters take something from you or say something bad about you. When you bring it up, they'll not only deny they did anything wrong, but they'll insist that you're the one that did something wrong. This makes you feel guilty and question your own values.

Manipulative behavior is often so subtle that you don't recognize it until the next day. This means convincing you to do something that'll benefit them, but at your expense. Sometimes, they'll add a made-up reward for doing the request for them. They'll manipulate you by judging and criticizing you to make you feel guilty for not helping them.

Blaming behavior is easy to recognize because you are the one that is often blamed for something. Gaslighting behavior is blaming someone else for not helping them get what they want. It's your fault. They'll say they had a bad day because of you. They'll blame you for ruining their lives. If they make a bad decision or a wrong decision, it's not their fault, they'll blame you or someone else. They'll blame you in public at a meeting or social gathering.

Gaslighting behavior consists of lying, manipulating, criticism, and blame. Learn to recognize this behavior as fast as possible to protect yourself and prevent unhealthy consequences. Obtain eight hours of sleep every night, have a healthy nutrition lifestyle, and one hour of exercise every day to prevent this behavior in yourself.

Be your true authentic self when faced with a gaslighting situation. Think from the heart with kindness to yourself and self-compassion and think from the mind with creative ways to help yourself.

*   *   *

Responding to a worldwide disaster. People all over the world have lived through a global pandemic that has restructured our lives on every level. Is there a "right way" to respond? And how can we prepare for the next worldwide altering event? People have catastrophic events in their lives. They get fired. They get thrown out of school. They're in a devastating life-threatening natural disaster or war.

There are three responses during a worldwide catastrophic event. A small percentage of people become super achievers, most people have a normal response with recovery over time, and a small percentage of people will respond poorly with ongoing stress for months and maybe a lifetime.

Super achievers develop and use healthy habits that include eight hours of sleep every night, daily exercise, and healthy nutrition. They learn something new every day. They avoid negative energy from people and join other super achievers for learning and inspiration. They remove themselves from toxic environments in their lives. They challenge themselves every day. They take responsibility for their actions. They don't blame or criticize.

They have unwavering commitment. They prioritize and execute. They have learned the discipline to say no to friends and at work if they are not able to complete the request. They eliminate stress by learning to bypass and stay out of the anger center and the self-thinking stress center.

For most people who experience a catastrophic event in their lives, recovery is a slow process where they gradually return to their normal routine over time. They return to their work and daily events to move forward. They replace thinking about the event. Eventually the event fades from active memory and is forgotten.

A small percentage of people don't want to forget and dwell on themselves for months and even for years and years. This is a major problem. Some people can't stop thinking about the event. They continually think from their anger center and their stress center every day, sometimes for hours. This is unhealthy, unproductive, and takes away from happiness. They're irritable, quick to lose their temper, and can be unfriendly and mean to people.

They're always on edge in public, watchful of impending danger. They may have recurrent flashbacks and nightmares about the event. They don't want to return to enjoyable activities that gave them happiness. They're always doing negative thinking from their cingulate self-centered stress center.

If these feelings persist for more than a few months and interfere with their lives and others, professional help can be a useful option.

Prolonged stress is the problem. For example, Greta, a wonderful caring woman, finds herself standing in the check-out line at the grocery store with tears rolling down her face from level-10 stress. She has been caring for her husband who has progressive debilitating Alzheimer's disease. While in line, she is angry with herself because she isn't smart enough to help him. She's upset with herself because she doesn't spend enough time with her husband. This is self-destructive thinking from the stress center. She is not being kind to herself.

She needs to think from the heart with kindness to herself and self-compassion. She can do this by realizing that being with him and helping him as much as she does is sufficient. She does not need to be at his side 24 hours a day. If the condition is so severe that this type of monitoring is needed, then he should be in a chronic care facility under the care of medical professionals.

Finally, Greta has a terrible thought that she would be better off if he died. She feels terrible that she could think such a thing. Here's an option for her at this point. She can feel the stress of this thought, realize it's not thinking from the heart, let it peak within ten seconds, and move on. She can stop this thought from activating the stress center.

Once again, she should be kind to herself from the heart with no other self-centered thoughts from the stress center. Think from the heart with kindness to herself. She's an amazing person. She's giving her time and help as much as she can to keep her husband alive at home.

The call to action for people going through a catastrophic event in their lives is minimize thinking from the anger center and stress center. Acknowledge you're thinking from these two brain regions and stop thinking from them.

If self-thinking behavior with self-destructive thoughts and self-pity thoughts develop, do the opposite, be kind to yourself, think from the heart. Make a mistake? Acknowledge it. Obtain the benefit. Move on to thinking about something else, creative thinking from the mind to solve the problem.

Post-disaster stress is from self-centered thinking. Manage this stress by knowing who you are moment by moment. Be your true authentic self and think from the heart with kindness to yourself and think from the mind for a creative way to thrive in a miserable situation.

* * *

Ghosting awareness. Ghosting is social weakness. Be your true authentic self and have deep conversations that may be painful in the short term but prevent anguish and suffering long term so people can move on with their lives.

Life is better when you know what ghosting means. I call this ghosting awareness. Learn to recognize the ghoster so you don't spend your time being hurt, stressed, and not knowing the future. Ghosting means not answering a text, email, or a call.

Ghosting began in the dating world when boyfriends and girlfriends wanted to break up. They would go silent, intentionally not responding to the text. It was an easy way out.

The ghoster felt good; however, the ghosted person is left not knowing what's going on, frustrated, and stressed. They will go to any extreme to get a response. This can go on for weeks or even months. The ghoster person has completely forgotten. The ghosted person is stressed, unhappy, and can't move forward.

Ghosting has spilled over to the business world. John began working at a financial startup with a very pleasant CEO founder. John worked extremely hard with the promise of a large financial future closing deals. He enjoyed the work and enjoyed interacting with the CEO.

At six months, John sent an email to the CEO for an update on several deals. He didn't hear for a few hours and sent a text. Still nothing, he talked with the cofounder who said the CEO was spending hours into the night negotiating a big deal.

John sent an email two days later with no response, and he sent another three days later with no response. He sent a text asking if he could help with the deal. Nothing. John made a call that was immediately sent to voice mail.

This was unusual and had never happened before. Now John became extremely worried. He thought the CEO had become a friend and something bad may have happened. He called the cofounder to find out any news, and the cofounder was also worried and couldn't connect with the CEO. John was also stressed because nothing was happening with the deals, which meant he was not going to make any money. He sent a fifth email, pleading for a return answer, nothing.

John talked to his son about the situation, "You're being ghosted."

"What? What does that mean?" John asked, confused.

"He's ghosting you. He quit and shut down the business long ago, and he's not going to tell you," explained his son.

John didn't see this coming, and it was unexpected. The six months of work was for nothing. He didn't get paid. All the deals fell through, and he was never going to get any money. The good thing for John is that he found out in seven days. He immediately found a new job with a stable company.

This wasn't the situation for the cofounder who didn't know about ghosting and couldn't believe he was deceived and scammed. This took him three months of stress and making no money trying to connect with the CEO to keep the company going.

Another example of ghosting in business occurs when the ghoster doesn't tell the truth. For example, an enterprising cancer research doctor presented a proposal in the hospital CEO's office. This would benefit patients and bring more revenue for the hospital with no expense as the doctor had external financing. The CEO agreed with everything the cancer doctor said and was excited about going ahead with the program as soon as possible.

The cancer doctor left the meeting and closed the door. The hospital CEO told the chief of medicine, "there's no way in a million years I'm going to help that doctor."

The chief of medicine was in disbelief, he had never seen this behavior before. Why wasn't the CEO honest with the cancer doctor? Because the CEO is weak. This doctor was unusually aggressive and intimidating, so the easy way out was to agree with everything. This would shorten the meeting, create no stress with the CEO, and no drawn-out arguments back and forth.

This is social weakness by the hospital CEO. Just like ghosting, the hospital CEO was unwilling to experience the short-term pain and stress caused by having a deep conversation.

This is self-centered thinking from the primitive brain region and not thinking from the heart with caring and compassion for others. People that ghost have no concern about the recipient's feelings or situation. Regardless of the situation, good or bad, people should be given an answer and the basis for the answer. This is thinking from the heart.

Saying no and giving the basis for the decision is useful information. If convincing, this can be used to abandon the project resulting in no more stress, time, or money. The result can be the opposite, the information provides a clue for a successful project.

Breaking up, dissolving a company, and being honest are painful conversations, but the pain is short-lived for both individuals. This is not the same in a ghosting situation where the recipient is left confused, stressed, and hurting for days, weeks, and sometimes longer. In a ghosting situation where loss of massive amounts of money is involved or in an obsessive romantic relationship, the consequence can be extreme.

> *"Ghosting is social weakness."*

There are several types of ghosters. Some people may be shy and say to themselves that they don't want to cause pain in the other person. Instead, it's the opposite they can cause severe pain by ghosting. They need to use empathy by thinking about the other person's situation. They need to be their true authentic selves and take the consequences of a short-term painful conversation.

Some ghosters are narcissistic controllers and enjoy ghosting because it's fast and they don't have to listen to the other person's painful conversation.

Everyone often ghosts one time given the barrage of spam and other unwanted incoming emails. Two times indicate questionable ghosting. Three attempts with no response is ghosting, and five is confirmation of a 'no' or a 'rejection.'

Ghosting can have dire consequences. The bride or groom who ghosts the day before the wedding. The CEO who ghosts in the middle of a $50M capital raise. The government official who ghosts in the middle of a hostage situation.

It's important to be aware of ghosting so that you can make the determination quickly, accept the rejection, and move on with no regret or stress.

*   *   *

Self-healing. We are our own best self-healers. We can learn self-healing by creating an environment for healing with strategies that will transfigure how we approach injury and illness. Approaching these challenges with a positive mindset will yield greater outcomes.

You have a tremendous capacity for self-healing. Apply principles of the Eplerian Life Philosophy by approaching illness and injury in a positive manner. Healing is a state of mind. It's restoring physical health and emotional health from injury or disease.

Your body has an almost unlimited ability to heal itself. You need to know how to let this happen because this ability may be dormant or blunted by the intensity of daily living. It's using your mind to manage injury and disease.

Several years ago, I was returning home from work in my car listening to someone playing the piano live on the Public Broadcasting Service radio. At the end of his playing, I listened to the piano player talking with the commentator. The piano player was dying from a progressive deadly infection that caused blindness and incurable blood loss, yet when asked how he was coping with the illness, he calmly replied that he was healed. He died the next day.

How could this piano player say he was healed when he had a terminal illness? This is because healing is a state of mind. He used his mind, which is outside the body. He didn't think about himself from the stress center, and he had no anger toward himself or anyone else because of his illness. He learned how to live moment by moment by eliminating self-thinking thoughts and anger. He lived through the mind and from his heart with kindness and giving.

Self-healing is learning how to manage your injury or disease. There are five steps.

First, learn everything you can about what you're facing. Ask your doctor questions and make sure you understand the answers. Learn about your disease and its natural course. What happens if pills, surgery, or other medical interventions are not used? Search medical educational sites for anatomy of the injury and process of the disease. Remember to stay close to primary source information such as PubMed and University sites. Listen to opinions with caution, as after several levels of discussion, valuable information is left out and confusing information may be added.

Second, learn about the diagnostic testing used to confirm the extent of the injury and the diagnosis. Learn the benefits and risks of testing. Some tests are simple with no risk, while other diagnostic studies or procedures can be risky and lead to complications. Ask questions about the testing or procedures until you fully understand the answers. Then consider your situation to determine whether the benefit is worth the risk.

Third, explore all treatment options. There are always options. Compare these to the natural history of the illness or injury with no medical intervention. For example, deep muscle therapy and physical therapy for low back pain may be preferred to pills and surgery. Learn the benefits and risks of each option and choose the best one for you.

Fourth, monitor the injury or disease with symptoms or objective measurements. Use the 48-hour rule, if the symptoms are improved, keep doing the same treatment. If there is no change in symptoms, stay the course. If there is deterioration, contact the doctor for further direction.

Fifth, create an environment for healing. Approach the injury and disease in a positive way. This means saying, "I'm going to manage this situation," not "I can't deal with this or why did this happen to me?" Some people think disease is an enemy that needs to be defeated. This is dangerous thinking as fighting tactics fail, delay resolution of the natural process, and may have deadly consequences.

The disease is part of you, not a favorable part, but a part that needs to be managed and controlled. Curing the disease is desirable, but not necessary. Learn how to manage the situation, that's good enough. The disease won't control you. Managing the disease will let you live your life with creativity and enjoyment moment by moment. Approaching the illness or injury in a positive way sets up the body and defense system for healing.

Have compassion for the injured area. Have compassion for the diseased organ system. The system is functionally healthy. The disease is causing dysfunction.

Use controlled breathing for the calming effect and counters the adrenalin stress response. Trigger the relaxation reflex with a few belly breaths by deeply breathing in and moving your belly outward. Use yoga breathing that includes equal breath in and equal breath out, yoga square breathing, expanding the ribs, telescoping breathing, free-up-your-diaphragm, super shoulder shrug, and alternate nostril breathing.

Visualization is the last step for creating an environment to heal. Use visualization while in the alpha- or theta-brainwave state through traditional eyes-closed meditation or my preferred method of eyes-open meditation.

You can create a "healing place" in your mind. For example, using your own guided meditation, walk down 25 wooden steps either from a location above a beach or a mountain meadow. Feel your feet in the warm sand or soft grass. Visualize a comfortable chair under a canopy with a warm breeze in the air. Breathe in healing energy sending this to the injured area or dysfunctional organ system, and be specific, such as sending healing energy to heart arteries, heart muscle, or the heart electrical system.

Other visualization techniques include replacing dysfunctional cells. With the mind, replace dysfunctional cells beginning with one cell replacing the injured cell, and continue with two cells, four cells, and hundreds of cells. Every cell in the body is continually being replaced, some every few minutes and others every few weeks or months. Visualize healthy, strong cells replacing the inflamed or dysfunctional cells.

Use the mind to repair the RNA and DNA in your cells. You were born with DNA instructions for a healthy functioning body and organ systems. Over time, methylation of the DNA causes damage and sluggishness. With your mind, renew the DNA.

A final visualization involves your genome. Switch on your dormant healing genes. Epigenetics tells us the environment can greatly influence the activity of our genes. Over time, genes that generate enzymes and reactions in the healing process become switched off. Turn them back on with your mind. Be persistent, as these methods require repetition and time in terms of weeks, months, and years.

Fundamental requirements for healing include living a healthy life with a healthy nutritional lifestyle, eight hours of sleep, and a daily exercise program.

Healing during the end-of-life situation requires a special discussion regarding both the family and the individual with the terminal illness.

For example, a terminally ill person has progressive cancer after weeks of heroic failed treatments, the patient has long known the eventual outcome and family members have come to the realization with feelings of kindness, forgiveness, and love. However, there may be a family member who is angry and only thinks self-centered thoughts from the stress center. This person can create a toxic healing environment often taking away comforting and loving time with the loved one.

"Do everything!" the person demands, yelling loudly for everyone to hear. "Father can't die!" The person shouts at the doctors and nurses, disrupting the controlled ICU environment making the patient and other family members uncomfortable taking away loving time with the patient. This self-centered behavior is usually out of guilt from not spending enough time or having arguments with the father.

The doctors try expensive experimental treatments taking time away from interacting with the patient and making the situation worse by the day. However, the family member continues demands and self-centered angry behavior. Severe complications develop with multiple irreversible organ failure, yet this person continues to scream for anything that might save the father's life. Finally, the doctor tells everyone the patient is going to die soon. All tubes are pulled, and all tests stopped. The family has 24 hours to share the last moments without interruption and without thoughts of hope, anger, or fear.

This is a sad option that happens too frequently. There is a much better approach. For example, a women has widespread ovarian cancer and admitted to the hospital weak, bedridden, and a high fever. The first step is for the medical team to determine if the disease has reached an irreversible stage. Doctors and patients have faced this issue for centuries. In some situations, it may be difficult or even impossible to make this determination. Yet there often comes a time along the continuum when everyone knows that the process is terminal.

If caregivers confirm that this is a terminal event, then it's helpful to talk about the concept of death as a journey where bags need to be packed and a destination chosen. This is where the healing process begins for both the patient and the family.

What does packing bags mean? It means creating a peaceful mind and coming to peace with the person who is dying. It means coming to terms with guilt. It means resolving anger and resentful feelings toward the person. It means resolving lingering doubts that you wished you had done things differently. It means resolving emotional issues with the spouse and children.

What does destination mean? Determining a destination depends on a person's beliefs and spiritual perspective. For some, it may be heaven, and for others, a different destination. When the bags have been packed and the destination known, then it's time to depart. The journey will be peaceful and comforting, not fraught with breathing machines, kidney machines, surgical invasion, powerful antibiotics, harsh chemotherapy, and the gnawing and constant anger and emotional upheaval of trying to deal with the issues. The patient's family and friends have no bitterness or anguish about the final days. They have no hostility or resentment toward the doctors and nurses. Instead, they are left with memories of a loving and wonderful life.

This is one approach for a terminally ill person. It's important to remember that this is a time in life where the ill person and the family need to think from the heart with kindness, forgiveness, empathy, and love. There is no place for self-centered thinking from the head anger center and stress center.

Self-healing decreases anxiety and increases speed of recovery. Deep breathing training and relaxation training can decrease fatigue and anxiety, which will eliminate the harmful effect of the stress inflammation response. Self-healing using meditation decreases stress and strengthens hereditary genes.

Use self-healing by creating an environment to heal. Approach your injury or illness in a positive way, learn everything you can about what you're facing, learn and use controlled breathing, and use visualization.

You are in charge. Learn self-healing. You can do this better than anyone else. Your chances of success are unlimited.

Chapter 10

Health is Life

"Health is the greatest wealth."

— Aristotle

Without health, you can't do what you want, you can't go where you want, and you can't enjoy life moment by moment. Optimal health is based on fundamental health habits, being your true authentic self, and thinking from the heart with kindness, and the mind with creativity to help others and inspiration to improve the world. Health is a state of mind.

The traditional definition of health, "The absence of disease," is negative and not specific. Health is not the opposite of disease. My definition of health is "Living an optimal life with high energy, creativity, and enjoyment." This means living a healthy life by eliminating bad health habits and embracing good health habits.

There are ten primitive brain health habits that must be eliminated

(1) **Eliminate anger.** Anger is triggered when someone or something has been taken from you and often in an unfriendly or abusive personal way. These triggers are out of your control and can happen at any time. One approach is to recognize the anger, try to learn something, and then feel the anger for less than ten seconds until it is neutralized by the calming system.

Have no thought about the source or cause of the anger and no second thought, only feeling. Feel the anger without thinking. You can scrunch your face and clinch your hands if you need to for feeling rather than thinking.

Remember to breathe deeply and slowly. Fast shallow breathing will make you nervous and make the situation worse.

Feel the anger, let it peak in six to eight seconds. You'll find yourself gradually thinking about something else. If you think about the person or anger situation with the second or third thoughts and the bad story, then the anger will continue and worsen resulting in grave consequences for you and others.

Once you're able to manage anger for less than ten seconds, then learn to stop activating or triggering the anger center from negative thoughts or actions. The ultimate solution is live in the mind at a slower brainwave frequency not allowing thoughts of anger.

(2) **Eliminate stress.** This is more difficult than anger because stress is from the primitive cingulate brain region and is massive compared to the small almond-shaped amygdala anger region.

Anger occurs from a single cause when something's been taken from you. Stress occurs from thinking about yourself with almost unlimited sources of thoughts, some of which people don't even recognize as thinking about themselves.

Fortunately, there are many ways to stop primitive brain thinking causing stress. Regardless of the technique, you can only experience stress for six to eight seconds before it becomes harmful to your health and others.

First, use the six to eight second anger rule, feel the stress, try to learn something, let the stress peak, and let it go in six to eight seconds. The primitive brain translates self-centered thoughts into stress for humans.

Second, as soon as you realize you're thinking about your problems or other self-centered thoughts, you can actively change your thinking. You can be kind to yourself with self-compassion by thinking from the heart. You can also say "love and peace" over and over which will stop all thinking from the stress center.

Third, use the parasympathetic calming system to neutralize the stress within a few seconds. Activate this system with belly breaths, drink of water, or a 12-minute walk. You can also activate the calming system with yoga breathing techniques such as equal breaths in and out, yoga square breathing, expanding the ribs, telescoping your breathing, free-up-your-diaphragm technique, super shoulder shrug, and the alternate nostril breath technique.

Fourth, stimulate endorphins, which are neurotransmitters or messengers the brain releases resulting in a natural pain reliever and neutralizing stress. Endorphins give you a feeling of not caring about your own problems and not caring about other people's problems. Endorphins will neutralize stress. Running, such as a six-mile run, can result in endorphin release. It's the "runner's high" that has been known about for many years. This may take several months before you recognize the feeling, and a short jog is not sufficient.

The 10-second freezing cold shower technique will induce endorphins by the 'diving reflex.' The instant freezing water hits your face, your eyes are wide open, and you don't have a care in the world. It's a good feeling and starts the day with high energy.

Endorphin release can occur at a workout facility running on the treadmill or elliptical combined with lifting weights. This will happen with a vigorous class workout such as hot flow yoga, spin class, or dance class. Other activities that trigger endorphins such as enjoyment from music, a delicious festive meal, laughing out loud, and social interaction with special people.

Once you're able to limit thoughts about yourself from the primitive brain region to less than ten seconds, then learn to stop these self-centered thoughts activating the primitive brain. This will take weeks or months of practice. If accomplished you will live a life free of stress allowing you to think from your heart and explore the mind for indescribable positive feelings. As with anger, living in the mind will not allow negative thoughts to cause stress.

(3) Eliminate self-criticism and self-pity. Eliminate negative thoughts about yourself. Challenges give people's lives richness and fulfillment. Sometimes, failed challenges and mistakes leave people upset and angry with themselves. This is thinking from the primitive brain and must be eliminated.

Thinking about other people being successful or why did the person win and you didn't. This self-centered thinking can be instantly eliminated by thinking from your heart with kindness to yourself with self-compassion. You're successful, this was a one-time problem that you will learn from and move on to success. Think from your heart with kindness to yourself. Love yourself.

(4) Eliminate complaining, criticism, and judgment. People who have pessimistic and rigid minded tendencies see the world filled with problems. This view results in incessant complaining and criticism driving friends and people away from them. Criticism spills over to judging people. This is self-directed thinking from the primitive brain, and difficult to eliminate because it becomes a habit and part of a person's character.

For healthy people who find themselves complaining, criticizing, or judging, they need to recognize this as soon as possible and learn to stop. Think from your heart with empathy and compassion for others.

(5) Eliminate blame and excuses. Blaming a person or a company or an event for a bad personal outcome is unhealthy and stressful. This is primitive brain self-centered thinking. Eliminate blame by realizing blame is not accepting personal responsibility.

When you take responsibility for yourself, a project, or for others, most of the time, it's a good outcome. Sometimes, there's a bad outcome. If so, take the blame. Take the blame as soon as the bad outcome is known with no delay, then you can help develop a plan to fix the problem before long-term damage takes place. Eliminate blaming others, it's stressful and takes time and enjoyment away from you and everyone else.

Eliminate excuses. Take personal responsibility. If you are your true authentic self, there is no need for excuses. They're extra words with no meaning. If you're late, don't say anything, or say you're late and tell the truth. You forgot. You didn't give yourself enough time. You didn't want to come to the meeting. Whatever it is. Tell the truth.

The truth may be painful in the short term, but it will have huge payoffs in the long term. People will trust you and will be able to depend on you. They know who you are. You're not trying to be someone else and making excuses. Take responsibility. It's healthy. It feels good.

(6) Eliminate trying to be other people and trying to be your job title.
Trying to be someone else or comparing yourself to others is thinking from
the primitive brain and causes stress.

People try to be someone else because they don't like who they are, they
don't think they're good enough, or they want to be someone better than
themselves. Some people develop the perfect successful person in their
head that they keep comparing themselves to. They will never attain this. It's
primitive brain thinking.

The solution for eliminating this type of thinking is to believe that you're
a unique person and are the best version of yourself. Be kind to yourself.
Love yourself.

A special discussion is needed for people who try to be their job title, and
people don't realize they're doing this until someone tells them. This causes
personal stress and stress in people around them. This results in lost productivity, lost innovation, and drives employees away. People at work need to be
their true authentic selves including the CEO, executives, managers team
leaders, and employees.

Trying to be the best team leader is going to fail for the person and for the
team. Teams and situations are different. There are no 'book' instructions for
being the best team leader. People need to be themselves, and they will be
the best and most productive team leader. Trying to be the best father or the
best mother won't work. Be your true authentic self, and you'll be the best
parent for your children.

Trying to be someone else is unhealthy, stressful, and unproductive. Always
be your true authentic self at home, at work, and in public.

(7) Eliminate resentment, jealousy, and revenge. This is self-centered
thinking from the primitive brain because people are comparing themselves
to others. Resentment means you're angry and unhappy because you think
you've been treated unfairly, you've been insulted, or you've been offended.
People who have resentment think about themselves from the primitive
brain. Feelings aren't facts. People are angry from something that someone
said, but most of the time, the words were not deliberately chosen to upset

anyone. The words were used as part of a normal conversation intended no harm or being offensive to anyone. The feelings are anger, but facts show a normal conversation intending no anger. Feelings are not facts.

If you're on the receiving end of an angry outburst by someone claiming you offended them, then you need to have empathy from the heart, explain the situation, apology if needed, and move on.

If you are being your true authentic self, there is no need for feeling resentment. If you think someone offended you, then talk about it and clarify. If someone meant to insult you to your face, do not engage, feel the anger in yourself, let it peak in six to eight seconds, and leave the situation. Think from your heart with kindness to yourself with self-compassion. Do not engage, get over your anger in a few seconds, and move on. It's the healthiest long-term response. Do the same thing for a nasty rejection, get over it in a few seconds.

Some people feel resentment toward others who have a bigger house or make more money. This is self-centered thinking trying to be someone else. Eliminate this type of feeling by thinking from your heart with kindness to yourself.

Jealousy means being unhappy because someone has something you want or does something you can't do. This is primitive brain thinking. You're stressed because you're comparing yourself to others. Be content with what you have in the moment and like yourself as you are with no need to think about what others have.

In a romantic situation, jealousy means an unhappy feeling and sometimes anger because you think someone you love is attracted to someone else or someone is attracted to the person you love. This too is primitive brain thinking. Be confident in who you are. Be your true self. Feelings aren't facts. Clarify the situation to your full understanding. If there is no issue, talk about your feelings, forgive yourself and your close relationship, and move on. If there is an issue, confront the situation, develop a plan moving forward for establishing trust, or take the consequences of going your separate ways.

Revenge means something you do to hurt or punish someone because they hurt you or someone else. This is dangerous primitive brain thinking that can have a disastrous outcome. There is no place for this feeling or situation for people who are being their true authentic selves. Don't engage and move on or think from the heart with forgiveness.

(8) Eliminate thinking about the negative past and negative future. Everyone has heard, "don't think about the past." This is too general, don't think about the "negative" past and don't think about the "negative" future. This is unhealthy, stressful, and nonproductive. This is primitive brain thinking.

How can people stop this bad habit? Understanding and knowing these negative thoughts causes harmful stress. Train yourself to recognize these thoughts and change the topic to the moment and think from the heart about the magical times and the good times. Engage life in the moment. There's no thinking about the negative past or negative future.

(9) Eliminate worry and guilt. These two ways of thinking have the same origin, which is self-directed thoughts from the primitive brain. Worry is thinking about something that may happen in the future. It's negative thinking about future events out of your control. This thinking is unhealthy and unproductive causing stress. Worry should be eliminated for improved health.

Worrying about someone may be harmful and stressful to the other person. For example, "I worry about you falling asleep driving home" or "I worry about you getting into trouble at the party." These negative statements send people off with negative feelings. They can potentially cause life-threatening danger because they will be thinking negative thoughts and may be distracted while driving. Worry must be eliminated.

Guilt is similar. It's self-centered thinking from the primitive brain. This thinking and feeling needs to be abandoned. Guilt is caused by people not being their true selves. Guilt is caused by lacking self-confidence. Guilt is caused by not accepting and liking everything about yourself.

At the Santa Monica Beach, two women walking by Arnold Schwarzenegger during his prime physical condition said aloud to each other, "I never want to look like that." Instead of being ashamed or feeling guilty about his appearance, Schwarzenegger instantly replied, "You never will."

People do something they regret or verbally hurt someone or don't do something they promised to others. These events have happened to everyone, and they will continue to happen. Not enough sleep or not feeling well clouds prefrontal lobe judgment, and accidentally or unconsciously doing something they would not do during optimal healthy conditions. This is normal behavior with no need for guilt.

Guilt is also related to personal responsibility. Something bad happens because of your actions. Acknowledge to yourself what you did wrong and develop a solution to prevent this from happening in the future. If the situation is appropriate, give the three-component apology. Say you're sorry. Say what you did wrong. Ask what you can do to make it right.

Having the feeling of guilt is unhealthy by causing stress and taking joy out of life. Eliminate the guilty feeling.

(10) Eliminate trying to please others. You don't need to think about pleasing anyone. This is primitive brain thinking from the stress center. You are your own person. There is no need to do what self-centered people want you to do or do something that goes against your values.

Do what's right in your heart and take the consequences. Almost all the time, this will make life enjoyable. Short-term, sometimes this could end in negative comments, but long term, it's so much better being your true self than trying to be someone people want you to be.

Remember, do what you want to do. Don't do what others want you to do.

Trying to please others and trying to have people like you is self-centered thinking from the primitive stress center. Doing something you don't want to do to please others will cause stress and negative behavior that can be a lifetime of regret. Be your true self with no need for negative outside influences to change the way you are.

There are 20 good health habits

(1) Be your true authentic self. The benefit of being your true authentic self is lifechanging. You have no need to be what people and society tell you to be. You make the choice of who you are. You don't spend time thinking from the anger center or self-thinking thoughts from the stress center. You feel good thinking from your heart with kindness and giving. You feel good thinking from the mind solving problems and helping others.

You're not trying to be anyone else or comparing yourself to others. You have no need to please others. You have no negative thoughts about the past or the future. It feels good not to complain, criticize, judge, or blame others. You take advantage of fear and manage sadness. You don't wallow in self-criticism and self-pity. You have no need for resentment, jealousy, or revenge. It feels good to have no worries and no guilt.

You enjoy strong personal leadership by making instant decisions, taking responsibility, and having unwavering commitment. You have a healthy posture, eight hours of sleep, a healthy nutritional lifestyle, and one hour of daily exercise.

You're happier and more productive. You have high energy. You're creative and innovative. You're engaged in life. You enjoy living in the moment. You're trustworthy. People want to be with you.

You live in the moment. This expression has been talked about for thousands of years. What does this mean? This means being engaged in the moment and being your authentic self with no distractions from external negative forces. This means paying attending to the moment with no thoughts about your problems, negative thoughts about the past or future, and no thoughts about things out of your control. This means no primitive brain thinking.

For example, in troubling times, take time to reflect your feelings at any given moment, such as a moment before going to sleep. At that moment, you're safe, you have no money problems, you have no job problems, and you have no relationship problems. Those are all in the past or in the future, not in the moment.

Be your authentic self by eliminating primitive brain thinking, and think from the heart with kindness and the mind with creativity to help others. Be your true self and everything else falls into place.

(2) Obtain eight hours of sleep every night. Obtain eight hours of sleep every night which includes six hours to restore brain energy and two hours for feelings of kindness from the heart and social judgment from the pre-frontal lobe for doing what's right.

(3) Have a healthy nutritional lifestyle. This means eating the right food in the right amount at the right time prepared in a healthy manner.

The right foods have no added sugar, no added salt, and no processed foods with omega-6 fats. The right amount is sufficient to provide energy for each meal, no more and no less. Prepared in a healthy manner means foods in their natural state, steamed, boiled, or medium heat with no fried or charred foods.

(4) One hour of exercise every day. This will provide energy for the entire day. Mix it up with walking, running, treadmill, swimming, or elliptical; weights for all muscle groups; yoga stretches; and group classes.

(5) Have a healthy posture. This means chin straight, eyes forward, shoulders down, and back straight. Interacting at work, during a meeting, or a social event, a healthy posture looks good, gives you a look of confidence and trust, and gives you energy.

A slumped shoulder and head down appearance looks bad. People don't want to interact. This gives a not-interested-in-anything look. Everyone has heard about the importance of body language. Your posture and your body speak volumes of information about you, good and bad. Remember, your face tells the world who you are. Be your true authentic self by thinking from your heart with kindness. Your face will tell the world you are successful, resourceful, trustworthy, and someone everyone needs to know.

Your outstretched palms say welcome, and you're open to having an enjoyable interaction. Palms out tells people you're a kind person while the back of your hands tells people to go away. Having your palms facing someone tells them you have an open mind and willingness to listen. Cross your arms, then you're finished, not interested in anything. Have a good posture for success.

(6) Make instant decisions. If a decision is needed big or small, then make the decision immediately. This is better for you and everyone else. You have enough information. In addition, you have the mind with unlimited knowledge, use it. Saying no is helpful. This allows the other person or organization to move forward to obtain more information, make a better case, or abandon the request.

Indecision or putting off the decision can be a disaster and even cost lives in some situations because terrible things can happen during the delay. There are no bad decisions, only bad outcomes. If the decision is made quickly and results in a bad outcome, then the problem can be fixed fast before irreversible damage.

(7) **Take responsibility and mean it.** Develop the personal responsibility habit. Take every opportunity to be responsible for a project or new product at work or a new home or community activity because challenges are healthy and result in advancing to bigger challenges with bigger rewards. The important consideration of responsibility is knowing the consequences of a bad outcome, accepting the blame, and fixing the problem.

If you are lacking the skill, resources, or interest, don't take the responsibility. A positive outcome from taking responsibility feels good. It's an accomplishment. Others feel good too because you improved people's lives.

(8) **Have unwavering commitment.** If you say yes to a request at home or at work, then do what has been asked no matter what it takes. This requires the discipline to say no to family, friends, and the boss. If you can't do the request because of lack of skills, resources, or interest, then say no regardless of the consequences.

It's better to say no than not fulfill a commitment. People keep track of these negative events, and they won't trust you. They won't ask you to participate in important work opportunities and won't invite you to enjoyable social activities.

(9) **Use positive social communication and interaction at home, at work, and in public.** This means both participants feel better after an interaction with no put-downs, no one-ups, and no destructive comments. For example, someone tells you about an exciting event, rather than saying "that sounds stupid" or "wait until you hear what I did." You can say, "sounds great, tell me more."

Consider other people's feelings with your comments, no one likes to feel weak or frail because of comments that you think may be helpful. There's no need for empty words or fillers. Although presumed meaningless, in some situations, these words can create a negative feeling in the other person or may make the other person uncomfortable.

Use positive communication at home, in the office, and in public. Both people feel good after the interaction.

(10) Have daily slow-brainwave meditation time. The benefits of meditation include decreasing stress, release of feel-good neurotransmitters and hormones, balances the brain regions, and happiness. You can also experience total calmness, acceptability, and unconditional love.

You can use traditional eyes-closed mantra meditation, eyes-open relaxation method, or yoga techniques. Learn to be in the alpha-brainwave state spontaneously so you can use your creativity and innovation, solve problems, and help others.

(11) Learn something new every day. Learn something new, preferably outside your daily work and home life. For example, learn about world economics and global impact, learn about science and energy from particle physics, or learn a new recreational activity. Over the years, you'll learn new ways to solve problems, help others, and live a healthy life.

(12) Be grateful for the day and the positive people in your life. Reflect on what you have and be grateful. This will make you feel better about your life and what you have. People can be overwhelmed by the negative forces in their current lives which causes stress. Taking a break and reflecting on what you have, especially the people in your lives who take nothing from you, feels good and gives you energy to improve the situation.

(13) Understand and use self-healing. People have an almost unlimited capability of healing. This is often blunted and masked by so much primitive brain stress that healing can't take place. Therefore, eliminating stress is a starting point. Healing is a state of mind with a positive approach to the situation. You can manage this illness or injury. That's all you need to do. Manage the situation, and you can live a healthy invigorating life.

A major component of self-healing is using breathing techniques for calming the system so energy can be used for the healing process. These include yoga breathing techniques such as equal breaths in and out, yoga square breathing, telescoping your breathing technique, and a good one for healing is the alternate nostril breath technique.

Use the slow-brainwave state and visualization for healing. While in the alpha- or theta-brainwave state, center your thoughts on healing. You can visualize a healing place on the beach or in a meadow by experiencing a warm day with a gentle breezing sitting in a comfortable chair surrounded by a canopy of soft linen. Breathe in healing energy and send it to the disease organ system or injured region. Visualize healthy cells pushing aside injured or dysfunctional cells. Visualize repairing DNA in genes of cells to displace inflamed cells.

We have a huge capacity for self-healing. Eliminate stress and approach the situation in a positive way. Use breathing techniques, slow brainwave state, and visualization. Exercise your way back to life.

(14) Managing fear and sadness. Fear and sadness are positive emotions. Fear is protective and sadness is based on love.

The feeling of fear comes from the gut. You can experience this by thinking about something that frightens you. Where do you have the feeling? It's not in your head and not in your heart. It's in your gut. The function of the gut belly brain is acting as a risk management system that began with avoiding eating or drinking poison. This function expanded to risk in physical and mental situations such as walking near a cliff or saying yes to a risky proposition.

Listen to your gut for nutrition advice including choosing healthy foods and eating the healthy amount for you. Listen to your gut when interacting with people or being asked to participate in a potentially risky project or event. In intensive situations, add listening to your heart and using the mind for successful analysis and a solution.

(15) Have compassion for yourself and others. Be kind to yourself, especially during troubling times. Love yourself. Think from the heart with kindness to yourself. If you make a mistake, your decision has a bad outcome, or you unintendedly cause pain, then it's common to blame yourself, call yourself stupid, and think your life is over. This is the time to be kind to yourself. Think from the heart by being kind to yourself and saying you're a good person, you'll continue to be a good person, and life is good.

What would you say to a friend or a family member if they made the mistake? You would give them forgiveness, support, and encouragement. You wouldn't yell at them for being stupid. Have self-compassion. Think from your heart with kindness to yourself.

Have compassion toward others. Use empathy by putting yourself in their situation. Give your support and encouragement. Volunteering exemplifies having compassion for others. Do something without getting paid. Give without expecting anything in return. It feels good and you help others too.

(16) Have meaning in your life. Give outside yourself. Volunteer your time, energy, and help. This gives you a sense of value and worth. This feels good and improves your wellbeing.

Have meaning in your life through volunteering, community activities, or a positive social cause. Meaning is guided by personal values. People who have a purpose in life have greater life satisfaction and are healthier. Get involved in a nonprofit organization. Create a way to use your passion and strength to help others. Spending time with people you care about gives you meaning in life.

(17) Maintain high level happiness. This means being content with your current situation moment by moment especially during bad times such as a financial downturn, job loss, or loss of a close relationship. This is the time more than ever you need to maintain high-level happiness for creating a solution. People avoid unhappy people and don't take the time to help them. Maintain high level happiness in any way you can. Being grateful is a good starting point.

Jon Clifton at Gallup in the book, *Blind Spot: The Global Rise of Unhappiness,* has shown the global rise of unhappiness has reached an all-time high, and Dave Allman at Gallup has shown the low rates of wellbeing across the globe. The unhappiness level is measured with the negative experience index which is a composite of five negative experiences including anger, stress, sadness, physical pain, and worry.

This measure of happiness is related to experiencing negative feelings of anger, stress, and worry, all negative feelings from the primitive brain. Eliminate this thinking and be your authentic self which will give you time to think from your heart with kindness and happiness. Be grateful for the people in your life who don't take anything from you. Be grateful for being alive because you can have high energy, creativity, enjoyment, experience positive experiences, and know extraordinary people.

(18) Have daily accomplishments, big and small. Accomplishments provide well-being because this produces a feeling from the mind. Go through the day expecting a good day so you're open to accomplishments. Finding the good in people and events.

Many people have a bad habit of thinking about what doesn't get done for the day. "I didn't do anything today," is a common expression from people who are stressed and live their lives with a negative outlook. They don't think about the good things and only the bad. It's a matter of attitude toward life.

Think about everything you did during the day, not about what you didn't do. Pay attention, engage in life, and enjoy accomplishments.

(19) Think, write, text, and say positive words. Positive words give people a good feeling. Negative words cause stress. Negative words come from the primitive brain. Positive words come from the heart.

There's an expression, "think positive" to succeed in life. This doesn't work. It's forcing you to think a certain way. There's no benefit in forcing your thoughts. Instead, think from the heart with kindness to yourself and others, and you will automatically use positive words that will make you feel good and others too.

(20) Be engaged in life at all times. Being engaged in life is one of life's pleasures. You have healthy interactions and experience magical moments. This means paying attention to life in front of you. This means knowing what you want, what you're doing, and where you're going. It's having purpose in life.

Cellphone dependency has changed the world in a negative way causing stress, taking away enjoyment, and disconnecting from life. Stage-3 cellphone dependency is people always having the phone in their hand and placing the phone face up. Looking at negative events and distressing images causes stress. Texting negative thoughts and texting bullying comments causes anger and stress. Stage-3 cellphone dependency is primitive brain behavior.

Negative cellphone use is out of control. The percentage of these phone-dependent non-engaged people is increasing at an astonishing rate to where people don't talk to each other and have lost healthy conversations, especially deep meaningful conversations. It's an unwanted intrusion.

This situation has decreased engagement in life and eliminated positive social interaction taking enjoyment along with it. Look at mothers and fathers with their children in a restaurant, not one single word will be spoken. The parents will have their heads down with a lifeless look on their faces staring with a far-away look at their phones. The children have the same look and inwardly pleading for attention from their parents. These are magical moments never to be repeated. This scene occurs among adults in social gatherings, business meetings, workout facilities, and from pre-school to graduate school.

Don't be a cell phone Zombie. Leave the phone out of site when interacting with family, friends, and in public.

Always engage in life. It feels good. It's healthy. People want to be with you.

Know and eliminate the ten bad health habits. Know and thrive with the twenty good health habits.

*   *   *

Eplerian Life Philosophy for a new human civilization. The Eplerian Life Philosophy is simple: Know who you are moment by moment. Know where you're thinking from. The five locations are the head, heart, gut, body, and the mind, which is outside the body. Be your true authentic self. Think from your heart with kindness. Think from the mind with creativity to help others, courage to be your true authentic self, and inspiration to improve the world. We are healthier. We are happier.

The two words carved in granite 3400 years ago, "Know Thyself." The idea of knowing who you are can have a profound positive influence on your life. My own experience in being my true authentic self has proven this beyond all expectations by giving me the freedom to think what I want and do what I want with no outside force or influence. This has allowed me to say no to unfulfilling opportunities and to say yes to extreme challenges. Other benefits include no anger and stress by eliminating primitive brain thoughts and behavior, enjoyment in the moment, and thriving with responsibility.

In my health habit seminars, being your true self became the most important health habit for living your best life at home, at work, and in the community. At a seminar, several years ago, someone asked, "How do you become your true authentic self?" At the time, I had no answer. I had no way to tell people how to become their authentic self. I do now, after developing the Eplerian Life Philosophy in December 2019.

I made this discovery after many years of research that culminated in functional MRI research showing the specific brain region where people think from. This showed that stress is from people thinking about themselves. Eliminating stress is a fundamental way to be your true authentic self.

For me, being my true authentic self was the process of life. I had probably always been my true self during childhood and beyond, but I didn't recognize this and understand the implications until many years later.

Knowing that I was being myself would have been useful much earlier because I could have used this to my advantage growing up by understanding why I did what I did and why people sometimes disagreed with my actions. I was being my true authentic self by making decisions and doing what I wanted to do rather than trying to be someone people wanted me to be. I would have eliminated stress, worry, guilt, and judging others.

I had to find the answer to the question, how do you be your true authentic self? Years and years of research and iterations led to discouragement and almost giving up because more and more academic psychologists and others recommended abandoning the idea of knowing who you are, and I agreed. It was too general and not useful as we're all types of people during the day.

Then in December 2019, my research showed something that will change the world. It's the development of innovative technology called functional MRI (fMRI). This technology was not available to Socrates or Aristotle. For the first time ever, fMRI tells doctors and scientists where people think from.

I thought that we think from the brain in our heads when we take tests or try to solve a problem. The first thing I learned from fMRI studies is that I was wrong and so was conventional thinking about the brain. These studies showed several independent brain regions, not one single brain, and you can only think from one region at a time. This was new to me. I never knew we have different brains in our head.

Some of these brain regions are primitive and will take over your life 24 hours a day. Furthermore, they're negative and require no sleep because they function by instinct.

This new discovery didn't stop there. It gets better. Scientists had people do the fMRI scan and asked them not to think about themselves. A red light will shine if they do. Their task is to turn off the red light and keep it off. It's a simple request, but almost everyone spends a large part of the day thinking about themselves in one form or another. People have been conditioned to think about themselves since childhood.

The fMRI technician behind the glass controls the red light. Remember, the fMRI scan shows the technician where people think from. The technician realizes when people think about themselves, the primitive brain region called the posterior cingulate cortex lights up, and the technician pushes the button for the red light. As this part of the brain cools down, the technician turns off the red light because the person is no longer thinking from the cingulate brain region.

A massive surprise occurred! Something no one has ever known before. Whenever people were thinking from the primitive cingulate brin region, they were stressed. If people are stressed, they're thinking from the primitive cingulate brain region.

After three weeks or 21 days, people learn to keep the red light off during the entire fMRI sessions. Check in on them, six months or a year later. These people are healthier with lower blood pressure and pulse, two-times more productive, three-times more creative, enjoy life more, and are better friends and citizens.

This is a profound study for me. Not thinking about yourself increases productivity and creativity and gives you an enjoyable life. It's free costing no money. There are no life-threatening side effects and no pills or professional intervention.

I call this cingulate region, the stress center, and it's part of the primitive brain. It's the reptilian or crocodile brain, and some people call it the "monkey brain." In humans this translates to anger from the amygdala brain region and stress from the cingulate brain region. The cause of stress in humans is thinking about yourself. When you think about yourself, you're stressed.

There are three negative brain regions. So far, the anger center and the stress center are two unhealthy brain regions to think from. The accumbens pleasure center is the third region. How could this be unhealthy? This is because this region is instant chemical pleasure from the dopamine neurotransmitter produced by the brain. The function of this independent brain region has its origins for reproduction of the species. It's the intoxicating pleasure from having sex. And it's habit forming and addicting, fulfilling its function of proliferation and continuation of the species.

This region too is a primitive region requiring no thinking. It's an instinctive response. The problem occurs when people find out this feeling of pleasure can be triggered by an almost unlimited source. For example, this may begin with sugar and advance to alcohol and drugs, especially cocaine which has a direct and instant route to the accumbens.

The pleasure feeling from the accumbens pleasure center is short-lived, less than 20 seconds from sugar, and followed by a crash if not sustained. Seeking to maintain this feeling with drugs and alcohol has disastrous consequences for the person and society.

The conclusion from this added information for me is that thinking from these head brain regions needs to be eliminated. You can only think from one region at a time so eliminating thinking from these regions will allow you to think from other locations such as the heart with kindness and the mind with creativity to help others.

Remember that the anger center wants to control your life and requires no sleep. This is true for the stress center and the pleasure center too. They want to control your life. Unfortunately, too many people let this happen. Don't let this happen to you. Be your true self, and it won't happen.

To put all of this into words, I developed the Eplerian Life Philosophy. "Knowing who you are" is too general so I added a time element with three words. "Know who you are moment by moment." This means knowing where you're thinking from and that's who you are.

Using these seven words, I began to develop a simple practical way to know who you are.

Continued research showed there are four other locations to think from. This was a huge breakthrough because there are alternative places to think from rather than the three unhealthy head regions. These are the heart, gut, body, and the mind, which is outside the body.

The function of the heart is to keep itself healthy. The heart does with kindness, giving, empathy, forgiving, and being grateful. The heart also keeps itself healthy by having the capacity to make decisions that are best for your health.

The function of the gut is to provide healthy nutrition advice and risk management by fear. Use the feeling as a warning for using the mind for analysis and an answer.

The function of the body is to physically enable us to do things we need to do for ourselves and others. Thinking from the muscles and joints while exercising improves and maintains the body for optimal functioning.

The function of the mind is creativity to solve problems and help others. The feelings from the mind include calmness, acceptance, and unconditional love.

Considering this information, you now know the answer to the seminar question. "How can I be my true authentic self?" It's easy. Stop thinking about yourself.

"The less you think about yourself, the more you are your true authentic self."

The benefits of knowing who you are begin with freedom. During childhood, you're told who you are by your parents and teachers. During college, you're told who you are by your professors and friends. Then you're told who you are by your boss. During all this time, you're being told who you are by society. All of this is necessary for becoming a person to fit into the current culture, but over time this is stressful, and you need to be free from this. It's time to be your true self.

Other benefits include feeling good. You like yourself. You're your own person. You're happier and more productive. You have high energy. You're creative. You're engaged in life. You enjoy living in the moment. You don't criticize, complain, or blame. You have no guilt, worry, or jealousy. You have zero-level stress. You're trustworthy. People want to be with you.

What are some applications of the Eplerian Life Philosophy? In addition to freedom from being told who you are, these applications include eliminating the harmful effects of stress and anger and eliminating trying to be someone else and trying to please others. They include discarding thinking about yourself, thinking about the negative past, and thinking about the negative future. The applications include managing fear and sadness and eliminating self-criticism and self-pity. Productivity, creativity, and innovation can be improved.

Additional applications include eliminating resentment, jealousy, revenge, judgment, complaining, criticism, blame, and eliminating worry and guilt. The applications include personal leadership, making instant decisions, enjoying responsibility, and unwavering commitment. They also include developing a healthy sleep program, healthy nutrition lifestyle, a daily exercise program, and healthy posture. Live in the moment and be your true self. The Eplerian Life Philosophy is for people to live their best lives at home, at work, and in the community.

There are three groups of people who are not their true authentic selves

Group one. People are afraid to be their authentic selves because they fear the consequences. They fear ridicule, criticism, or failure. Like me, they may not think they're smart enough. Use courage from the mind to overcome fear. The Eplerian Life Philosophy can serve as a guide.

Group two. People don't know how to be their true selves. The Eplerian Life Philosophy has been created to show how to become your true authentic self.

Group three. People don't want to be their true selves because their self-centered behavior through deception and manipulation has provided everything they want. They also experience four seconds of chemical pleasure making people feel bad about themselves. They become enraged if their behavior is challenged. This is not human behavior.

For people in group one and two, there's only one thing you need to do to be your true authentic self. Stop thinking about yourself. Learn and train yourself to avoid triggering the primitive brain region. Stop activating the primitive brain, and you'll have a life with no anger and no stress. Recognize these 50 primitive brain-thinking behaviors and stop them.

Primitive brain thinking behaviors. (1) Thinking about your problems. (2) Negative thoughts about yourself, angry at yourself, and self-destructive thoughts. (3) Feeling sorry for yourself and self-pity. (4) Complaining. (5) Criticizing. (6) Judging. (7) Excuses. (8) Blame. (9) Lying. (10) Manipulation. (11) Wrongly blaming yourself. (12) Talking about problems instead of solutions. (13) Comparing yourself to others. (14) Trying to be someone else. (15) Trying to be your job title. (16) Trying to please others. (17) Thinking about what people think of you. (18) Jealousy. (19) Retaliation and revenge. (20) Worry. (21) Guilt. (22) Seeking immediate gratification. (23) Seeking status. (24) Seeking control over people. (25) Seeking power. (26) Negative thoughts about the past. (27) Negative thoughts about the future. (28) Negative thoughts about work. (29) Negative thoughts about a close relationship. (30) Negative thoughts about money. (31) Having the cellphone in your hand at all times. (32) Jumping to conclusions. (33) All-or-nothing approach. (34) Tunnel vision. (35) Fear of missing out. (36) Imagining the worst-case situation (37) Using emotions to make decisions. (38) Not able to delay gratification. (39) Avoid taking responsibility. (40) Not able to make decisions. (41) Over generalization. (42) Difficulty with change. (43) Difficulty with abstract thinking. (44) Difficulty with ambiguity (45) Perfectionism and having regrets. (46) Fear of failure (47) Giving expecting something in return (48) Undisciplined. (49) Pessimism. (50) Egocentric thinking.

Here are several more primitive brain behaviors. (1) Nutrition – eating foods with added sugar, added salt, and processed foods, eating too much food, and eating while standing. (2) Sleep – not getting eight hours of sleep, naps longer than ten minutes, requiring sleeping pills, falling asleep watching TV, and looking at the lighted cellphone before sleeping. (3) Exercise – cellphone in the hand while working out, poor form, and poor posture. (4) Driving – self-centered impatient driving, non-emergency honking, remote locking with the car-horn sound, and tailgating (5) Negative social and communication interaction – one-ups, put-downs, and destructive comments with family, friends, coworkers, neighbors, and in public.

Break the primitive brain thinking habit. Learn and understand the primitive brain and the need to stop thinking from there. Then recognize when you have a primitive brain thought and stop. Do this for three weeks, and you may find yourself living a life with no anger and no stress.

> *"Be human. Stop thinking about yourself from the primitive brain."*
> *"Think from your heart with kindness and your mind with creativity."*

Human behaviors from the heart include kindness to yourself and others, giving without expecting anything in return, unconditional love, gratitude, appreciation, forgiving, and empathy.

Human behaviors from the gut include choosing and eating healthy foods. This means eating foods that do not cause inflammation such as no added sugar, no added salt, and no processed foods especially foods with manufactured omega-6 fat. Gut belly brain behavior includes choosing anti-inflammatory foods that contain omega-3 fats and fiber. The gut feeling of fear keeps us healthy. It's a human behavior keeping us safe and preventing us from doing a physical activity or social activity that has excessive risk.

Human behaviors from the body include the good feeling from exercising all the muscle groups that include the biceps; triceps; neck, back, and abdominal muscles, quadriceps, hamstrings, and calves. Human behavior can use the mind to combine with the body to perform extraordinary athletic feats that no other species can perform. Human behavior from the body enables a healthy positive posture.

Human behaviors from the mind include creativity to solve problems and help others, innovation to develop new products and services, courage, attention, discipline, persistence, inspiration, awe, total calmness, feeling of not needing to do anything, acceptance, belonging, joy, and bliss.

> *"Primitive brain thinking is about yourself."*
> *"Human thinking is about everyone else."*

Benefits of being your true authentic self. (1) You are your own person. (2) You don't have to listen to anyone telling you what to do if you don't want to. (3) You don't need to listen to anyone telling you who you're supposed to be. (4) You have no need to please people so they will like you. (5) You chose who you are, no one else. (6) You don't think from the primitive brain anger center. (7) You have zero-level stress (8) You feel good thinking from your heart with kindness and giving. (9) You feel good thinking from the mind solving problems and helping others. (10) You feel good from feelings of the mind that include total calmness, acceptance, happiness, and unconditional love. (11) You're not trying to be anyone else or comparing yourself to others. (12) You're not trying to be your job title. (13) You have no negative thoughts about yourself, no self-criticism, and no self-pity. (14) You don't feel sorry for yourself. (15) You don't think about your problems. (16) You don't worry. (17) You don't feel guilty and you have no regrets. (18) You have no negative thoughts about the past. (19) You have no negative thoughts about the future. (20) You don't complain. (21) You don't criticize or judge. (22) You don't blame. (23) You don't have excuses. (24) You use fear to keep you safe and healthy. (25) You use sadness to replace someone or something you lost. (26) You have no resentment or jealousy (27) You have no retaliation or revenge. (28) You make instant decisions (29) You thrive on personal responsibility. (30) You have unwavering commitment. (31) You have a healthy, confident posture. (32) You have eight hours of sleep every night. (33) You have one hour of exercise every day. (34) You have a healthy nutritional lifestyle. (35) You are always your true authentic self.

How do you obtain the benefits of the Eplerian Life Philosophy? Know where you're thinking from and be your true authentic self.

There are three phases for eliminating primitive brain thinking

First. Learn about the primitive brain and understand its function. The primitive brain is needed during infancy for survival, for reproduction of the human species, and life-saving instinctive reactions as an adult. These are important primitive brain functions, but the primitive brain is not useful for anything else. Thinking from the primitive brain results in unhealthy and harmful behaviors for you, other people, and society.

Second. Manage primitive brain behavior to less than the ten seconds because this is too brief to activate the harmful adrenaline cortisol response. Here's a list of eight ways to do this, and you can use one or more of them depending on the situation. Create your own way to stop thinking from the primitive brain.

1. The six- to eight-second technique. Feel the anger or stress without thinking, let it peak and move on to something else.
2. Self-technique. Recognize when you're thinking from the stress center and think from the heart or the mind.
3. Neuro-bypass and 'love and peace' technique. Repeat "love and peace" to yourself for 30- to 90-seconds.
4. Think from the heart. Be kind to someone. Give something to someone. Help someone.
5. Think from the mind. Think about your project or upcoming positive experience. Feel deep calmness, total acceptance, or extraordinary joy.
6. Trigger the parasympathetic system. Use belly breaths, drink water, go for a 12-min walk and yoga breathing techniques.

7. Trigger endorphins. Prolonged running or exercise; and the 10-second freezing- cold-water on-your-face shower technique.
8. Distraction. Instantly listening to upbeat music, a festive meal, laughing out loud, or positive social interaction with people.

You need to think in positive ways. For example, think and say more positive words than negative words. See the good in people and events. See the positive in events that occur during the day instead of seeing problems. Eliminate overthinking by not thinking a second negative thought about an event or a person.

Third. Eliminate primitive brain thinking. In the past, I thought it was impossible to eliminate anger and stress. However, I was wrong. Primitive brain thinking can be totally and forever eliminated from your life. Imagine what your life would be like. Image what the world would be like. It would be a new human civilization!

How do you eliminate primitive brain thinking? Stop the thought or action from activating the primitive brain. This can be accomplished with persistent practice. Use the mind with courage, attention, and inspiration.

There are two activation triggers of the primitive brain that must be eliminated. They are negative thoughts and negative actions.

Negative thoughts will trigger primitive brain thinking instinctively. Learn to ignore these negative thoughts or learn to stop thinking negative thoughts, and you will eliminate primitive brain thinking and behavior.

Negative actions from the senses will activate the primitive brain. These include seeing or hearing a potential threat; someone taking away your enjoyment, your values, or your opinions; someone insulting you or offending you; or someone criticizing you, blaming you, or ridiculing you. All these actions will instinctively trigger primitive brain thinking and behavior. You need to prevent activating the primitive brain.

Ultimately for being human, you want to live in the mind. You can't think from the primitive brain with negative thoughts, anger, or stress when you're in the mind.

Use the Eplerian Life Philosophy by knowing where you're thinking from. Think from your heart with kindness to yourself and giving. Think from the mind with creativity and innovation to solve problems and help others, courage to be your true authentic self, and inspiration to improve the world.

Be exceptional by being your true self. Thrive on your uniqueness. You have an unlimited capacity for living an extraordinary life.

About the Author

Dr. Gary Epler is an internationally known Harvard Medical School professor and opinion leader in optimal health, peak performance, and leadership. He improves people's lives through transformational thinking and being their true selves. Dr. Epler is a successful serial entrepreneur as a founder and CEO of three companies including a biotech company, a nutraceutical company, and a health consulting company. He is an award-winning speaker and a bestselling author who has impacted businesses and the lives of people throughout the world through his speaking, books, teaching, and business consulting. He has developed the Eplerian Life Philosophy for a new healthy way of life at home, at work, and in the community.

Dr. Epler has been recognized yearly since 1994 in *The Best Doctors in America*. He believes personalized health empowers people. He has written four health books in the critically acclaimed "You're the Boss" series about people taking charge of their health *including Manage Your Disease, BOOP, Asthma*, and *Food*.

Dr. Epler has been called upon by individuals from around the globe who have a rare lung disease called BOOP that he discovered. He discovered a new lung parasite in South America. He was at the Centers for Disease Control (CDC) in Atlanta where he chronicled the nutritional needs of North African children and managed the tuberculosis refugee program in Southeast Asia. He was Chief of Medicine at the New England Baptist Hospital for 15 years. He has written more than 110 scientific publications and given more than 500 seminars and workshops around the world. In addition to conducting clinical and research work, Dr. Epler strives to educate. He became editor-in-chief of an internet-based educational program in critical care and pulmonary medicine offered by the American College of Chest Physicians. *Business Week* acclaimed him for his development of e-health educational programs that enable patients to manage their health and diseases. Dr. Epler was recognized as one of *Boston Magazine's* "Top Doctors in Town."

Dr. Epler ran several marathons including Boston, New York, and proposed to his wife, Joan at the start of the Paris Marathon; and for their first anniversary, they ran the original Greek marathon together. He delivered the 20th baby from a mother who named the baby after him. He's been one of the Boston Celtics team doctors. He has taught medicine throughout the world and was fortunate enough to save a dying infant in South America from an overwhelming parasitic infection by using the sap from a fig tree. He is a radio and television personality. He is a Hollywood screenwriter and has written a medical thriller movie, a medical drama TV show, and a lifestyle reality TV show. He is active in the community. He coached soccer, basketball, hockey, baseball, and club baseball at Boston College. He lives in the Boston area with his wife Joan, and they have two sons, Greg and Brett.

www.ingramcontent.com/pod-product-compliance
Lightning Source LLC
Chambersburg PA
CBHW032041090426
42744CB00004B/77